FORMULA ONE 2024

Copyright © 2024 Welbeck Non-Fiction Limited
First published in 2024 by Welbeck

An Imprint of HEADLINE PUBLISHING GROUP

10 9 8 7 6 5 4 3 2

ISBN 978-180279-711-4

Editor: Conor Kilgallon
Design: Russell Knowles and Luke Griffin
Picture research: Paul Langan
Production: Rachel Burgess

Printed at Bell & Bain Ltd, UK

MIX
Paper | Supporting
responsible forestry
FSC® C104740

HEADLINE PUBLISHING GROUP
A Hachette UK Company
Carmelite House
50 Victoria Embankment
London EC4Y 0DZ

www.headline.co.uk
www.hachette.co.uk

All stats and facts correct as at December 2023.

Above: Max Verstappen splashes through the puddles to qualify in pole position for the Canadian Grand Prix.

FORMULA ONE 2024

TEAMS | DRIVERS | TRACKS | RECORDS

BRUCE JONES

WELBECK

CONTENTS

ANALYSIS OF THE 2024 SEASON — 8

RED BULL RACING	10	ASTON MARTIN	30	SAUBER	48
Max Verstappen	12	Fernando Alonso	32	Valtteri Bottas	50
Sergio Perez	13	Lance Stroll	33	Zhou Guanyu	51
MERCEDES-AMG	14	ALPINE	34	HAAS	52
Lewis Hamilton	16	Pierre Gasly	36	Nico Hulkenberg	54
George Russell	17	Esteban Ocon	37	Kevin Magnussen	55
FERRARI	20	WILLIAMS	38		
Charles Leclerc	22	Alex Albon	40		
Carlos Sainz Jr	23	Logan Sargeant	41		
McLAREN	24	'ALPHATAURI'	44		
Lando Norris	26	Yuki Tsunoda	46		
Oscar Piastri	27	Daniel Ricciardo	47		

TALKING POINTS 2024

| The Andretti Clan Throws Its Hat Into the Ring | 56 | Can F1 Academy Produce Another Female F1 Racer? | 60 |
| It Was Hit and Miss as Las Vegas Joined the F1 Circus | 58 | | |

KNOW THE TRACKS 2024 — 62

Sakhir	64	Montreal	72	Baku	82
Jeddah	65	Barcelona	73	Marina Bay	83
Melbourne	66	Red Bull Ring	76	Circuit of the Americas	84
Suzuka	67	Silverstone	77	Mexico City	85
Shanghai	68	Hungaroring	78	Interlagos	86
Miami	69	Spa-Francorchamps	79	Las Vegas	87
Imola	70	Zandvoort	80	Losail	88
Monaco	71	Monza	81	Yas Marina	89

REVIEW OF THE 2023 SEASON — 90

Bahrain GP	92	Austrian GP	102	Qatar GP	112
Saudi Arabian GP	93	British GP	103	United States GP	113
Australian GP	94	Hungarian GP	104	Mexico City GP	114
Azerbaijan GP	95	Belgian GP	105	Sao Paulo GP	115
Miami GP	96	Dutch GP	106	Las Vegas GP	116
Monaco GP	97	Italian GP	107	Abu Dhabi GP	117
Spanish GP	100	Singapore GP	110		
Canadian GP	101	Japanese GP	111		

FINAL RESULTS 2023	118
FORMULA ONE RECORDS	120
2024 SEASON FILL-IN CHART	126

Opposite: It was a matter of when, not if, Max Verstappen would wrap up his third F1 title and the deed was done in the Qatar sprint race.

A moment of introspection for Lando Norris on the grid before the Monaco GP.

/// ANALYSIS OF THE 2024 SEASON

Red Bull Racing was on remarkable form through 2023 and, with no regulated technical changes mandated, there is no reason why it shouldn't be anywhere other than at the front of the field in the season ahead. The big question is whether any of the other top teams can not only produce a quick car but one that is consistently quick across the 24-race season.

It's hard to know which is the more daunting task in 2024: competing in a record 24 Grands Prix or taking on Red Bull Racing. The former task will be draining, mentally, physically and logistically, but the latter has troubled rival designers and engineers for the past two years since the last round of technical changes that Red Bull mastered and they didn't.

Adrian Newey continues to lead the brains trust at Red Bull, but he has lost chief engineering officer Rob Marshall to McLaren, so nothing stays still forever. The chief concern, however, for team principal Christian Horner will be the progress of their rivals and whether Sergio Perez can return to

form in 2024 to ensure that they can land a third constructors' title in a row.

Chief technical officer Mike Elliott left Mercedes last autumn, so there has been a change to the design crew and both Lewis Hamilton and George Russell will be praying that they can have a consistently competitive car, especially Russell, who joined the sport's golden team just as it lost its Midas touch.

Ferrari also needs to find consistent form as Frederic Vasseur settles into his second year as team principal, with both Charles Leclerc and Carlos Sainz Jr craving a car that performs best in the race, rather than just in qualifying. One win last year was one

better than Mercedes managed, but neither team will be happy with those returns.

McLaren has been too far from the front for too long and its dire early-season form last year suggested that the malaise had worsened, but the MCL60's drastic gain in performance suddenly put both Lando Norris and Oscar Piastri in the spotlight. One of the stories of this season is going to be whether Norris can contain his talented team-mate as the Australian settles into his second year in F1.

As big guns Mercedes, Ferrari and McLaren go after Red Bull Racing in 2024, it's hard to know whether Aston Martin will be able to shine to the same extent as last year. Clearly no one has had the temerity to point out to Fernando Alonso that being in his 40s might be a good time to slow down, as he was sensational, but the team's chances of tilting at podium positions again might be slimmer.

Alpine is looking to have a less frenetic and spiky season, keeping on both Pierre Gasly and Esteban Ocon, but the French duo know that their team's Renault power unit will continue to hamper their best efforts.

F1 prides itself on being a fast-moving entity, a sport that thinks on its feet, but turning around a struggling team takes years rather than months. The good news for long-suffering Williams fans is that the team is pointing in the right direction again. Alex Albon will surely continue to get the best out of whatever car he is given, while Logan Sargeant will continue learning from the second seat.

Yuki Tsunoda and Daniel Ricciardo ought to make a formidable pairing for the team that raced last year as Scuderia AlphaTauri and will pick up whatever scraps fall from F1's high table. The same will be true for Sauber, but Valtteri Bottas and Zhou Guanyu know that their best hope will be in the early races, before the Swiss team's traditional decline sets in, a trend that will need to be sorted when it partners with Audi from 2026.

With Michael Andretti anxious to land an entry for 2026, Haas will be looking to maximise its position as America's team before then, but it really needs to raise its game and produce a car that can do more than just quick laps in qualifying and design one that can maintain speed through a Grand Prix distance to give Nico Hulkenberg and Kevin Magnussen any hope at all.

// RED BULL RACING

Red Bull Racing could well be set for its third consecutive season of domination of F1, as no other team has risen to its challenge and Max Verstappen has been untouchable as he spearheads the team's attack.

Max Verstappen was all but unstoppable in 2023, starting with victory in the first round in Bahrain, and it will be a major feat to beat him.

Jackie Stewart was that rare racing driver who knew how to retire at the top. He had won three F1 titles in the space of five years and was set to bow out after his 100th Grand Prix at Watkins Glen. Sadly, the death of team-mate Francois Cevert in qualifying meant that he stopped there and then. However, he has never stopped attacking life with the same vigour and Red Bull Racing is a product of that.

Firstly, while being a roving ambassador for blue-chip multinationals, Jackie took the time to ensure that when elder son Paul wanted to go racing in Formula Ford that he had the best people around him. Thus, Paul Stewart Racing was created, moving up swiftly to Formula 3 then Formula 3000 before Paul stood back from racing and the team pushed on into F1.

Stewart Grand Prix made its debut in 1997 and was immediately a midfield team but then had its greatest day in tricky conditions at the Nurburgring in 1999 when Johnny Herbert triumphed.

The Stewarts realised that it would need more money to advance and so sold the team and its base in Milton Keynes to Ford in 2000, with Ford electing to enter the team as Jaguar Racing. This certainly brought in investment but, alas, management interference too, and

KEY PERSONNEL & 2023 ROUND-UP

HELMUT MARKO

A driver good enough to reach F1, peaking with eighth at Monaco, Helmut's career was ended in 1972 when he was blinded in one eye by a stone at the French GP. He then ran his own F3 and F3000 teams before fellow Austrian Dietrich Mateschitz wanted to use motor racing to promote his Red Bull brand. Acting as a consultant, Helmut oversaw its scholarship drivers in the junior categories, taking a hard-edged approach to discarding those he didn't think good enough.

RACING TO A RECORD F1 CLEAN SWEEP

McLaren nearly did it in 1988, but it fell short by winning only 15 of the season's 16 Grands Prix. With a campaign extended to 22 Grands Prix, thus making the challenge all the harder, no one expected Red Bull to win every race as the season roared into life last year. Yet, Max Verstappen and occasionally Sergio Perez early in the year, were seldom challenged. Perez struggled in qualifying, reducing his race chances, but Verstappen was uniformly excellent, whatever the conditions, and gathered and kept on winning to end up with double Perez's tally.

2023 DRIVERS & RESULTS

Driver	Nationality	Races	Wins	Pts	Pos
Sergio Perez	Mexican	22	2	285	2nd
Max Verstappen	Dutch	22	19	575	1st

this held the team back despite the best efforts of Eddie Irvine and Mark Webber. There were flashes of speed, but no wins, and it was a blessing when the team was given new impetus for 2005 from its purchase by Red Bull energy drinks founder Dietrich Mateschitz.

The idea was to throw its net wide to help a number of promising drivers in the junior single-seater categories and then select the best of these for its F1 team. Initially, though, and wisely so, it wanted experience and signed David Coulthard from McLaren. This had its merits, especially when he coaxed ace designer Adrian Newey to join him.

It took until 2009 for Red Bull Racing's first victory, when Sebastian Vettel won in China and he would go on to win a four-way title shoot-out, against drivers including team-mate Webber, in Abu Dhabi in 2010. And so began a run of four drivers' titles until 2013.

The increasing challenge from Mercedes from 2014 meant that Red Bull Racing reverted to the role of chaser and there was a change in the team's internal dynamic as Daniel Ricciardo took over the second seat and outscored Vettel at his first attempt. However, Ferrari began to outstrip it in 2015, and Williams too. Then Ricciardo was joined by Max Verstappen midway through 2016, with the Dutchman winning on his first attempt after stepping up from Red Bull's junior team, Scuderia Toro Rosso, and this helped to propel the team back to second overall.

What followed was a quest to ally Newey's chassis with competitive engines, as its TAG Heuer-badged Renault engines couldn't match the power output of the rival Mercedes and Ferrari units. While Lewis Hamilton notched up title after title with Mercedes, Verstappen added experience to his natural speed and increasingly became a threat.

With the Honda engines that the team used from 2019 onwards offering a step forward, Verstappen began to challenge Mercedes more and more, helping Red Bull Racing to be runner-up to Mercedes in 2020 and again in 2021 when Verstappen clinched the drivers'

FOR THE RECORD

Team base:	**Milton Keynes, England**
Active in Formula One:	**As Stewart GP 1997–99, Jaguar Racing 2000–04, Red Bull Racing 2005 on**
Grands Prix contested:	**503**
Wins:	**114**
Pole positions:	**96**
Fastest laps:	**95**
Constructors' titles:	**6**
Drivers' titles:	**7**

THE TEAM

Team principal:	**Christian Horner**
Motorsport consultant:	**Helmut Marko**
Chief technical officer	**Adrian Newey**
Chief engineer, car engineering	**Paul Monaghan**
Chief engineer, technology & analysis	**Guillaume Cattelani**
Technical director:	**Pierre Wache**
Head of performance engineering:	**Ben Waterhouse**
Head of race engineering:	**Gianpiero Lambiase**
Sporting director:	**Jonathan Wheatley**
Chassis:	**Red Bull RB20**
Engine:	**Honda RBPT V6**
Tyres:	**Pirelli**

title with a one-lap dash in Abu Dhabi.

There were new technical regulations for 2022 and Red Bull Racing started with the most competitive car. Verstappen did the rest, adding the 2022 and 2023 titles.

Sebastian Vettel and Adrian Newey celebrate in India in 2013, another win in his fourth title-winning year.

"I hardly have to say anything [to race engineer Gianpiero Lambiase] anymore. If I report that I have understeer or oversteer, he immediately knows what he needs to adjust."

Max Verstappen

It appears unlikely that anyone will stop Max Verstappen from making it four titles in a row for Red Bull. He was in such imperious form last year, winning 19 of the 22 Grands Prix, that he must surely be heading for another title.

Max scored a record 19 wins last year, so his only target can be to try to beat that in 2024.

Max was born to race, with a mother – Sophie Kumpen – who followed her father into racing and excelled in karting plus a father, Jos, who shone for Benetton in F1 in the mid-1990s.

Not surprisingly, Max began racing karts as soon as he was old enough and there was little that young Max didn't win on the way up through the karting ranks, peaking with the World and European KZ titles in 2013 as he turned 16. Top kart racers often bypass the first rung of single-seaters, Formula 4, and go straight to Formula Renault. Max didn't do that, but skipped directly to racing's third level, Formula 3, taking an incredible ten wins to rank third in a European championship that was won by Esteban Ocon.

Everyone suggested a campaign in Formula 2 would prepare him further, but Jos encouraged Max to try to go straight to F1. And this is what he did, joining Scuderia Toro Rosso for 2015 to become F1's first 17-year-old driver. Many watched on with concern that he wouldn't be ready for this giant leap, but it never fazed Max and he bagged a couple of fourth places before the year was out.

Just five races into 2016, Red Bull Racing decided that Max would do better than Daniil Kvyat and they swapped drives. Not only that, but Max then shocked everyone by winning on his debut for Red Bull Racing in the Spanish GP.

Although Max drove increasingly well over the next few years, it was always in pursuit of Lewis Hamilton and Mercedes. Then, after claiming nine wins in 2021, he was handed victory in strange circumstances in the Abu Dhabi finale to pip Lewis Hamilton to the crown.

Then, after Red Bull adapted the best to 2022's new technical rules, Max made it two titles in a row.

TRACK NOTES

Nationality:	**DUTCH**
Born:	**30 SEPTEMBER 1997,**
	HASSELT, BELGIUM
Teams:	**TORO ROSSO 2015–16,**
	RED BULL RACING 2016–24

CAREER RECORD

First Grand Prix:	**2015 AUSTRALIAN GP**
Grand Prix starts:	**185**
Grand Prix wins:	**54**

2016 Spanish GP, 2017 Malaysian GP, Mexican GP, 2018 Austrian GP, Mexican GP, 2019 Austrian GP, German GP, Brazilian GP, 2020 70th Anniversary GP, Abu Dhabi GP, 2021 Emilia Romagna GP, Monaco GP, French GP, Styrian GP, Austrian GP, Belgian GP, Dutch GP, United States GP, Mexico City GP, Abu Dhabi GP, 2022 Saudi Arabian GP, Emilia Romagna GP, Miami GP, Spanish GP, Azerbaijan GP, Canadian GP, French GP, Hungarian GP, Belgian GP, Dutch GP, Italian GP, Japanese GP, United States GP, Mexico City GP, Abu Dhabi GP, 2023 Bahrain GP, Australian GP, Miami GP, Monaco GP, Spanish GP, Canadian GP, Austrian GP, British GP, Hungarian GP, Belgian GP, Dutch GP, Italian GP, Japanese GP, Qatar GP, United States GP, Mexico City GP, Sao Paulo GP, Las Vegas GP, Abu Dhabi GP

Poles:	**32**
Fastest laps:	**30**
Points:	**2586.5**
Honours:	2021, 2022 & 2023

F1 WORLD CHAMPION, 2013 WORLD & EUROPEAN KZ KART CHAMPION, 2012 WSK MASTER SERIES KF2 CHAMPION, 2011 WSK EURO SERIES CHAMPION, 2009 BELGIAN KF5 CHAMPION, 2008 DUTCH CADET KART CHAMPION, 2007 & 2008 DUTCH MINIMAX CHAMPION

SUCCESS AT ALMOST EVERY TURN

It didn't appear to matter to Max what sort of circuit he was competing on. Whether high-downforce, low-downforce or something in between, Max was able to win on them all. He was in such strong form that there were clear reasons for the few races he didn't win. In Jeddah, he had a driveshaft failure in qualifying and started down in 15th on the grid and could make it back only to second place behind team-mate Sergio Perez by flag fall. Then in Baku he was called in for a pit stop at a less than optimal time, consigning him to second place behind Perez again. All his other finishes, bar in Singapore when Ferrari's Carlos Sainz Jr came out on top, were victories. As the season advanced, Red Bull's quest to become the first team to win every round became more and more beguiling but, once this was ended, it was time for Christian Horner and the team to bathe in the glory of their achievement. Max just kept on winning to take a record number of wins in a season, 19.

SERGIO PEREZ

Last year was one that Sergio will want to forget, as his form plummeted after a promising start and he was left so far behind team-mate Max Verstappen that he was of little use to the team. This season might be his last at Red Bull Racing.

If Sergio doesn't rediscover his form in 2024, don't expect him to stay on with the team.

Sergio headed for the USA as soon as he could and graduated to single-seater racing at the tender age of 14. Starting in the Skip Barber Dodge Series, he then took an even larger step for 2005 by heading to Europe. This was so that he could learn the circuits as he contested the largely German-based ADAC Formula BMW series and it turned into a two-year project.

Formula 3 came next, with Sergio moving to England to contest the British championship in 2007, starting in the national class in which he won the title. Staying on for 2008, Sergio moved up to the senior class and was roundly beaten by Jaime Alguersuari, ranking only fourth.

Going for glory in more powerful GP2 in 2009, he started the year well with two wins in the Asian series but his main campaign in Europe wasn't much of a success and so he stayed on for a second year, doing better to win five races and be runner-up behind Pastor Maldonado.

An appreciable budget from Mexican sponsors landed Sergio his F1 break with Sauber in 2011 and he progressed well. He claimed a pair of second places in 2012, with the former, at the Malaysian GP, one of his greatest ever performances as he harried Fernando Alonso's Ferrari on a wet track.

There followed a move to McLaren, but this didn't go well and so he joined Force India for 2014 and was easily outscored by team-mate Nico Hulkenberg. However, he was clearly highly rated by the team

as it kept him on for the next six years, including the final two seasons after it had changed its name to Racing Point.

At the last race of 2020, in what many thought might be his final race in F1, Sergio scored a famous win in the Sakhir GP and earned a move to Red Bull Racing as a result.

Selected as a number two to Max Verstappen, Sergio took one win in 2021 then two in 2022 to rank fourth then third, albeit seldom challenging his Dutch team-mate.

LIVING PERPETUALLY IN MAX'S SHADOW

Any driver who picks up two wins, a second place and a fifth in a season's first four Grands Prix might feel pleased with themselves, especially if they had won only the same number of Grands Prix across the previous season's 22 rounds. However, Sergio's challenge petered out after that as there were to be no more wins and precious few podium visits. The root cause for the Mexican's decline was that his form in qualifying was abysmal – he frequently couldn't even get F1's most competitive chassis into Q3 for the final ten qualifiers. Although Sergio would typically then advance up the order through the course of a Grand Prix, the damage had been done. Red Bull Racing were absolutely aware that if they had been pushed harder by their rivals, his poor record could have denied them the constructors' title and so his seat has come under threat. Although Sergio enjoyed a wonderful late-race scrap with Fernando Alonso in Brazil, being pipped in that did his reputation more harm.

TRACK NOTES

Nationality:	**MEXICAN**
Born:	**26 JANUARY 1990, GUADALAJARA, MEXICO**
Teams:	**SAUBER 2011–12, McLAREN 2013, FORCE INDIA 2014–18, RACING POINT 2019–20, RED BULL RACING 2021–24**

CAREER RECORD

First Grand Prix:	**2011 AUSTRALIAN GP**
Grand Prix starts:	**257**
Grand Prix wins:	**6**
	2020 Sakhir GP, 2021 Azerbaijan GP, 2022 Monaco GP, Singapore GP, 2023 Saudi Arabian GP, Azerbaijan GP
Poles:	**3**
Fastest laps:	**11**
Points:	**1486**
Honours:	**2023 F1 RUNNER-UP, 2010 GP2 RUNNER-UP, 2007 BRITISH FORMULA 3 NATIONAL CLASS CHAMPION**

MERCEDES-AMG

Unless the team has made strong gains with its new chassis, this could be the third season in a row in which Lewis Hamilton and George Russell have to chase after the Red Bulls, as they try to be the best of the rest.

Lewis Hamilton and George Russell (above) had to endure a slow start to last year in which Lewis's pole in Hungary was a rare high spot.

So strong is the identity of the Mercedes F1 team thanks to its remarkable run of titles from 2014 to 2020 that it is sometimes hard to remember that the team's previous life in three different guises was less illustrious.

The team from Brackley to the west of Silverstone started life as BAR when Craig Pollock and his former skiing pupil Jacques Villeneuve got together with British American Tobacco to take over the World Championship arm of the fading Tyrrell team. That was in 1998 and the all-new BAR (British American Racing) team burst forth in 1999 complete with the much-derided strapline of 'a tradition of excellence'.

Alas, the team's maiden campaign was very poor. Even getting to the end of a Grand Prix was too much for its cars at most races. No one expected instant success, despite the high calibre of personnel it had enticed from rival teams, but BAR's first year was a flop, as there was no tradition and no excellence.

In time, BAR made strides and Jenson Button would have won several races in 2004 had it not been for Michael Schumacher's superior Ferrari. Then, with Honda wanting to increase its involvement beyond just supplying engines, the team was renamed Honda Racing for 2006 and Button scored a remarkable win in a wet/dry Hungarian GP.

KEY PERSONNEL & 2023 ROUND-UP

HYWEL THOMAS

Bath University is a powerhouse for British engineers and Torquay-born Hywel is in its vanguard as managing director of Mercedes AMG's HPP (High-Performance Powertrains) division. Starting at Perkins Engines on graduation, he moved to Cosworth for his first taste of motor racing and then joined HPP in 2004. Starting as an engineer, Hywel rose through the ranks as Mercedes began to make waves in F1, eventually becoming MD. HPP is involved in other Mercedes projects, including its Project 1 Hyper ultra car.

SWITCHING THE FOCUS EARLY TO 2024

Mercedes's 'zeropod' concept was hoped to be the cure for the team's performance shortfall in the second year of the new technical rules, but it wasn't. Indeed, as the team chased improved performance, the drivers were keen that the W14 would bounce less and offer handling that was more predictable. Hamilton's podium finish in Australia suggested that all was not lost, but it took until the second half of the season for Mercedes to find form.

2023 DRIVERS & RESULTS

Driver	Nationality	Races	Wins	Pts	Pos
Lewis Hamilton	British	22	0	234	3rd
George Russell	British	22	0	175	8th

FOR THE RECORD

Team base:	**Brackley, England**
Active in Formula One:	
	As BAR 1999–2005, Honda Racing
	2006–08, Brawn GP 2009, Mercedes
	2010 on
Grands Prix contested:	**468**
Wins:	**125**
Pole positions:	**137**
Fastest laps:	**100**
Constructors' titles:	**9**
Drivers' titles:	**8**

THE TEAM

Head of Mercedes-Benz Motorsport:	
	Toto Wolff
Technical director:	**James Allison**
MD, Mercedes-AMG High Performance	
powertrains:	**Hywel Thomas**
Chief designer:	**John Owen**
Performance director:	**Loic Serra**
Sporting director:	**Ron Meadows**
Trackside engineering director:	
	Andrew Shovlin
Chief trackside engineer:	**Simon Cole**
Chassis:	**Mercedes F1 W15**
Engine:	**Mercedes V6**
Tyres:	**Pirelli**

A combination of the next two seasons offering meagre results and then the global economic slump meant that Honda pulled out after 2008 and only an 11th-hour management takeover led by team principal Ross Brawn got the team on to the grid for 2009; but what a season that was. Button and Rubens Barrichello were given a performance advantage as their cars had a double-decked diffuser and Button's six wins in the first half of the year before rivals understood and then caught up with this aerodynamic advantage, were enough to secure the team's first crown.

To attain financial security, Brawn agreed to the team being financed by Mercedes and changing its name in the German manufacturer's honour from 2010, with Michael Schumacher stepping back into F1 to lead its attack.

It took until 2012 for the silver-liveried team to win again, then it was given a boost when Lewis Hamilton was coaxed across to partner Nico Rosberg from 2013.

Then the titles flowed from 2014 as the British driver began a seven-year run of success for the team in which he won six drivers' titles, with Rosberg champion in 2016, and the team pocketed the constructors' title in each of those years. Mercedes also won the constructors' title in 2021 when Hamilton was beaten in controversial fashion by Red Bull Racing's Max Verstappen at the season-closing Abu Dhabi GP – F1 restart protocol was not observed before a one-lap sprint to the finish after a safety car deployment.

One of the reasons for the team's remarkable success was its excellent group of designers, aerodynamicists and engineers, clear leadership from Toto Wolff and, in its early days, the influence of former world champion Niki Lauda, who acted as an astute buffer between the team and the manufacturer.

Red Bull Racing mastered new technical regulations in 2022 and remains on the top of the pile, with Hamilton and George Russell, who joined just at the time Mercedes stopped being the dominant force in F1, to struggle in Verstappen's wake. Russell did have one moment of delight, though, when he won at Interlagos in the penultimate race of the season. In 2023, Mercedes, if anything, fell further away from Red Bull's pace, its F1 W14s less competitive than the McLarens and the Ferraris by the end of the season.

Valtteri Bottas joined at the 11th hour in 2017 and is shown here racing to his first win, at the Russian GP.

"It was a great end to our fight with Ferrari to finish 2023 second. George's driving was exceptional and Charles showed sportsmanlike behaviour not to slow at the end."

Toto Wolff

After two years without a win, the seven-time world champion has eschewed all talk of retirement and is back for another crack, praying that Mercedes will provide him with a car with which he can challenge the best from Red Bull Racing.

Lewis had to call on his experience to sort last year's car and deserves better for 2024.

There isn't a driver who has made it into F1 in the past decade without an illustrious karting pedigree and Lewis was certainly one of the best as he ascended the ranks. Key to his further progress, though, was meeting McLaren's then boss Ron Dennis at an awards dinner and getting him to agree to help him towards F1.

The British Formula Renault title was claimed in 2003 and then the European Formula 3 crown two years later, before Lewis stepped up the pace and landed the GP2 title at his first attempt in 2006.

Then came F1 and Lewis was straight on to the podium on his debut in Melbourne. That third place was followed by four second places and his first win, in Canada. This meant that he was able to challenge team-mate Fernando Alonso and he came within a point of becoming a rookie world champion but fell one point short of Ferrari's Kimi Raikkonen.

At the second time of asking, Lewis was crowned after edging out Ferrari's Felipe Massa. Frustratingly, other teams moved ahead of McLaren, and it took a move to Mercedes in 2013 to get back on track, scoring win after win to add six more world titles between 2014 and 2020, only having this run broken in 2016 when he was pipped by team-mate Nico Rosberg.

Then came the dramatic 2021 Abu Dhabi GP in which most feel that a decision by FIA race director Michael Masi did not follow the rule book and so handed the title to Max Verstappen. Since 2022, with a new set of F1 technical regulations, Mercedes has fallen off the pace.

PRESSING ON JUST TO REACH THE PODIUM

It was clear from the outset of the 2023 season that Mercedes had failed to become any more competitive in the second year of F1's new regulations and that Red Bull Racing still seemed to be operating on another level. This would have been dispiriting for any driver, but especially so for a multiple world champion. It was obvious that an eighth F1 title would have to wait. The first aim for Lewis was to get his Mercedes F1 W14 to be wieldy enough to achieve a podium finish. That came with second place in Melbourne, but it took another four rounds until he was on the podium again, in Barcelona. But there were never going to be any wins, not with Verstappen in such scintillating form. It was interesting to see Lewis really striving to get the maximum performance from his car in a way that he seldom had to, but it impressed all who witnessed his pole lap in Hungary or his run to second (before disqualification on a technicality) at COTA.

TRACK NOTES

Nationality:	**BRITISH**
Born:	**7 JANUARY 1985,**
	STEVENAGE, ENGLAND
Teams:	**McLAREN 2007–12,**
	MERCEDES 2013–24

CAREER RECORD

First Grand Prix: **2007 AUSTRALIAN GP**

Grand Prix starts: **332**

Grand Prix wins: **103**
2007 Canadian GP, United States GP, Hungarian GP, Japanese GP, 2008 Australian GP, Monaco GP, British GP, German GP, Chinese GP, 2009 Hungarian GP, Singapore GP, 2010 Turkish GP, Canadian GP, Belgian GP, 2011 Chinese GP, German GP, Abu Dhabi GP, 2012 Canadian GP, Hungarian GP, Italian GP, United States GP, 2013 Hungarian GP, 2014 Malaysian GP, Bahrain GP, Chinese GP, Spanish GP, British GP, Italian GP, Singapore GP, Japanese GP, Russian GP, United States GP, Abu Dhabi GP, 2015 Australian GP, Chinese GP, Bahrain GP, Canadian GP, British GP, Belgian GP, Italian GP, Japanese GP, Russian GP, United States GP, 2016 Monaco GP, Canadian GP, Austrian GP, British GP, Hungarian GP, German GP, United States GP, Mexican GP, Brazilian GP, Abu Dhabi GP, 2017 Chinese GP, Spanish GP, Canadian GP, British GP, Belgian GP, Italian GP, Singapore GP, Japanese GP, United States GP, 2018 Azerbaijan GP, Spanish GP, French GP, German GP, Hungarian GP, Italian GP, Singapore GP, Russian GP, Japanese GP, Brazilian GP, Abu Dhabi GP, 2019 Bahrain GP, Chinese GP, Spanish GP, Monaco GP, Canadian GP, French GP, British GP, Hungarian GP, Russian GP, Mexican GP, Abu Dhabi GP, 2020 Styrian GP, Hungarian GP, British GP, Spanish GP, Belgian GP, Tuscan GP, Eifel GP, Portuguese GP, Emilia Romagna GP, Turkish GP, Bahrain GP, 2021 Bahrain GP, Portuguese GP, Spanish GP, British GP, Russian GP, Sao Paulo GP, Qatar GP, Saudi Arabian GP

Poles:	**104**
Fastest laps:	**65**
Points:	**4639.5**

Honours: **2008, 2014, 2015, 2017, 2018, 2019 & 2020 F1 WORLD CHAMPION, 2007, 2016 & 2021 F1 RUNNER-UP, 2006 GP2 CHAMPION, 2005 EUROPEAN F3 CHAMPION, 2003 BRITISH FORMULA RENAULT CHAMPION, 2000 WORLD KART CUP & EUROPEAN FORMULA A KART CHAMPION, 1999 ITALIAN INTERCON A CHAMPION, 1995 BRITISH CADET KART CHAMPION**

GEORGE RUSSELL

No wins and a degree of frustration marked George's second year with Mercedes, a team that he joined hoping to become world champion. All he can do is pray that the team can rediscover its winning formula for 2024 so that he can realise the success he craves.

George was outscored by Lewis and must redress that if he is to become the team's leader.

Having made himself into someone to watch by winning the European KF3 kart crown in 2012, George showed that his skills transferred to single-seaters by winning the British Formula 4 championship title two years later, and performing well on a few outings in the European Formula Renault series. George earned the accolades and F1 test drive that came with the McLaren Autosport BRDC Young Driver award.

George elected not to campaign in the European Formula Renault title in 2015 but to advance to Formula 3. He won a round for Carlin but had to make do with sixth place in the rankings and George's highlight was probably finishing second behind Antonio Giovinazzi in the Masters F3 invitation race at Zandvoort.

Returning for a second year in European F3 didn't produce the title, though, as George's two wins were enough only for third overall.

Moving to GP3 in 2017 was a success, as George not only won that title easily but also impressed in F1 test outings for Mercedes. He was ready to step up to the FIA Formula 2 Championship for 2018 and was successful from the start, taking seven wins for ART Grand Prix and defeating Lando Norris and Alex Albon.

Having done well on more test outings for Mercedes and Force India, George was more than ready to step up to the World Championship in 2019 and made his debut with Williams. This was a team in decline at this point and was nowhere near competitive enough to have a chance of even a top-ten finish, but George

impressed nonetheless and continued to show his merit.

Then, for the penultimate round of 2020 at Sakhir, Lewis Hamilton felt unwell, and George was brought in to substitute for him; he showed that he was quicker than Mercedes number two Valtteri Bottas and might have won had his car not suffered a puncture.

Then, he replaced Bottas for 2022, just as Mercedes lost its form, although George did win the Sao Paulo GP from pole position.

TREADING WATER UNTIL 2024

Although George outscored multi-titled team-mate Lewis Hamilton in 2022, he had expected more, with wins at the very least and perhaps even the drivers' title. That was not to be the case and the big question was whether the team could master the regulations to give him a better shot in 2023. It was soon apparent that they could not, and he had to make do with high points like third place in the Spanish GP and a strong but unrewarded drive in Canada. Mercedes had a choice to make: to work flat-out on developing its F1 W14s into more competitive packages or to allocate some of the team's brains to work solely on getting it right for 2024, and, anxious to become winners again, they chose the latter. Later in the year, as Mercedes found in qualifying if not in races, George showed better form but would remain frustrated. This was especially evident in Singapore after his efforts to get past Lando Norris and go after race leader Carlos Sainz Jr ended up in the wall.

TRACK NOTES

Nationality:	**BRITISH**
Born:	**15 FEBRUARY 1998,**
	KING'S LYNN, ENGLAND
Teams:	**WILLIAMS 2019–21,**
MERCEDES 2020 (one race) & 2022–24	

CAREER RECORD

First Grand Prix:	**2019 AUSTRALIAN GP**
Grand Prix starts:	**104**
Grand Prix wins:	**1**
	2022 Sao Paulo GP
Poles:	**1**
Fastest laps:	**6**
Points:	**469**
Honours:	**2018 FIA**
F2 CHAMPION, 2017 GP3 CHAMPION, 2015 F3 MASTERS RUNNER-UP, 2014 BRITISH F4 CHAMPION & McLAREN AUTOSPORT BRDC YOUNG DRIVER AWARD, 2012 EUROPEAN KF3 KART CHAMPION	

The mechanics wait for instruction before a practice session as the engineers analyse data in the Mercedes AMG garage.

FERRARI

It had looked at the start of last year that Ferrari would be the team pushing Red Bull Racing hardest, but the Italian marque will have to think hard about how it squandered its performance and ensures that it performs to its potential this year.

The Ferrari drivers had seasons of both form and failure in 2023 and will only succeed if the team can help them more in the campaign ahead.

Ferrari entered the first World Championship in 1950, but its racing history goes back to when Enzo Ferrari moved from being a mechanic to racing driver in the 1920s. When he quit racing himself, he formed his own team, Scuderia Ferrari. He had wanted to call it Scuderia Mutina (the Latin name for home town Modena), but people convinced him otherwise. In 1932, his team assumed control of the Alfa Romeo racing programme, but early successes were then overtaken by the phenomenal form shown by Auto Union and Mercedes.

After World War Two, despite the success of the Alfa Romeo 158 designed by Gioacchino Colombo, Enzo decided that he would rather go it alone. So he started to run his own cars, following his father's maxim that 'a company is perfect when the number of partners is uneven and less than three.'

Engines were everything and Enzo would later say that aerodynamics were

needed only by those who couldn't build good engines. He had good grounds to say that as Alberto Ascari won two Grands Prix in 1949. The Ferraris had no answer to

the pace of the Alfa Romeos in the World Championship's first year, but Jose Froilan Gonzalez scored Ferrari's breakthrough win at Silverstone in 1951. Following a

KEY PERSONNEL & 2023 ROUND-UP

ENRICO CARDILE

Enrico's passion was clear when he wrote his thesis on the Ferrari wind tunnel and he became a Ferrari employee in 2005. Using his qualifications in aerodynamics, Enrico worked on the design of Ferrari's GT racing cars, gaining plaudits as they won titles in the World Endurance Championship and other series. Appointed as head of aero development for Ferrari's F1 team in 2016, he was promoted to be vehicle project manager the following year and then put in charge of its chassis from 2021.

FAST BUT NOT QUITE FAST ENOUGH TO CHALLENGE

It's never enough for Ferrari just to be gathering points and securing podium positions intermittently, so 2023 was a disappointment for the Maranello outfit. Having been second behind Red Bull Racing in 2022, the team's fall to third overall last year was disappointing. There were high points, like Carlos Sainz Jr's pole for the Italian GP and Charles Leclerc's second place in Austria, but too often the team made a mess of reading a race, especially when conditions changed, and it cost them valuable points. Victory in Singapore put much of this right.

2023 DRIVERS & RESULTS

Driver	Nationality	Races	Wins	Pts	Pos
Charles Leclerc	Monegasque	21	0	206	5th
Carlos Sainz Jr	Spanish	21	1	200	7th

FOR THE RECORD

Team base:	**Maranello, Italy**
Active in Formula One:	**From 1950**
Grands Prix contested:	**1074**
Wins:	**243**
Pole positions:	**249**
Fastest laps:	**259**
Constructors' titles:	**16**
Drivers' titles:	**15**

THE TEAM

Chairman:	**John Elkann**
Team principal:	**Frederic Vasseur**
Technical director, chassis & aerodynamics:	**Enrico Cardile**
Technical director, power unit:	**Enrico Gualtieri**
Head of aerodynamics:	**Loic Bigois**
Sporting director:	**Diego Ioverno**
Head of supply chain:	**Enrico Racca**
Driving academy director:	**Jock Clear**
Head of track engineering:	**Matteo Togninalli**
Chassis:	**Ferrari SF24**
Engine:	**Ferrari V6**
Tyres:	**Pirelli**

change to F2 regulations in 1952, Ferrari got its first world champion that year with Alberto Ascari and he repeated the feat in 1953.

A change to larger engines and the arrival of Mercedes left Ferrari hunting for form, but Juan Manuel Fangio landed the 1956 crown after Ferrari had taken over Lancia's chassis. Mike Hawthorn became Ferrari's third different champion in 1958, but a new threat was surfacing from the active, revolutionary minds of the people leading the small British teams like Cooper and Lotus who Enzo would dismiss as 'garagistes'.

Ferrari was ready for the next rule change, reducing engine size to just 1500cc in 1961, and Phil Hill not only took the title but the form of his team-mate Wolfgang von Trips, up to his death at Monza, was enough to give Ferrari its first constructors' title.

By this time, Cooper and Lotus had been joined by BRM at the head of the field and it took the British nous of former motorbike racing world champion John Surtees for Ferrari to take the 1964 crown.

Surtees would later leave after clashing with the team management, and perhaps this showed how Enzo had allowed too many people to work beneath him. Indeed, it took until the arrival of Niki Lauda and his establishing a relationship with team manager Luca di Montezemolo for Ferrari to become competitive again, with the Austrian landing the 1975 and 1977 titles either side of his fiery accident.

Two years later, despite Ferrari not having mastered the ground effects that Lotus had honed so successfully in 1978, the Ferraris at least had an engine good enough not only to make Enzo smile as it kept them in the hunt, but for Jody Scheckter to lead home Gilles Villeneuve in a Ferrari one-two.

Then came the wilderness years when British teams Williams and McLaren moved ahead of Ferrari, leaving Enzo decreasingly in control of operations until his death in 1988.

A new dynamic began in 1996 when Michael Schumacher joined the team, and over the next few years he would form another axis with Rory Byrne and Ross Brawn, this time with team principal Jean Todt augmenting its power base. The result was five titles in a row from 2000 to 2004. Since then, Kimi Raikkonen took the title in 2007, Felipe Massa just missed out on being world champion in 2008 and only the arrival of Charles Leclerc and Carlos Sainz Jr in recent years has given the *tifosi* reasons to cheer.

> **"After last year's summer break, we made constant progress and were the only team other than Red Bull Racing to have won a race. We are determined to continue this progress."**
>
> Frederic Vasseur

Michael Schumacher takes the last of his 13 wins in his 2004 title-winning season, his fifth in a row.

CHARLES LECLERC

The Monegasque driver's fifth year with Ferrari was not his best; points went begging as he and the team failed to gel. This, in turn, led to greater pressure to succeed. This year, Charles will need to do better.

Charles failed to win even once in 2023, despite starting from pole position at four races.

Charles is a driver who seemed to glide through the karting and junior single-seater categories without having to make too much effort as his natural speed was plentiful and his race craft strong. Either titles or top rankings fell at Charles's feet in karts, from cadet karts through Euro KF karts and the World KZ karts. Then this pattern repeated itself when he advanced to racing single-seaters in 2014 when he

was 16 and immediately was a frontrunner in Formula Renault, finishing as runner-up in a regional series.

This set Charles up for Formula 3. He won four rounds of the European series, then was runner-up in the end of-season Macau GP.

Then came GP3. Charles followed Esteban Ocon in winning that title, then stepped up to F2 for 2017 and won that one too, his seven wins putting him way clear.

F1 was next and Ferrari eased his graduation by placing Charles with Sauber, to whom it supplied engines. His results, in qualifying in particular, made people look up and pay attention. After peaking with sixth place, Charles was assigned a Ferrari race seat for 2019 and would probably have won on his second outing at Sakhir but for an intermittent engine problem. He would win later in the year, however, at Spa-Francorchamps and Monza to help him to outscore team-mate Sebastian Vettel.

Charles was less competitive in the 2020 season, dropping four places in the rankings to eighth overall as Mercedes

dominated, then the incoming Carlos Sainz Jr settled in well at Ferrari to rank above him in 2021. The 2022 season was better, as Charles won the opening race at Sakhir, the third at Melbourne's Albert Park and then again at the Red Bull Ring midway through the season. These victories helped him to pip Red Bull's second driver Sergio Perez to finish second overall as Max Verstappen cantered towards his second successive F1 title.

TRACK NOTES

Nationality:	**MONEGASQUE**
Born:	**16 OCTOBER 1997,**
	MONTE CARLO, MONACO
Teams:	**SAUBER 2018,**
	FERRARI 2019–24

CAREER RECORD

First Grand Prix: **2018 AUSTRALIAN GP**
Grand Prix starts: **123**
Grand Prix wins: **5**
2019 Belgian GP, Italian GP, 2022 Bahrain GP, Australian GP, Austrian GP
Poles: **23**
Fastest laps: **7**
Points: **1074**
Honours: **2022 F1 RUNNER-UP, 2017 FIA F2 CHAMPION, 2016 GP3 CHAMPION, 2015 MACAU F3 RUNNER-UP, 2014 FORMULA RENAULT ALPS RUNNER-UP, 2013 WORLD KZ KART RUNNER-UP, 2012 UNDER 18 WORLD KART RUNNER-UP & EURO KF KART RUNNER-UP, 2011 ACADEMY TROPHY KART CHAMPION, 2010 JUNIOR MONACO KAT CUP CHAMPION, 2009 FRENCH CADET KART CHAMPION**

LOSING HIS FERRARI PRE-EMINENCE

Having finished the 2022 drivers' championship behind only Red Bull Racing's Max Verstappen and three places ahead of Ferrari team-mate Carlos Sainz Jr, Charles started 2023 with high hopes, especially when Mercedes and Alpine appeared to have lost form. There was promise aplenty in the early-season races, but poor race strategies and mistakes of his own cost him. Taking pole in Azerbaijan was a step forward but both Red Bull drivers usurped him. That third position in Baku was bettered only by second place at the Red Bull Ring, then equalled with another third place from pole in the Belgian GP. But, when Ferrari finally broke Red Bull Racing's winning streak on the streets of Singapore, it was team-mate Sainz Jr who took the plaudits. By this point of the season, the Spaniard had become the apparent team leader, and it was tricky for Charles to regain his position of pre-eminence within the team with further frustration coming when he was disqualified at COTA before grabbing third in Mexico.

CARLOS SAINZ JR

Last year was important for Carlos as he came on strongly during the season. He began to match Charles Leclerc for supremacy at Ferrari before moving past him to become Ferrari's leader, helped by a famous win in Singapore. This year, he will want more.

Carlos seemed to take some steps forward last year to put pressure on his team-mate.

Carlos Sainz fleetingly raced single-seaters, but it was his ability on looser surfaces for which he is known, becoming World Rally Champion in first 1990 then 1992 for the Toyota works team.

Carlos Jr started racing karts as soon as he could and won the Madrid cadet kart title when he was 11, then raced ever more high-performance karts until he was runner-up in the 2009 European KF3

championship. This proved that Carlos Jr was more than ready for the step up to single-seaters; he was a race winner in European Formula BMW in 2010 before landing the Northern European Countries Formula Renault title and finishing second in the Euro series in 2011.

Signed as a Red Bull scholarship driver, Carlos Jr was a race winner in European F3 in 2012 but ranked only fifth and so changed tack to compete in GP3 in 2013. Ranking only tenth in GP3 was a near disaster for his career, putting him at risk of losing his Red Bull backing. However, he showed sufficient pace in a handful of outings in more powerful Formula Renault 3.5 and this was the category to which he devoted himself in 2014 to beat Pierre Gasly to the championship title.

Thus, Carlos Jr earned his F1 break for 2015, with Red Bull placing him in its junior team, then known as Scuderia Toro Rosso. He settled in well and was soon scoring points, with fourth place in Singapore, his best result before Renault took him on late in 2017 as a replacement for Jolyon Palmer.

The next step was joining McLaren for

2019 and he came third at Interlagos. He went one better at Monza in 2020, crossing the finish line just 0.4 seconds behind the AlphaTauri of surprise winner Pierre Gasly.

Signed by Ferrari for 2021, he finished second at Monaco and did well enough to outscore team leader Charles Leclerc. Then in 2022, Carlos Jr landed that first win, at Silverstone. That wasn't enough, though, for Carlos to remain ahead of Leclerc in the rankings.

TRACK NOTES

Nationality:	**SPANISH**
Born:	**1 SEPTEMBER 1994, MADRID, SPAIN**
Teams:	**TORO ROSSO 2015–17, RENAULT 2017–18, McLAREN 2019–20, FERRARI 2021–24**

CAREER RECORD

First Grand Prix: **2015 AUSTRALIAN GP**
Grand Prix starts: **183**
Grand Prix wins: **2**
2022 British GP, 2023 Singapore GP
Poles: **5**
Fastest laps: **3**
Points: **982.5**
Honours: **2014 FORMULA RENAULT 3.5 CHAMPION, 2011 EUROPEAN FORMULA RENAULT RUNNER-UP & NORTHERN EUROPEAN FORMULA RENAULT CHAMPION, 2009 MONACO KART CUP WINNER & EUROPEAN KF3 RUINNER-UP, 2008 ASIA PAC IFIC JUNIOR KART CHAMPION, 2006 MADRID CADET KART CHAMPION**

WIN IN SINGAPORE IS A BIG BOOST

The second win of Carlos's F1 career, in Singapore, was very tight and he had Lando Norris to thank for holding the Mercedes of a charging George Russell at bay. However, it was confirmation that he was now hitting top form, following a dip in confidence after some poor tactical calls in the first half of the season. Always smooth in style, Carlos kept his nerve and appeared to grasp the in-season development of the Ferrari SF23 better than team-mate Charles Leclerc. At Monza, this helped the Spaniard to find the upper hand to qualify on pole, and lead, until caught and passed by the Red Bulls. But he did enough to finish third and claim his first podium of the season. Next time out he was also in superior form at Singapore's Marina Bay circuit and went two better to win. Carlos then followed this by outgunning Leclerc at Suzuka too, this time finishing fourth to open a temporary points lead in their intra-team battle. A non-start in Qatar hurt, but third place in the United States GP boosted his advantage.

// McLAREN

It really was a season of two halves for McLaren last year, but the upswing in competitiveness combined with an excellent driver pairing suggested that this once great team will soon be among the leading group vying to topple Red Bull Racing.

If McLaren can build on the form that Lando Norris (above) and Oscar Piastri enjoyed in the second half of 2023, they could win again.

Bruce McLaren was a remarkable man. Firstly, he didn't let a mobility-limiting disease suffered in childhood hold him back. Instead, he turned his mind to racing and how he could make a simple Austin Seven Ulster go faster, then trying it out at beach races near his native Auckland. Having displayed obvious ability, he headed from New Zealand to Europe in the late 1950s and shone with Cooper, winning the United States GP in 1959 at the age of 22 – the then youngest winner of a round of the World Championship.

After watching former team-mate Jack Brabham start a business building racing cars alongside his racing programme, Bruce decided to do the same, albeit with more of a hands-on approach.

The first McLaren to start a Grand Prix was in 1966, at Monaco, and the basis for what followed was built on the sales success of giant sports cars designed to compete in the lucrative North American Can-Am series; Bruce and team-mate Denny Hulme dominated the Can-Am and thereby encouraged the sale of a great number of customer cars.

Based near Heathrow, the number of McLaren employees was tiny, with all expected to muck in and improvise. Once McLaren had got its hands on the Ford Cosworth DFV in 1968, it finally

KEY PERSONNEL & 2023 ROUND-UP

ROB MARSHALL
Rob worked for Red Bull Racing for 17 years, starting as chief designer under Adrian Newey and rising to be chief engineering officer, but then he was coaxed to take over as McLaren's technical director for 2024. After a spell using his mechanical engineering degree at Rolls-Royce, he began in motor racing with Benetton in 1994, helping the team to make its breakthrough with Michael Schumacher before joining Red Bull in 2006 as the team worked towards its golden spell with Sebastian Vettel from 2010.

CHOPPING, CHANGING AND ADVANCING
The MCL60 was all at sea at the start of the season, but found enough form for both drivers to score in the third round, in Melbourne. However, there were backward steps too and it was frequently hard to predict how they might fare. Fortunately, changes led to the MCL60 finding form for the second half of the season, with notable progress on low-downforce circuits, and this helped Lando Norris and Oscar Piastri to get right into the mix.

2023 DRIVERS & RESULTS

Driver	Nationality	Races	Wins	Pts	Pos
Lando Norris	British	22	0	205	6th
Oscar Piastri	Australian	22	0	97	9th

FOR THE RECORD

Team base:	**Woking, England**
Active in Formula One:	**From 1966**
Grands Prix contested:	**946**
Wins:	**183**
Pole positions:	**156**
Fastest laps:	**164**
Constructors' titles:	**8**
Drivers' titles:	**12**

THE TEAM

Chief executive officer:	**Zak Brown**
Team principal:	**Andrea Stella**
Technical director, engineering & design:	**Rob Marshall**
Technical director, aerodynamics:	**Peter Prodromou**
Technical director, car concept & performance:	**David Sanchez**
Chief operating officer:	**Piers Thynne**
Deputy technical director, engineering & design:	**Neil Houldey**
Director, race engineering:	**Hiroshi Imai**
Director, driver development:	**Emanuele Pirro**
Chassis:	**McLaren MCL61**
Engine:	**Mercedes V6**
Tyres:	**Pirelli**

had a competitive engine and Bruce raced to the marque's first F1 win at Spa-Francorchamps. Sadly, he would die in a crash when testing his latest Can-Am car at Goodwood in 1970. The team still couldn't topple Matra, Lotus, Tyrrell or Ferrari, but it was becoming ever more competitive and the combination of the excellent M23 plus Emerson Fittipaldi yielded a first drivers' title in 1974, with James Hunt winning a scrap with Ferrari's Niki Lauda in 1976 to land a second title.

Ron Dennis took over the team in 1980, and his professional approach combined with TAG Porsche engines and the phenomenal driver pairing of Lauda and Alain Prost led to three titles in a row from 1984 to 1986.

Williams was strong at this time, with Nigel Mansell and Nelson Piquet at the forefront, but they were cowed when Ayrton Senna moved from Lotus to join Prost at McLaren and they won every round bar one in 1988 as the Brazilian took the crown. Keeping with the two best drivers in the two best cars, Prost won the 1989 title, but left for Ferrari as

he found the atmosphere within the team too noxious, leaving Senna to land titles in 1990 and 1991.

Then Williams moved in front, and it took until the end of the decade and the arrival of Mercedes engines for McLaren to shine again. At the start of 1998, no one could hold a candle to the team's pairing of Mika Hakkinen and David Coulthard in their Adrian Newey-designed MP4-13s, and although Michael Schumacher began to take them on in his Ferrari, Hakkinen clinched the crown at Suzuka. The Finn did it again in 1999, albeit having the pressure taken off him when Schumacher broke a leg at the British GP.

All the teams needed to regroup after Michael Schumacher's control of the first five World Championships of the 21st century for Ferrari. McLaren was back on song in 2007 with Fernando Alonso and rookie Lewis Hamilton, but they were pipped at the final round by Ferrari's Kimi Raikkonen, and it took until the end of the following season for Hamilton to give McLaren its most recent world title.

Since then, there have been some uncompetitive years with Honda power and some false dawns, like Daniel Ricciardo beating team-mate Lando Norris to win the Italian GP in 2021, but the feeling now is that the good times might be about to return.

25

> **"I was proud of every single person at McLaren last year. They worked incredibly hard from our challenging start through to being in a position to fight for not only points but podiums."**
>
> Andrea Stella

The ultimate McLaren line-up: boss Ron Dennis with Alain Prost and Ayrton Senna in 1988.

// LANDO NORRIS

Last year was Lando's best season in F1 yet, once the McLaren MCL60 sorted out its early problems. There was added pressure from within, too, as rookie Oscar Piastri began to challenge for supremacy, which would certainly have sharpened Lando's focus.

Lando did everything but win in 2023 and will aim to go one better than his run of seconds.

Lando's rise through the karting ranks owed everything to major financial backing. So, after gathering title after title as he climbed the karting ladder, including the World KF Junior and Senior titles in consecutive years, he stepped up to single-seaters.

The plan was to enter as many races as possible, across multiple championships, to gain extensive experience. So it was that Lando won the MSA Formula title in 2015, at the age of 15, before starting his 2016 season in New Zealand, landing the Toyota Racing Series title as a preparation for a blitz of the European junior single-seater scene. This was a huge success as he claimed the northern European and pan-European Formula Renault titles. He also won the McLaren Autosport BRDC young driver award, earning him a future F1 test.

Clearly a young man in a hurry, Lando powered to the FIA Formula 3 title at the first attempt, then stepped up and came close to repeating this feat in Formula 2 where he was part of a three-way title battle, ending up second to George Russell but ahead of Alex Albon.

McLaren had seen enough and so Lando broke into F1 in 2019, going well enough for a team that wasn't on the top of its form to score a pair of sixth-place finishes.

His second year with McLaren started with a bang, as he made it to the podium at the opening race in Austria by defeating Lewis Hamilton's usually dominant Mercedes on the last lap. It would be his best result all year, but he advanced two championship places to end the season ranked ninth overall, three places behind team-mate Carlos Sainz Jr.

In 2022, now armed with Mercedes engines, Lando peaked with second place at Monza and outscored team-mate Daniel Ricciardo to rank sixth and establish himself as the team leader.

TRACK NOTES

Nationality: **BRITISH**
Born: **13 NOVEMBER 1999,**
GLASTONBURY, ENGLAND
Teams: **McLAREN 2019–24**

CAREER RECORD

First Grand Prix: **2019 Australian GP**
Grand Prix starts: **104**
Grand Prix wins: **0 (best result:**
2nd, 2021 Italian GP, 2023 British GP,
Hungarian GP, Singapore GP, Japanese
GP, United States GP, Sao Paulo GP)
Poles: **1**
Fastest laps: **6**
Points: **633**
Honours: **2018 FIA F2**
RUNNER-UP, 2017 EUROPEAN F3 CHAMPION,
2016 EUROPEAN FORMULA RENAULT
CHAMPION & NORTHERN EUROPE FORMULA
RENAULT CHAMPION & TOYOTA RACING
SERIES CHAMPION & McLAREN AUTOSPORT
BRDC YOUNG DRIVER AWARD, 2015 MSA
FORMULA CHAMPION, 2014 WORLD KF KART
CHAMPION, 2013 WORLD KF JUNIOR KART
CHAMPION & EUROPEAN KF KART CHAMPION
& KF JUNIOR SUPER CUP WINNER

LEARNING FROM A DIFFICULT START

Life in F1 is only comfortable if you have competitive machinery and, last year, Lando most certainly did not. In the early stages of the season, he had to fight the car to get it to go where he wanted, yet he adapted and extracted the maximum. Later in the season, there were tracks that suited the car and tracks that didn't, meaning a real up and down nature to his campaign. Yet, through perseverance from all sides, the MCL60 became less of a handful. Fourth place in Austria heralded better things, and a pair of second places in the next two rounds at Silverstone and the Hungaroring finally gave him reason to smile, as did two more consecutive second-place finishes in Singapore and at Suzuka. Having a team-mate as rapid as rookie Oscar Piastri added another dimension and certainly brought the best out of Lando as he fought to maintain supremacy. By completing his season with more visits to the podium, Lando moved up the order to rival Fernando Alonso and Carlos Sainz Jr.

OSCAR PIASTRI

The Australian rookie showed enough pace in his first year of F1 to suggest that he could become one of the sport's leading players for the next decade. Now, he needs machinery competitive enough to allow him to take a shot at his first GP win.

Oscar proved to be one of the best rookies for years and will keep Lando on his toes again.

Australians love a winner in any sport and for the first time in many decades, they can get excited about a driver of their own who ought not only go on to become a Grand Prix winner to boost their love of motorsport but has the ability to become the nation's first world champion since Alan Jones in 1980 and in so doing outstrip all that Mark Webber achieved.

Oscar's pedigree is little short of phenomenal, not just for the titles it includes but for the fact that he won the championship crown in each of the three levels beneath F1 in consecutive years. No one else has managed to do that before.

Oscar learnt his driving skills in karting and was good enough to rank sixth overall in the FIK World OK Junior series. That was in 2016 and he ended that year, while still 15, by contesting the United Arab Emirates Formula 4 series as his step up to single-seaters.

He then headed to England to race in the British F4 series, ending the season as runner-up. Oscar's next stop was Formula Renault, learning the European circuits with Arden in 2018, then winning seven races for R-ace GP in 2019 to land the title.

After this, one year per category was clearly enough as Oscar stepped up to the FIA Formula 3 series, won the first race he contested and then the title too, albeit only after a final round shoot-out with Theo Pourchaire and Logan Sargeant, showing that he not only had

the speed to come out on top but the mindset too.

His extraordinary title hat-trick was clinched in 2021 when he remained with Prema Racing as he stepped up to Formula 2. He won six races to end up not just as champion but more than 60 points ahead of his closest rival.

Oscar's 2022 season was spent as reserve driver for the Alpine F1 team. Then came negotiations as Alpine wanted him to fill one of its race seats alongside Esteban Ocon for 2023, but Oscar had weighed up his options and elected to join more settled McLaren instead.

TRACK NOTES

Nationality:	**AUSTRALIAN**
Born:	**6 APRIL 2001,**
	MELBOURNE, AUSTRALIA
Teams:	**McLAREN 2023–24**

CAREER RECORD

First Grand Prix:	**2023 BAHRAIN GP**
Grand Prix starts:	**22**
Grand Prix wins:	**0 (best result: 2nd,**
	2023 Qatar GP)
Poles:	**0**
Fastest laps:	**2**
Points:	**97**
Honours:	**2021 FIA F2**
CHAMPION, 2020 FIA F3 CHAMPION, 2019 EUROPEAN FORMULA RENAULT CHAMPION, 2017 BRITISH FORMULA 4 RUNNER-UP	

IMPRESSING IN HIS ROOKIE SEASON

It came as no surprise that Oscar impressed in his first year of F1, as his track record on his ascent through the single-seater categories was sensational. The 22-year-old Australian not only managed to tackle the initially wayward McLaren MCL60 but was soon really pushing team leader Lando Norris on a regular basis. Results were slow to come by at first, but there was a rare moment of hope when both drivers scored in the third round in his home city of Melbourne. That eighth-place finish was followed by tenth in Monaco. However, it was the mid-season upgrade package that gave Oscar hope, and he responded by finishing fourth at Silverstone then fifth at the Hungaroring. Better was to follow when Oscar qualified slower only than the dominant world champion Max Verstappen's Red Bull at Suzuka, a circuit on which he had never raced before, and he went on to harry Norris before settling for third place. The very next race, in Qatar, Oscar did better still and finished second.

Oscar Piastri puts his McLaren MCL60 through its paces at the Hungarian Grand Prix, finishing fifth.

ASTON MARTIN

Last year was a major step forward for this team based at Silverstone, with Fernando Alonso gathering podium finishes for fun to help drive it towards fourth place in the rankings. Repeating this feat will be a major task in 2024.

Aston Martin will be looking to build on the form that made it competitive in the first half of 2023 and keep it going all season this time.

Aston Martin's ambitions in the 1950s, beyond selling as many of its sports cars as possible, were centred on the prestige that it would gain if it could win the Le Mans 24 Hours. It was a hard nut to crack, but it was finally achieved in 1959.

Aston Martin also widened its focus that same year to take in F1. However, its DBR4 design was already on the verge of being outmoded, as its engine was under its lengthy snout rather than tucked behind the driver's shoulders as was becoming the accepted practice. Roy Salvadori was able to finish second in the non-championship International Trophy at Silverstone and then sixth on a couple of occasions in World Championship rounds, but it was clear that Aston Martin had no long-term F1 plans and it withdrew midway through 1960.

Decades later, after his racing career was petering out, Eddie Jordan turned to running his own team, first in F3 and then in F3000. He was successful in that and

guided Jean Alesi to the crown in 1989. Jordan has never been a man to stand still, though, and he not only stepped up to F1 in 1991 but did so with a beautiful

and very effective chassis designed by Gary Anderson, a car good enough for Jordan to rank fifth. The current Aston Martin team stems from Jordan.

KEY PERSONNEL & 2023 ROUND-UP

DAN FALLOWS

The team's technical director joined Jaguar Racing as an aerodynamicist 22 years ago, but shifted across to work for chassis builder Dallara when parent company Ford pulled the plug on its involvement at the end of 2004. After the team turned into Red Bull Racing, Dan returned and remained with the team until June 2021, rising through the ranks through Sebastian Vettel's four title-winning seasons to become the team's head of aerodynamics. Then his most recent move brought him to Aston Martin F1.

GETTING UP AMONG THE BIG NAMES

Aston Martin's first foray into F1 in 1959 and 1960 didn't amount to much and neither did the return of Aston Martin green in 2021 or 2022, but last season was different as Fernando Alonso joined the driving line-up and stormed to third, first time out. Then he did it again and again, racing to six top-three results in the first eight rounds. Life became harder after that, and team-mate Lance Stroll could never match his pace, but the team had its best run for years and enjoyed it.

2023 DRIVERS & RESULTS

Driver	Nationality	Races	Wins	Pts	Pos
Fernando Alonso	Spanish	22	0	206	4th
Lance Stroll	Canadian	21	0	74	10th

FOR THE RECORD

Team base: **Silverstone, England**

Active in Formula One: **As Jordan 1991–2005, Midland 2006, Spyker 2006–07, Force India 2008–18, Racing Point 2019–20, Aston Martin 2021 onwards**

Grands Prix contested: **601**

Wins: **5**

Pole positions: **4**

Fastest laps: **8**

Constructors' titles: **0**

Drivers' titles: **0**

THE TEAM

Chief executive officer: **Martin Whitmarsh**

Team principal: **Mike Krack**

Chief technical officer: **Andrew Green**

Technical director: **Dan Fallows**

Sporting director: **Andy Stevenson**

Engineering director: **Luca Furbatto**

Head of trackside engineering: **Bradley Joyce**

Chief operating officer: **Bob Halliwell**

Chief designer: **Akio Haga**

Performance director: **Tom McCullough**

Operations director: **Mark White**

Chassis: **Aston Martin AMR24**

Engine: **Mercedes V6**

Tyres: **Pirelli**

First seasons are often a lot easier than second ones at the sport's top level, as the focus is on the immediate situation and not on what is required for the next campaign. Yet, the team matured and Rubens Barrichello and Eddie Irvine raced to second and third in the 1995 Canadian GP to really put down a marker.

Changing to Mugen Honda engines was a step up from previous Peugeot power and finally the team got its breakthrough win, at a wet Belgian GP in which not only did Damon Hill win but team-mate Ralf Schumacher finished second. Life got better still the next year, with Jordan ranking a career-best third overall behind Ferrari and McLaren thanks to two wins by Heinz-Harald Frentzen.

To be at the front of the grid in F1 was becoming ever more expensive and a run of name changes followed as more investment was sought to keep the team competitive; it was known as Midland in 2005, Spyker in 2007 and then Force India in 2008. Jordan had headed off to enjoy the spoils of creating an F1 team, with wealthy Indian Vijay Mallya becoming the man at the helm. The next decade was one of mixed fortunes, with a run of good drivers dragging results out of the cars under the pressure of increasing discontent within the team. The staff were loyal, but financial difficulties as the Indian tax authorities pursued Mallya wore them down and so it was a relief for all when a takeover deal was announced in August 2018.

Canadian tycoon Lawrence Stroll took over, named the team as Racing Point – which is how it ran for 2019 and 2020 – and placed his son Lance as one of the drivers, but it was always felt that he was seeking to strike a manufacturing deal. Finally, an agreement was put in place, as the cars were painted metallic mid-green and emerged badged as Aston Martin for the 2021 season.

Four-time world champion Sebastian Vettel joined Lance Stroll, not just to show the way but to mentor the young Canadian. A second-place finish for Vettel in Azerbaijan suggested things might come good, but that was a highpoint as the team ended the year seventh overall, three places lower than it had managed in 2020. Things failed to improve in 2022 when Aston Martin F1 ranked seventh again, as it failed to get to grips with new technical regulations.

Rubens Barrichello and Eddie Irvine on a big day for Jordan as they celebrate on the podium in Canada 1995.

"We cannot influence what other competitors are doing. The only thing that we have in our hands is to do the best possible and be at 100% at all times."

Mike Krack

FERNANDO ALONSO

This double world champion was back in fashion last year as his arrival at Aston Martin coincided with the introduction of a more competitive car. He showed that there is life for a driver aged over 40 as he grabbed podium finishes by the handful.

Fernando revelled in racing at the front again and will want to do the same in 2024.

This driver, who made his debut in F1 before some of his rivals were born, was always earmarked for greatness. National, international and world karting titles were garnered and he won the Formula Nissan title in his first year in single-seaters.

In 2000 Fernando then moved directly to the sport's second level, Formula 3000. This much more powerful category was mastered with ease and the way that he took his first win at Spa-Francorchamps when he blitzed the field still stands out.

Benetton's talent scouts already had his name on a contract and placed him at Minardi for his entry to F1. With no race seat available at newly rebranded Renault, his 2002 season was spent as the team's test driver before it gave him a ride for 2003. Fernando rewarded them with victory in Hungary. In his third season, he won seven times and took the title, then added the 2006 crown too.

A move to McLaren could have made it three titles in a row, but he and team-mate Lewis Hamilton were pipped by Ferrari's Kimi Raikkonen before Fernando returned to Renault for a less happy spell.

Joining Ferrari in 2010 gave him another title shot, but he was pipped again, this time by Red Bull Racing's Sebastian Vettel. The most recent of his wins came in Spain in 2013. If Fernando's second spell at Renault was less successful than his first, then so it proved again when he returned to McLaren, its Honda engines weak. Eventually, he went back to the team from Enstone, now racing as Alpine, for a third spell, before joining Aston Martin last year to add his experience to their attack.

TRACK NOTES

Nationality: **SPANISH**
Born: **29 JULY 1981, OVIEDO, SPAIN**
Teams: **MINARDI 2001, RENAULT 2003–06, McLAREN 2007, RENAULT 2008–09, FERRARI 2010–14, McLAREN 2015–18, ALPINE 2021–22, ASTON MARTIN 2023–24**

CAREER RECORD

First Grand Prix: **2001 AUSTRALIAN GP**
Grand Prix starts: **377**
Grand Prix wins: **32**
2003 Hungarian GP, 2005 Malaysian GP, Bahrain GP, San Marino GP, European GP, French GP, German GP, Chinese GP, 2006 Bahrain GP, Australian GP, Spanish GP, Monaco GP, British GP, Canadian GP, Japanese GP, 2007 Malaysian GP, Monaco GP, European GP, Italian GP, 2008 Singapore GP, Japanese GP, 2010 Bahrain GP, German GP, Italian GP, Singapore GP, Korean GP, 2011 British GP, 2012 Malaysian GP, European GP, German GP, 2013 Chinese GP, Spanish GP
Poles: **22**
Fastest laps: **24**
Points: **2267**
Honours: **2019 DAYTONA 24 HOURS WINNER, 2018/19 WORLD ENDURANCE CHAMPION, 2018 & 2019 LE MANS 24 HOURS WINNER, 2005 & 2006 F1 WORLD CHAMPION, 2010, 2012 & 2013 F1 RUNNER-UP, 1999 FORMULA NISSAN CHAMPION, 1997 ITALIAN & SPANISH KART CHAMPION, 1996 WORLD & SPANISH KART CHAMPION, 1994 & 1995 SPANISH JUNIOR KART CHAMPION**

FERNANDO ISN'T FINISHED YET

Fernando finished third behind the two Red Bulls in the opening round at Sakhir. This was his first visit to a podium since his third place at the 2021 Qatar GP and only his second podium visit since 2014. It was clearly no fluke result, as the Spanish veteran then achieved five more podium finishes in his next seven outings, including a season's best of second place at Monaco. This was repeated two races later in Canada. There was a slight drop in performance as the season approached its summer break, with the AMR23 seemingly not gaining from in-season development as much as rival entries, but Fernando then slotted in second place and fastest lap at the Dutch GP to stay in the mix. A worse slump for Aston Martin then followed, with the races at Monza, Marina Bay, Suzuka and Losail not offering even a sniff of a podium result. Worse came with a pair of retirements before he bounced back to be third in Brazil.

LANCE STROLL

This Canadian driver started last season strongly as Aston Martin had a competitive car, but he couldn't get close to team-mate Fernando Alonso and his form fell away through his seventh year in F1. He needs a big season to get his mojo back.

Lance will be looking to become more consistent to relieve the pressure he felt in 2023.

Lance took the traditional route taken by almost all racing drivers in the 21st century by going karting as soon as he was old enough to participate. With his father Lawrence busy at weekends racing in the North American Ferrari championship, there was racing at every turn.

Lance advanced through the kart ranks, peaking with sixth place in the World KF series at the age of 14 and stepped up into single-seaters when he graduated to the Ferrari-backed Florida Winter Series. He followed this by entering the Italian F4 Championship in 2014, starting with a bang by winning the title. As 2014 became 2015, he went down to New Zealand and won the Toyota Racing Series crown.

This meant that he had a good deal of racing mileage under his belt when he stepped up to F3 for 2015. Running in the European championship, he placed fifth, but his season had been peppered with the sort of accidents that only those with a billionaire father could afford. So, it was a wise move to have a second year in F3 and Lance had a great season, allying his clear pace with a more mature approach. The result was 14 wins and the title.

So, with a budget to help ease his way into F1, and no desire to risk this career momentum by competing in F2, Lance lined up for the 2017 Australian GP in a Williams. He then collected a surprise third-place finish in Baku in a race of incident interrupted by a red flag stoppage. But Williams was a team in decline, so Lance moved on to Racing Point for 2019, as the Silverstone team was renamed after evolving from Force India.

Learning from experienced team-mate Sergio Perez, Lance collected a couple of third-place finishes in 2020, in the Italian and Sakhir GPs, then he continued learning from four-time world champion Sebastian Vettel in 2021, by which time the team had been renamed again, this time to Aston Martin as his father assumed control of the sports car manufacturer. With seven years of tutelage, the F1 world waited to see if Lance could finally deliver.

TRACK NOTES

Nationality:	**CANADIAN**
Born:	**29 OCTOBER 1998,**
	MONTREAL, CANADA
Teams:	**WILLIAMS**
	2017–18, RACING POINT 2019–20,
	ASTON MARTIN 2021–24

CAREER RECORD

First Grand Prix:	**2017 AUSTRALIAN GP**
Grand Prix starts:	143
Grand Prix wins:	0 (best result: 3rd,
	2017
Azerbaijan GP, 2020 Italian GP, Sakhir GP)	
Poles:	1
Fastest laps:	0
Points:	268
Honours:	**2016 EUROPEAN**
F3 CHAMPION, 2015 TOYOTA RACING SERIES	
CHAMPION, 2014 ITALIAN F4 CHAMPION	

NOT UP TO SUFFICIENT PACE

It had been thought that Lance would miss the start of last season, after breaking a hand, but he was able to make the race at Sakhir, only to infuriate the Aston Martin team by clipping team-mate Fernando Alonso on the first lap before racing on to finish sixth. A fourth place two rounds later, in Melbourne, helped by the Alpine drivers clashing, was to be the highpoint of his season. However, Lance was almost invariably too far from Alonso's pace and so wasted the first half of the year when the Aston Martin AMR23 was at its most competitive. For a driver with more than 120 Grands Prix to his name at the start of the season, more could have been expected of Lance, and there were rumours that his focus was swaying towards playing tennis instead. Then Lance suffered a setback when he had to miss the Singapore GP after suffering an accident in qualifying and he was clearly frustrated through the remainder of the season, even taking it out on one of his team members before going on to take fifth in Brazil.

ALPINE

Alpine was not a happy place to be last year with key management departures and boardroom unrest, and the team is going to need to show strong leadership to get the stability required to provide Esteban Ocon and Pierre Gasly with the machinery to move forward.

Esteban Ocon raced to third at Monaco last year, but he and team-mate Pierre Gasly should be more encouraged by late-season form.

The step up from winning in F2 to joining the F1 circus used to be a simple one back in the 1980s. This is what the Toleman team did in 1981, albeit without much initial success. Indeed, with a large number of F1 entries then, it was usually a struggle even to qualify, and drivers Brian Henton and Derek Warwick managed it just once each. Yet, with Rory Byrne working wonders on the cars' design, the team had a frontrunner when Ayrton Senna made his F1 debut in 1984, even coming close to victory at Monaco. This team has since been renamed five times, in the following order: Benetton, Renault, Lotus (but with no connection to the original Lotus), Renault again and then as Alpine.

Extra impetus was provided when Benetton money bought naming rights in 1986. Harnessing the explosive horsepower from BMW's turbocharged engines led to some spectacular runs in qualifying, and then to the team's first victory in the season's penultimate round

in Mexico when Gerhard Berger was able to run non-stop on his Pirelli tyres while those on Goodyears needed to pit.

The team then stabilised as a good midfield outfit that would land occasional wins for Nelson Piquet and Alessandro Nannini. It ranked third in both 1988 and 1990.

KEY PERSONNEL & 2023 ROUND-UP

BRUNO FAMIN

This French engine specialist joined Peugeot in 1989 and moved to motorsport in 2005 when he was made Peugeot Sport's technical director, becoming involved with its Le Mans, Pikes Peak, Dakar Rally and rallycross programmes. Moving to the sport's governing body in 2019, Bruno became FIA director of operations. He came to F1 in 2023 as director of Alpine's power unit project, then was promoted to the post of acting team principal after Otmar Szafnauer departed last July as well as being made vice-president of Alpine Motorsports.

A SEASON OF INTERNAL UNREST

It had been feared that the pairing of long-time adversaries Pierre Gasly and Esteban Ocon would result in fireworks as they fought for supremacy. However, the fireworks came instead from the team management. First CEO Laurent Rossi criticised the drivers and then moved elsewhere within the Alpine group and both team principal Otmar Szafnauer and long-standing sporting director Alan Permane were shown the door. A third place apiece was unexpected.

2023 DRIVERS & RESULTS

Driver	Nationality	Races	Wins	Pts	Pos
Pierre Gasly	French	22	0	62	11th
Esteban Ocon	French	22	0	58	12th

FOR THE RECORD

Team base:	**Enstone, England**
Active in Formula One:	**As Toleman 1981–85, Benetton 1986–2001, Renault 2002–11 & 2016–2020, Lotus 2012–15, Alpine 2021 on**
Grands Prix contested:	**737**
Wins:	**50**
Pole positions:	**36**
Fastest laps:	**56**
Constructors' titles:	**3**
Drivers' titles:	**4**

THE TEAM

Chief executive officer:	**Philippe Krief**
Alpine Motorsports Vice President:	**Bruno Famin**
Technical director:	**Matt Harman**
Chief aerodynamicist:	**Dirk de Beer**
Interim sporting director:	**Julian Rouse**
Operations director:	**Rob White**
Head of trackside engineering:	**Ciaron Pilbeam**
Team manager:	**Paul Seaby**
Chassis:	**Renault A524**
Engine:	**Renault V6**
Tyres:	**Pirelli**

However, the arrival of Michael Schumacher took Benetton on to another level as he became a winner in 1992 when the team was third in the rankings again, then rattled off a pair of drivers' titles in 1994 and, without resorting to driving into Damon Hill, in 1995. It was very much a one-man team back then, with the likes of Jos Verstappen and Johnny Herbert suffering in his shadow, unable to break into the Schumacher–Byrne–Ross Brawn axis.

Then Schumacher left for Ferrari and Benetton fell back.

Acquired by and renamed Renault for 2002, it continued in the same vein, until being dragged back towards the front by rising star Fernando Alonso. The Spaniard did as Schumacher before him by first taking his breakthrough win and then bagging a pair of titles, in 2005 and 2006, with Giancarlo Fisichella, on his return to the team, winning a race each year to rank fifth and fourth.

The rise of Red Bull Racing pushed it back down the order and, bizarrely, it was then renamed for a second time

as a former F1 team with which it had no connection. This time, it became known as Lotus from 2012 until 2015 when it reverted to Renault again. Kimi Raikkonen returned from a spell away from F1 and gave it a win apiece in 2012 and 2013.

Tired of that name, the team from Enstone had a second spell racing as Renault from 2016, watching on as Mercedes dominated. Then it was rebadged to become Alpine from 2021 in deference to Renault's boutique sporting arm. There was a desire not only to boost the image of Alpine as it pushes its range of sports cars but also to make the team seem more French, even though it continued to be based in England. This coincided with some near instant success as Esteban Ocon won the Hungarian GP, but neither he nor Alonso, in his third spell with the team, could do anything about the pace of the Red Bulls and the team ended up ranked only fifth.

Alpine was more competitive in 2022 and moved ahead of McLaren to rank fourth, but Alonso and Ocon were

strangers to the podium and Alonso was lured away to join Aston Martin. Then Alpine's management fumbled its negotiations to promote rising star Oscar Piastri from its reserve driver role and he headed off to a race seat at McLaren. Inadvertently, this meant that Alpine got an all-French driver line-up as it brought in Pierre Gasly to join Ocon.

"My main concern is to work with Esteban, to make sure that we extract the maximum of the car, maximum out of the team and are both pushing in the same direction."

Pierre Gasly

Alpine started as Toleman in 1981, with Ayrton Senna coming second for the team at Monaco in 1984.

PIERRE GASLY

There were concerns that becoming team-mate with lifelong rival Esteban Ocon would prove a disaster, but both got on with the task of trying to propel their underpowered Alpines into the points wherever possible. Expect more of the same in their second year racing together.

Pierre defied expectations to settle into a working relationship with team-mate Esteban.

Pierre was always someone who stood out, whether that was when he started in karting, stepped up to racing single-seaters or raced to the GP2 title. He was clearly destined for F1, boosting his credentials with each further season. That said, the door to F1 doesn't open for everyone and it seemed for a time that Pierre might be one of those deserving drivers who miss out and don't have the financial backing to ensure that they get a ride.

The titles started flowing in karts and he stepped up to single-seaters to race in French F4 after he had been runner-up in the European KF3 series. Immediately a frontrunner, Pierre then spent two years in European Formula Renault, landing the title in 2013, two places ahead of his former karting rival Esteban Ocon.

Backing was essential to progress further, so it was a career-saver to become part of the Red Bull driver search programme. This helped him to step up into Formula Renault 3.5 for 2014 and he pushed champion Carlos Sainz Jr hard.

Two years were then spent in GP2, and Pierre landed the 2016 title with Prema Racing, finishing just ahead of Antonio Giovinazzi.

With no rides available in F1, Pierre was sent by Red Bull to contest the Super Formula series in Japan. This is where he really stood out, by winning a couple of races on circuits that he had never seen before to end the year ranked second. By then, though, he had made his F1 debut, with Scuderia Toro Rosso offering him a ride for five of the final six Grands Prix after it dropped Daniil Kvyat.

This led to a full-time ride in 2018, with a fourth place in Bahrain earning him promotion to Red Bull Racing the following year, but he couldn't match Max Verstappen and so was pushed back down to Toro Rosso to give Alexander Albon the ride.

For 2020, Toro Rosso was rebranded as AlphaTauri and Pierre had his day of days when he was victorious at the Italian GP, just as Sebastian Vettel had done when the team was Toro Rosso.

TRACK NOTES

Nationality: **FRENCH**
Born: **7 FEBRUARY 1996, ROUEN, FRANCE**
Teams: **TORO ROSSO 2017–18 & 2019, RED BULL RACING 2019, ALPHATAURI 2020–22, ALPINE 2023–24**

CAREER RECORD

First Grand Prix:	**2017 MALAYSIAN GP**
Grand Prix starts:	**130**
Grand Prix wins:	**1**
	2020 Italian GP
Poles:	**0**
Fastest laps:	**3**
Points:	**394**
Honours:	**2017 JAPANESE SUPER FORMULA RUNNER-UP, 2016 GP2 CHAMPION, 2014 FORMULA RENAULT 3.5 RUNNER-UP, 2013 EUROPEAN FORMULA RENAULT CHAMPION, 2010 EUROPEAN KF3 KART RUNNER-UP**

LOCKED IN AN INTERNAL BATTLE

The all-French driving line-up at Alpine was always going to provide a sideshow to Red Bull Racing's domination, with Pierre and quick compatriot Esteban Ocon both gritting their teeth as they attempted to achieve driver supremacy. They were close in terms of pace and results in the early races of the season and then Ocon finished third at Monaco, heaping extra pressure – in an already pressured environment – on to Pierre. Fortunately, he too claimed a third-place finish, much to his relief, in the Dutch GP at Zandvoort. A sixth place in the Singapore GP also put a smile on his face as he continued to focus on making sure that he scored more points than his team-mate. When Pierre followed this up two races later with a run to the six points for seventh place in the Sao Paulo GP at Interlagos, a race in which Ocon made a few errors, Pierre could finally feel that he had bragging rights within the team.

ESTEBAN OCON

Finishing on the podium at Monaco was a huge fillip for Esteban, but the lack of grunt from Alpine's Renault engines hurt him at circuits where horsepower was more important, and it left him aiming solely trying to outscore team-mate Gasly. Both deserve more in 2024.

Esteban will be looking to add more podium finishes to his tally with Alpine in 2024.

It wasn't a rarity in the 1960s for a driver to reach F1 having raced touring cars, yet Esteban is the only one of the current crop of 20 to have done so.

Initially, his career followed the now classic path of the various levels of karts through his teenage years, usually going head-to-head with Pierre Gasly, a rising star who was not just French but also from Normandy. Then came single-seaters, starting with Formula Renault and Esteban came third in the 2013 European championship, when Gasly took the title.

Stepping up to Formula 3 in 2014, Esteban really shifted up a gear and powered his way, not just to nine wins for the crack Prema Powerteam, but to the title at his first attempt as well – a feat that even Lewis Hamilton hadn't been able to achieve on his way to the top.

Like Valtteri Bottas before him, Esteban had to opt next for GP3 rather than F1's immediate feeder formula, GP2. And, like the Finn, Esteban grabbed the title. Mercedes liked what it saw and looked to find a way to put Esteban into F1 but, with no seats available, turned him into a touring car racer instead, entering him in the largely German-based DTM.

This would have felt like a backward step, but when Rio Haryanto was dropped midway through the season, Esteban was placed in the vacant seat at Mercedes-powered Manor and did enough for Force India to sign him for 2017.

His first full season in F1 was a good one, as he finished only a few points down on experienced team leader Sergio Perez in eighth overall, peaking with two fifth places.

Dropped for 2019 to make way for Lance Stroll, Esteban made his return to F1 with Renault in 2020 and enjoyed his first podium visit after finishing second behind Perez in the penultimate race of the year at Sakhir, but trailed team-mate Daniel Ricciardo across the season. For 2021, as Ricciardo moved on, Alonso arrived and the team was rebadged as Alpine, Esteban took his first win at the 2021 Hungarian Grand Prix.

A PODIUM LIGHTS UP A TRICKY YEAR

Esteban's third year with Alpine was his first without being team-mate to the evergreen Fernando Alonso. The dynamic changed as he was no longer trying to outstrip a double world champion but, instead, a driver he'd been racing against for pretty much all his career: Pierre Gasly. Their battle for superiority was always going to be worth watching and Esteban pulled ahead by racing to third place at Monaco, along with four other points-paying drives in the first eight rounds. Frustratingly for both drivers, the Alpine A523 wasn't getting enough horsepower from its Renault V6, and they struggled to get an otherwise decent car into the points as often as they would have liked. In the second half of the year, Gasly moved ahead as a run of retirements held Esteban back. The hardest thing to tell was just how well Esteban Ocon was getting on through the course of the 2023 season, having lost that most invaluable yardstick of Fernando Alonso, a driver that few can outshine, but his frustration grew as Gasly moved ahead.

TRACK NOTES

Nationality:	**FRENCH**
Born:	**17 SEPTEMBER 1996,**
	EVREUX, FRANCE
Teams:	**MANOR 2016,**
	FORCE INDIA 2017–18, RENAULT
	2020, ALPINE 2021–24

CAREER RECORD

First Grand Prix:	**2016 BELGIAN GP**
Grand Prix starts:	**133**
Grand Prix wins:	**1**
	2021 Hungarian GP
Poles:	**0**
Fastest laps:	**0**
Points:	**422**
Honours:	**2015 GP3 CHAMPION,**
	2014 FIA EUROPEAN F3 CHAMPION

// WILLIAMS

There were flashes of high-level performance last year as Alexander Albon achieved the occasional points-scoring drive and Williams moved forwards three places in the constructors' championship, but much rests on the bolstering of the team's technical side with Pat Fry as its new leader.

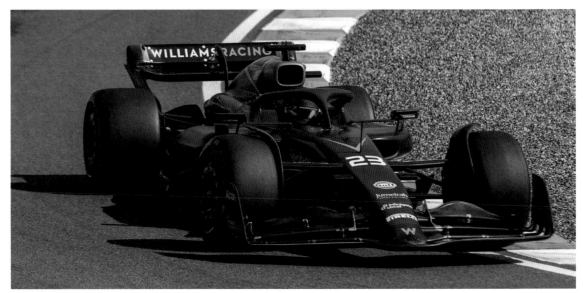

Williams advanced from 10th in 2022 to seventh last year and it will be down to Alex Albon to lead the team's attack for a third season.

Williams' road to becoming one of the most successful teams in F1 history was not an easy one. Indeed, Frank Williams' early attempts were largely derided. He was held back by a lack of budget and, excepting his time running a Brabham for Piers Courage in 1969 with second places in Monaco and at Watkins Glen, a lack of results. Yet, if ever sheer grit was rewarded, then this was the shining example.

Frank raced in F3, but the struggle to fund it was immense and he soon realised that his way to stay in motor racing was to run cars for others. Running Courage showed that he could do it, but Courage's death in the 1970 Dutch GP knocked Frank back and meagre funds meant that success was always going to be limited. Jacques Laffite at least finished second in the 1975 German GP, but this was soon followed by a tricky relationship with oil tycoon Walter Wolf in 1976.

Fortunately, Frank decided to do things differently in 1977 and teamed up with designer Patrick Head to form Williams Grand Prix Engineering. At last, progress appeared tangible, with Alan Jones taking second place in the US GP at the end of 1978.

The breakthrough came in the 1979

KEY PERSONNEL & 2023 ROUND-UP

PAT FRY

Having made his first steps in F1 with McLaren in 1987, as a race engineer, Williams' new chief technical officer ascended the ranks as the team enjoyed its heyday through the 1990s, helping Mika Hakkinen to his two titles. After 17 years with McLaren, Pat joined Ferrari as assistant technical director and rose to become director of engineering. A spell as a consultant at Manor was followed by a return to McLaren and then a move to Alpine in 2020 as chief technical officer.

THE FIRST APPARENT STEPS OF REVIVAL

At first, it was a shock when Alexander Albon showed well in practice or qualifying, but Williams' clear advances through the course of last year meant that it almost became expected. His ability to stretch the FW45's tyre life through the duration of the Grand Prix, in the second half of the year in particular, was a notable talking point outside of Red Bull's continued dominance. Rookie team-mate Logan Sargeant couldn't match Albon's skills.

2023 DRIVERS & RESULTS

Driver	Nationality	Races	Wins	Pts	Pos
Alex Albon	British/Thai	22	0	27	13th
Logan Sargeant	American	22	0	1	21st

FOR THE RECORD

Team base:	**Grove, England**
Active in Formula One:	**From 1971**
Grands Prix contested:	**815**
Wins:	**114**
Pole positions:	**128**
Fastest laps:	**133**
Constructors' titles:	**9**
Drivers' titles:	**7**

THE TEAM

Chairman:	**Matthew Savage**
Team principal:	**James Vowles**
Chief technical officer	**Pat Fry**
Chief operating officer:	**Frederic Brousseau**
Sporting director:	**Sven Smeets**
Chief aerodynamicist:	**Adam Kenyon**
Design director:	**Dave Worner**
Head of design:	**Jonathan Carter**
Head of vehicle performance:	**Dave Robson**
Team manager:	**David Redding**
Chassis	**Williams FW46**
Engine:	**Mercedes V6**
Tyres:	**Pirelli**

British GP at Silverstone. It had looked to be going to Jones, but a water pump failed and second driver Clay Regazzoni took Williams' first victory instead. Jones then won four races in the second half of the season and then won five times in 1980 to take the title, with Frank finally getting the accolades as Williams won the constructors' crown. The feat was repeated in 1981, with a second constructors' crown, but Carlos Reutemann faded at the Las Vegas finale and lost the drivers' title to Brabham's Nelson Piquet.

Keke Rosberg came out on top for Williams in 1982, but this time there was no constructors' title. That had to wait until 1986, a year in which a blow-out in the Adelaide finale cost Nigel Mansell the title. At least Piquet, with Williams in 1987, was able to land the drivers' crown and the Williams–Honda package continued to shine.

After the loss of Honda engines, it took until 1992 for Williams to prosper again when the combination of Nigel Mansell, Renault V10 engines and the amazing Adrian Newey-designed FW14B put its cars way out front.

Williams never liked its drivers to feel too comfortable, so Mansell was encouraged to make way for Alain Prost who was coaxed back from an F1 sabbatical, and he was the team's next champion. Then, for 1994, Williams got the man who had eluded the team when he stepped up to F1 in 1984: Ayrton Senna. Cruelly, he was killed at the third round, at Imola. Damon Hill kept the team focused, only to be denied the title by some unsportsmanlike driving from Benetton's Michael Schumacher in the final round.

In 1996, though, Hill got the job done, a feat repeated for Williams by Jacques Villeneuve in 1997. Then their fortunes wavered, as Newey had left for McLaren and it took a BMW engine deal to make Williams strong again, with both Juan Pablo Montoya and Ralf Schumacher becoming winners between 2001 and 2004. As other teams took turns to hit new heights, Williams began a gradual decline because its budget lagged behind. Then,

with Frank's health becoming less robust, daughter Claire took over until the team was finally sold during 2020.

Personnel changes since then show a renewing of the team's focus, with James Vowles coming in as team principal after Jost Capito's departure and then Pat Fry being signed from Alpine to take over as chief technical officer.

> **"It was fantastic to have (incoming chief technical officer) Pat Fry onboard with us at the Brazilian GP, seeing how the FW45 could be developed for this year's car."**
>
> James Vowles

Team chiefs Patrick Head and Frank Williams had their first title-winning year with Alan Jones in 1980.

// ALEX ALBON

If a top driver never drives uncompetitive machinery, they never get to show their true worth. The flip side is that Alex really needs a go with a top team, as he has shown that he is better than the cars that he has driven.

Alex continues to work wonders by making his tyres last, but deserves a competitive car.

After growing up around racing circuits when his father Nigel raced in the British Touring Car Championship and then in Asian Ferrari and Porsche series, it came as little surprise when Alex started in kart racing as soon as he was able. He was good, too, becoming European KF3 champion in 2010 and then runner-up in the World KF1 series the following year when he was 15.

Alex picked up Red Bull backing for his graduation to single-seater racing, which was no surprise because of his clear pace but also because his mother, Kankamol, is Thai, the same nationality as the co-founder of the energy drinks company.

Starting in Formula Renault in 2012, Alex didn't perform as expected and lost the Red Bull backing at the end of 2013. Fortunately, he made great progress in 2014 and, coming third, then showed decent speed in the following year's European F3 series. His next step was into GP3, and Alex won four races to end the year as runner-up to Charles Leclerc.

Formula 2 was next, and this turned into a two-year programme, advancing from 10th in the first year to third in the second – good enough for Red Bull to show renewed interest in its former scholar and place him with Scuderia Toro Rosso for his F1 debut in 2019.

Suddenly, Alex's career had momentum and he did so well early in the season that he, like Max Verstappen before him, was promoted midway through the campaign to Red Bull Racing, with Pierre Gasly being made to swap drives with him. The result

was a run of top-six finishes in eight of the remaining nine rounds.

In 2020, Alex reached the podium for the first time, for third at Mugello, then added another at Sakhir. However, he scored fewer than half of Verstappen's points and was dropped.

After spending 2021 racing a Ferrari 488 GT3, he got back into F1 with Williams in 2022. It was F1's tail-end team but he impressed with three point-scoring drives, each time displaying an incredible ability at preserving tyre life to help him stay with faster rivals.

TRACK NOTES

Nationality:	**BRITISH/THAI**
Born:	**23 MARCH 1996,**
	LONDON, ENGLAND
Teams:	**TORO ROSSO 2019, RED BULL**
	RACING 2019–2020,
	WILLIAMS 2022–24

CAREER RECORD

First Grand Prix:	**2019 AUSTRALIAN GP**
Grand Prix starts:	**81**
Grand Prix wins:	**0 (best result: 3rd,**
	2020 Tuscan GP & Bahrain GP)
Poles:	**0**
Fastest laps:	**0**
Points:	**228**
Honours:	**2016 GP3 RUNNER-UP,**
	2011 WORLD KF1 KART RUNNER-UP, 2010
	EUROPEAN KF3 KART CHAMPION, 2009
	SUPER 1 HONDA KART CHAMPION

THE TYRE-WHISPERER RACES ON

One of the sideshows last year, as Max Verstappen raced to yet another title, was to see how his former Red Bull Racing team-mate was managing to keep his Williams ahead of more competitive machinery. The Mercedes-powered FW45 was good on the straights but no match for the cars from F1's top teams in other aspects, and yet Alex was able to stay in the mix and challenge for points increasingly through the second half of the season. He did this by extracting the last metre of distance out of his rubber, sometimes turning a race that would be a two-stopper for most into a one-stopper to give himself a shot at a top 10 finish. After starting his campaign with 10th at Sakhir, Alex mastered mixed conditions to qualify well in Montreal and race to seventh. However, what became increasingly obvious was that he boosted his chances by qualifying well and then accrued more points in the races because of his gifts as a tyre-whisperer.

LOGAN SARGEANT

In what was a tricky rookie season in the World Championship, Logan made costly mistakes, scored a solitary point and was put in the shadow by team leader Alex Albon, but the 23-year-old American showed enough improvement to stay in the frame.

Logan crashed a little too much in his rookie year but deserves a second chance in 2024.

Logan and his older brother Dalton were karting hotshots and Logan made a name for himself when he ranked sixth in the European KF Junior series in 2014 when he was 13. A year later, he went better still, landing the World KF Junior title.

His next step was into single-seater racing, and he started in the United Arab Emirates F4 series that runs through the winter. Logan was immediately on the pace, stepping on to the podium for 15 of the 18 rounds to finish as runner-up.

Like so many racing hopefuls before him, Logan headed to England next, ranking third in the British F4 Championship. Then it was on to European Formula Renault in 2018 and he learned the circuits well enough to take three wins.

The FIA F3 Championship was his next step, but only a third place in the Macau street race at the end of the year saved a poor season in which Logan had to make do with best finishes of eighth place at Paul Ricard and the Hungaroring for Carlin Buzz Racing. Fortunately, 2020 went far better and Logan ranked third. Back for a third year of F3 in 2021, Logan had a poor season, ranking only seventh.

Fortunately, he had the budget to step up to F2 in 2022 and clearly relished the extra helping of horsepower, taking a maiden pole position and victory at Silverstone. This was followed by another victory at the Red Bull Ring, but there would be no more wins.

Towards the end of the season, Logan was given a golden opportunity when Williams let him run in the first practice sessions for the United States, Mexican and Brazilian GPs and this put him in position to become America's first F1 driver since Alexander Rossi's outings in 2015, providing that he could land a super licence.

Logan travelled to the final round in Abu Dhabi knowing that he would need to rank in the top five to be granted a super licence to step up to F1. Mastering the pressure, Logan did enough to rank fourth, just behind his Carlin team-mate Liam Lawson. And that was enough to land his F1 ride for 2023.

TRACK NOTES

Nationality:	**AMERICAN**
Born:	**31 DECEMBER 2000,**
	FORT LAUDERDALE, USA
Teams:	**WILLIAMS 2023–24**

CAREER RECORD

First Grand Prix:	**2023 BAHRAIN GP**
Grand Prix starts:	**22**
Grand Prix wins:	**0 (best result: 10th,**
	2023 United States GP)
Poles:	**0**
Fastest laps:	**0**
Points:	**1**
Honours:	**2016/17 F4 UAE RUNNER-UP, 2015**
	CIK WORLD KF JUNIOR KART CHAMPION

A ROOKIE YEAR OF LEARNING LESSONS

American F1 fans knew that they shouldn't expect podiums or wins in Logan's rookie year, as he was racing for the team that had ranked bottom in 2022. The more experienced fans also knew that it would be hard to get close to his impressive team-mate Alex Albon. However, with Logan perhaps feeling extra pressure to perform for F1's newest American fans, there were mistakes, crashes and retirements. Yet, with his drive not confirmed for 2024, Logan knuckled down and then, perhaps drawing inspiration from his home crowd, he finally landed his first point at the United States GP, coming home in tenth place. Hopes then soared at the inaugural Las Vegas GP when the Williams FW45 was clearly competitive on qualifying runs at least, putting Logan sixth on the grid, one place behind Albon. However, the race was less kind, and both fell out of the points, with Logan falling all the way down to 16th. His end of year tally of one point to Albon's 27 showed how much work there is to be done.

Alex Albon makes a pit stop during the Singapore Grand Prix. The Williams team used the Gulf Oil livery for three races in 2023.

Laurent Mekies has arrived from Ferrari to become team principal after Franz Tost's retirement, and he will be looking to guide the team under its new name towards a more consistent campaign in the year ahead.

New season, new name, but it will be intriguing to see whether it can score more than Yuki Tsunoda (above) and team-mates did in 2023.

By far the longest period of this team's oft-changing identity was the one it used when it stepped up to become an F1 team in 1985. This was as Minardi, named after team founder Giancarlo Minardi, and it arrived after spending several years as a frontrunner in Formula 2, with its greatest successes scored by Michele Alboreto in 1981 and later by Alessandro Nannini. However, Minardi didn't fancy making the change when F2 was to be replaced by F3000 for 1985 and so graduated to F1 instead, as teams were able to do in those far less expensive times. To say that Minardi's early F1 seasons were short on success would be an understatement, as money was tight and its drivers could get nowhere close to the pace of the dominant McLaren, Williams, Benetton and Ferrari teams of the day.

The first step forward came in 1988 when it dropped its heavy Motori Moderni engines for Ford units. The team's greatest day came at Silverstone in 1989,

when Pierluigi Martini came fifth and Luis Perez Sala sixth. The following year its Pirelli tyres were really competitive in qualifying, enabling Martini to place on the front row for the season opener in Phoenix. They weren't much use over a race distance, though, and so Martini fell to seventh.

KEY PERSONNEL & 2023 ROUND-UP

LAURENT MEKIES

Laurent has had a storied career in F1, starting with Arrows in 2001 before enjoying a long stint at Minardi, the forerunner to AlphaTauri. In 2014, he left his post as head of trackside operations to join the FIA as its safety director and later deputy race director. A desire to return to being with a team led to him joining Ferrari in 2018 as its sporting director, where he stayed until 2023. Laurent arrived to take over as team principal at the end of the season.

TWO CARS, FOUR DRIVERS

Yuki Tsunoda scrapped constantly for what was usually the final point on offer. When Nyck de Vries was dropped after ten rounds, many felt that, although he wasn't matching Tsunoda for pace, he deserved a longer time to settle in. Daniel Ricciardo was brought in as his replacement, but he drove in just two races before breaking a hand and opening the way for Liam Lawson to move across from Super Formula. He was immediately impressive. Ricciardo then returned and grabbed a welcome helping of six points by finishing seventh in Mexico.

2023 DRIVERS & RESULTS

Driver	Nationality	Races	Wins	Pts	Pos
Nyck de Vries	Dutch	10	0	0	22nd
Liam Lawson	New Zealander	5	0	2	20th
Daniel Ricciardo	Australian	7	0	6	17th
Yuki Tsunoda	Japanese	21	0	17	14th

With top results eluding the team, at least it could boast giving F1 debuts to Giancarlo Fisichella, Jarno Trulli and Fernando Alonso.

Then, with life in F1 becoming ever more expensive, Minardi was bought out with money from Red Bull and rebranded as Scuderia Toro Rosso in 2006. Still based in Faenza, it took a while to grow into its new identity, but its principal purpose was clear: it had been bought to try out the best of the young drivers from Red Bull's wide-based scholarship scheme. If they shone, they might have a chance to be promoted to one of the prized seats at Red Bull Racing. If they didn't, they would be unceremoniously dumped – which is what happened to the American driver, Scott Speed, in 2007.

Sebastian Vettel was clearly something different as the then baby-faced German not only went well with Toro Rosso but even had the audacity to guide it to victory in F1 before the senior team had managed it. This happened at a wet Monza in 2008 and he was duly promoted to Red Bull Racing.

Others, like Daniil Kvyat, were promoted to Red Bull Racing but then dropped back to Toro Rosso as the next big hope came through. None were more impressive, though, than Max Verstappen, as he was promoted after just four races of his second year with Toro Rosso and promptly won first time out, in Spain.

Fittingly for a team based in Italy, its second day of days came at Monza, just like its first with Vettel. This was in 2020, by which time the team had had a second rebrand and name change. Now racing as Scuderia AlphaTauri, to promote the fashion arm of the Red Bull empire, it provided Pierre Gasly with a car that shone in the Italian GP (as Vettel's had 12 years earlier) and he raced to an unexpected win.

Since then, the drivers have had one main task: to beat their team-mate and in so doing put themselves in the frame for the next opening at Red Bull Racing. But that's not easy when even getting into the top ten is a struggle.

Despite its strong connection to Faenza, Red Bull's secondary team is looking to upgrade its alternative base in the UK in an attempt to get more British engineers, designers and technical staff to join its forces.

Late team owner Dietrich Mateschitz celebrates the team's first win with Sebastian Vettel in 2008.

"We struggled with car performance at the start of last year, but were able to step it up through the year and improved from 10th to eighth in the final part of the season."

Yuki Tsunoda

YUKI TSUNODA

This popular Japanese driver is back for a fourth season, staying with the team that gave him his F1 break. He will be looking to deliver more drives of increasing maturity and seeing how he fares across a full season alongside the more experienced Daniel Ricciardo.

Yuki made strides in his third year with the team and will be seeking more consistent pace.

Yuki was a prodigy in kart racing who was good enough to finish as runner-up in the World FP Junior category in 2012 at the age of 12. Parental insistence on completing his schooling meant that it took a further four years until he was allowed to try single-seaters in the Japanese F4 championship and Yuki almost immediately finished on the podium. Falling short of landing the title

in 2017, Yuki returned for a second full season and got the job done.

Having caught the attention of talent spotters, Yuki became one of the Red Bull scholarship drivers in 2019, competing in Formula 3 in Europe, racing in two championships to gain experience of as many European circuits as possible. He did well enough to rank ninth in the FIA F3 Championship after coming on strongly in the second half of the campaign, winning one of the races at Monza.

Yuki spent 2020 in the FIA Formula 2 series, racing for the Carlin team. Three wins at Spa-Francorchamps, Silverstone and Sakhir impressed the sport's insiders and helped Yuki to end the year third as Mick Schumacher took the title. With F1 desperate to have a Japanese driver for the first time since 2014, it was decided that it was time for Yuki to step up.

In his first year of F1, 2021, Yuki showed that his selection by Scuderia AlphaTauri was a good one: he finished ninth on his debut at Sakhir and then raced to sixth place at the Hungaroring

later in the year. The highlight of his year came at the season-closing Abu Dhabi GP when he raced to an incredible fourth place, having advanced from an impressive eighth place on the grid. This helped him to end the year classified 14th overall with an impressive tally of 32 points, as AlphaTauri soared to sixth in the final reckoning.

Life proved a little harder in 2022, when Yuki peaked with seventh at the Emilia Romagna GP at Imola and AlphaTauri plummeted to ninth of the ten teams. There were quite a few errors, but he appeared to learn from them.

TRACK NOTES

Nationality:	**JAPANESE**
Born:	**11 MAY 2000, KANAGAWA, JAPAN**
Teams:	**ALPHATAURI 2021–24**

CAREER RECORD

First Grand Prix:	**2021 BAHRAIN GP**
Grand Prix starts:	**63**
Grand Prix wins:	**0 (best result: 4th, 2021 Abu Dhabi GP)**
Poles:	**0**
Fastest laps:	**1**
Points:	**61**

Honours: **2018 JAPANESE F4 CHAMPION, 2017 EAST JAPAN F4 CHAMPION, 2012 WORLD FP KART RUNNER-UP, 2011 & 2010 NEW TOKYO NTC KART CHAMPION, 2006 JAPANESE KID KARTS CHAMPION**

GAINING MATURITY IN HIS THIRD YEAR

Having picked up 12 points to rank 17th in his second F1 campaign for Scuderia AlphaTauri in 2022, Yuki improved to score 17 points last year. However, the Italian team gathered only 25 points in total, compared to its previous tally of 35. Yuki had a change of gear, though, when he raced for the first time without Pierre Gasly as a team leader and he grew into the role as he settled down. He put rookie Nyck de Vries into the shade, taking on more responsibility in developing the car than he had before and eliminating many of the errors that had dogged him in the past. With a car that was markedly less competitive than its predecessors, Yuki had to give his all even to score a point, with a trio of tenth-place finishes coming at Melbourne, Baku and Spa-Francorchamps, plus a run of drives that saw him miss out narrowly on scoring. Eighth place with fastest lap at COTA, ninth in Brazil and a spell as race leader in Abu Dhabi were just rewards and showed his improvement.

DANIEL RICCIARDO

This normally smiling F1 veteran was not smiling in 2022 as he endured a miserable time with McLaren and so stood down last year to regroup. He was then given a chance to step back in by AlphaTauri, with whom he is staying on in 2024.

Daniel returned from a year out, broke his hand, then bounced back again and went well.

Coming from Australia's west coast, Daniel realised that he would have to spend a lot of time travelling from his home in Perth to go racing, with distances of up to 2,300 miles (3,800km) to get to the east coast. Instead, his family decided that it would be better to contest South-East Asian series, as circuits like Sepang in Malaysia were closer to Perth than Bathurst or Albert Park. Third place in

Formula BMW convinced him that he had enough talent to try his hand at racing in Europe, a pursuit that would be helped when he became a Red Bull scholar.

Daniel tried Formula Renault in 2008 and impressed by being runner-up to Valtteri Bottas in the European championship. He then tackled the British F3 Championship and, driving for the pace-setting Carlin team, he landed the title in a year that produced six wins.

Keeping that momentum going, Daniel then raced in Formula Renault 3.5 in 2010 and, despite taking four wins, was pipped to the title. Staying on to try to go one better in 2011, his season changed course midway through when the F1 tail-end HRT team dropped Narain Karthikeyan and offered Daniel the drive. He took to F1 easily and was offered a drive with Scuderia Toro Rosso, doing well enough there to be promoted to Red Bull Racing for 2014. He then rewarded the team by taking the first of his eight F1 wins in Canada. Following many other good finishes he ended the year third overall behind the Mercedes drivers.

Although adding a few more wins over the next few years, he found himself

relegated in the team pecking order by Max Verstappen, so sought a change of team, first joining Renault, then agreeing to join McLaren for 2021. Although he had the honour of giving McLaren its first win since 2012, when he led a one-two finish in the Italian GP, Daniel ended the season two places and 45 points down on less experienced team-mate Lando Norris. In 2022, he ended the year four places and 85 points adrift and he clearly wasn't enjoying F1 anymore, so stood down to regroup.

TRACK NOTES

Nationality: **AUSTRALIAN**
Born: **1 JULY 1989, PERTH, AUSTRALIA**
Teams: **HRT 2011, TORO ROSSO 2012–13, RED BULL RACING 2014–18, RENAULT 2019–20, McLAREN 2021––22, ALPHATAURI 2023–24**

CAREER RECORD

First Grand Prix:	**2011 BRITISH GP**
Grand Prix starts:	239
Grand Prix wins:	8

2014 Canadian GP, Hungarian GP, Belgian GP, 2016 Malaysian GP, 2017 Azerbaijan GP, 2018 Chinese GP, Monaco GP, 2021 Italian GP

Poles:	3
Fastest laps:	16
Points:	1317
Honours:	**2010 FORMULA RENAULT 3.5 RUNNER-UP, 2009 BRITISH F3 CHAMPION, 2008 EUROPEAN FORMULA RENAULT RUNNER-UP & WESTERN EUROPEAN FORMULA RENAULT CHAMPION**

AN INTERRUPTED F1 RETURN

While he considered what it would take for him to enjoy F1 and be competitive again after a troubled time with McLaren in 2022, Daniel accepted a role with his former team, Red Bull Racing, as its reserve driver. The Australian said that he began to get his mojo back through the first half of the season. Then in July, Red Bull's second team, Scuderia AlphaTauri, dropped Nyck de Vries and asked Daniel to replace the Dutchman. Daniel finished ahead of team-mate Yuki Tsunoda first time out, at the Hungarian GP, which was impressive as he had not even had a test outing in the AT04. In the next race, the Belgian GP, he lost out by six places to the Japanese driver. Then came a hiccough, as Daniel had to relinquish the drive before the Dutch GP because he broke one of his hands in practice and had to be replaced by Liam Lawson. This was frustrating, but his charge to seventh place in Mexico City put a smile back onto his face.

// SAUBER

With the deal with Alfa Romeo having run its course, this Swiss team will be racing under its original name, Sauber, again. But even if the team does start the season brightly, you can expect lack of funding to see it fall back during the year.

Valtteri Bottas is staying for a third year as Alfa Romeo Racing's lead driver and will aim to score points whenever the top teams slip up.

When Alfa Romeo absolutely dominated the first ever World Championship in 1950 – filling the first four places on the grid at Silverstone and then claiming all three places on the podium, with their closest rival two laps in arrears – few would have thought that the Italian marque would disappear from the sport for decades. Yet this is what happened to Alfa Romeo and neither of its subsequent appearances in the World Championship have produced much to cheer about, with the added confusion of its third comeback in 2019 simply being a rebranding exercise for the Swiss Sauber team.

In 1950 and 1951, however, Alfa Romeo was dominant, with Giuseppe Farina landing the first drivers' title and Juan Manuel Fangio the second. In fact, the first win for any driver outside of the early 1950s' Alfa Romeo stranglehold only arrived at Silverstone in the fourth round of the 1951 season when Jose Froilan Gonzalez gave Ferrari its first F1 victory. Then, with a

change of regulations in the pipeline for 1952, Alfa Romeo shocked the racing scene by announcing that it was withdrawing.

That was that until the late 1970s, with Alfa Romeo focusing instead first on touring car racing and then, with considerable success, on sports prototypes, in which it won numerous

KEY PERSONNEL & 2023 ROUND-UP

ANDREAS SEIDEL
This German engineer got his start in motorsport with BMW and this led to F1 when Sauber became BMW Sauber and he ran trackside operations. A move to Porsche for 2010 had him overseeing the hybrid technology being pioneered in the top prototype class. A highlight was Porsche winning the 2015 Le Mans 24 Hours, but when the project closed, he joined McLaren in 2019. Andreas moved on from McLaren at the end of 2022, leaving his post to Andrea Stella before joining Alfa Romeo Racing as Group CEO.

DROPPING ONE POSITION TO NINTH
Valtteri Bottas's eighth place in the opening round at Sakhir was misleading, as it soon became clear that he and Zhou Guanyu were only going to get into the minor point-scoring positions if any of the cars from the leading teams hit trouble. For the remainder of the season, the team ran consistently as ninth best, ahead only of Haas, and the highlights were another eighth place for Bottas in Qatar before they lost a double points-score in Brazil when they retired.

2023 DRIVERS & RESULTS

Driver	Nationality	Races	Wins	Pts	Pos
Valtteri Bottas	Finnish	22	0	10	15th
Zhou Guanyu	Chinese	22	0	6	18th

races before taking the overall title in 1975.

Its second foray into F1 came in 1979 and there were occasional moments of promise for its bulky-looking red machines, such as when Bruno Giacomelli stormed into an early lead in the 1980 United States GP only to have an electrical failure.

A decade after this, Swiss sports car team boss Peter Sauber thought that he had Mercedes's backing to head into F1 after running its cars and its best young drivers, including Michael Schumacher and Heinz-Harald Frentzen, in the World Sports Car Championship and so he made the step. As it happens, Mercedes hesitated.

Mercedes provided Sauber with engines for its second season but not its third, as it offered McLaren the deal instead. So, Sauber pressed on regardless, his good-looking cars collecting the occasional third-place finishes through Frentzen, Jean Alesi, Johnny Herbert and Nick Heidfeld.

Money was always limited compared to the top teams, though, and Sauber always failed to attract the best F1 designers and engineers, who were unwilling to uproot from England to join the team at its Swiss base. So, it took the arrival of BMW money and BMW engines in 2006 for the team to achieve its greatest moment. This came at the 2008 Canadian GP when Robert Kubica led home Heidfeld in a most unexpected one-two when Lewis Hamilton crashed his McLaren out of the lead. Yet, there were other good results and BMW Sauber was classified third in the constructors' championship, behind only Ferrari and McLaren.

In time, the German manufacturer moved on and Sauber used Ferrari customer engines from 2010 with high points being Sergio Perez's second place in the 2012 Malaysian GP behind Fernando Alonso's Ferrari and Charles Leclerc's run of strong qualifying results through his rookie F1 season in 2018.

By this time, Peter Sauber had stood down and financial investment from Finn Rausing, whose family owns the Tetra Pak packaging empire, bolstered the team's funds in 2018, with the renaming project that put the Alfa Romeo name back in the F1 frame happening the following year to add further stability. Thus far, its five seasons under this revived name have failed to evoke memories of Farina and Fangio, or even Giacomelli pressing on for Alfa Romeo in 1980, but its best season in 2022 produced sixth in the constructors' ranking, putting it pretty much at the level at which the original Sauber used to operate.

FOR THE RECORD

Team base:	**Hinwil, Switzerland**
Active in Formula One:	**As Sauber 1993–2018 (as BMW Sauber 2006–2010) & 2024, Alfa Romeo 2019–2023**
Grands Prix contested:	**566**
Wins:	**1**
Pole positions:	**1**
Fastest laps:	**7**
Constructors' titles:	**0**
Drivers' titles:	**0**

THE TEAM

Owner:	**Finn Rausing**
Group CEO:	**Andreas Seidel**
Team representative:	**Alessandro Alunni Bravi**
Technical director:	**James Key**
CEO, Sauber Technologies:	**Axel Kruse**
Head of aerodynamics:	**Alessandro Cinelli**
Head of track engineering:	**Xevi Pujolar**
Chief designer:	**Eric Gandelin**
Head of aerodynamic research:	**Seamus Mullarkey**
Sporting manager:	**Beat Zehnder**
Head of race strategy	**Ruth Buscombe**
Chassis:	**Sauber C44**
Engine:	**Ferrari V6**
Tyres:	**Pirelli**

49

JJ Lehto was immediately onto the pace in Sauber's first season in 1993, finishing fifth on his first outing.

"Even though we have confirmed our driver line-up for 2024, Theo Pourchaire is part of it. We will have three drivers, not two official drivers and one reserve."

Alessandro Alunni Bravi

VALTERRI BOTTAS

It was a backwards step for Alfa Romeo Racing last year and Valtteri's first year honeymoon with the Swiss team in 2022 was followed by something far less rewarding. Unfortunately, he can't really expect a great jump in performance in 2024.

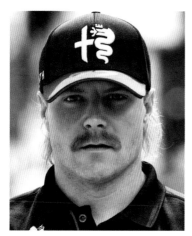

Valtteri brings experience to his 12th year in F1, but the challenge is staying on the pace.

50

Many of Valtteri's rivals had a smooth and serene passage to F1, which puts this affable Finn at odds with them as his route to the top was more problematic.

One of the main reasons for this was not so much a lack of skill, but a shortage of funds. He had enough money to move from karts to Formula Renault when he was 17, winning the European title at his second attempt. There was then enough

backing to move up to F3 and his two years in the Euro series marked him out as one of the top names; his third position ranking in both 2009 and 2010 were enough to prove that he was ready to make the step into the final category before F1, which was GP2 in 2011. However, he didn't have enough financial support.

It's often the manner in which sportspeople tackle a setback that shows their resolve, and Valtteri lowered his sights to GP3, knowing that anything less than the title might bring an end to his single-seater career. Not only did he land the title, but he made the most of the prize of a test run with Williams.

This was his biggest break, as he was snapped up to be the team's reserve driver, gaining valuable experience through 2012 and doing well enough for Frank Williams and Patrick Head to give him a race seat for 2013. A pair of second-place finishes in 2014 cemented his place in the team, but he suddenly shifted to Mercedes for 2017 after Nico Rosberg surprised everyone by announcing his retirement. This gave him a car with the potential to win races,

which he did over the next five years, but was never even close to the number won by team leader Lewis Hamilton. Bottas had to accept the role of being number two as Lewis landed title after title.

For 2022, Valtteri knew that his time with Mercedes had come to an end and joined Alfa Romeo Racing instead, accepting the less pressured but less successful atmosphere there, learning to enjoy not being in Hamilton's shadow.

TRACK NOTES

Nationality:	**FINNISH**
Born:	**28 AUGUST 1989, NASTOLA, FINLAND**
Teams:	**WILLIAMS 2013–16, MERCEDES 2017–21, ALFA ROMEO 2022–24**

CAREER RECORD

First Grand Prix:	**2013 AUSTRALIAN GP**
Grand Prix starts:	**222**
Grand Prix wins:	**10**
	2017 Russian GP, Austrian GP, Abu Dhabi GP, 2019 Australian GP, Azerbaijan GP, Japanese GP, United States GP, 2020 Austrian GP, Russian GP, 2021 Turkish GP
Poles:	**20**
Fastest laps:	**19**
Points:	**1797**
Honours:	**2019 & 2020 F1 RUNNER-UP, 2011 GP3 CHAMPION, 2009 & 2010 F3 MASTERS WINNER, 2008 EUROPEAN & NORTHERN EUROPEAN FORMULA RENAULT CHAMPION**

LIKE 2022, BUT LESS COMPETITIVE

Valtteri was given great cheer when he started his second season with Alfa Romeo Racing by securing eighth place in the opening Grand Prix in Bahrain. That put points straight into his account, but the increasingly relaxed Finn will have noted that this was a couple of places down on his opening performance in 2022 when he came sixth at the same venue. Tenth-place finishes in the Canadian and Italian GPs were brighter spots in a year that became increasingly difficult for the Alfa Romeo drivers; their C43 lost out in the battle for in-season development, just as so many cars from this Swiss team had failed to evolve through previous World Championship campaigns. A second eighth place result was achieved in the heat-sapping Grand Prix in Qatar as the season moved into its final rounds, and this would have been added to with more points in the Brazilian GP but both Valtteri and Zhou were brought in to retire with undeclared problems, which was frustrating.

ZHOU GUANYU

The timing of this Chinese driver's ascent to F1 could not have been worse, as it followed the COVID pandemic, meaning that he couldn't showcase his skills in front of a home crowd because the Chinese GP remained off the championship schedule until this year.

Zhou failed to really advance in his second year of F1 as Alfa Romeo lost ground to rivals.

The COVID years of 2020 and 2021 have concealed the strength of the burgeoning Chinese racing scene. Indeed, China stayed in isolation through 2022 as well. However, even before that, young Zhou had opted to go global in his quest for karting success, shining in the World and European series and moving into single-seaters when he was just 15.

This was in 2015 and he did well enough to rank second in the Italian Formula 4 series before heading down to New Zealand for the Toyota Racing Series, a championship known for attracting northern hemisphere talent wanting both to stay in race trim and also get noticed. The TRS champion at the start of 2016 was Lando Norris, with Zhou ranking sixth.

Back to Europe, with Ferrari having added him to its driver academy, Zhou contested the 2016 European Formula 3 series. Although he twice appeared on the podium, there was a great deal to learn for the youngster and it turned into a three-year project. He won races for Prema in the final year but ranked only eighth.

Aware that Zhou was their best hope of making it to the top, Chinese backers eased his way into Formula 2 for 2019, along with him signing as part of the Renault Sport Academy; he soon began to look at home, even winning a round in Sochi in 2020. However, he needed better results to merit graduation to F1 so stayed for a third season of F2, staying with UNI-Virtuosi. Although Oscar Piastri took the title, Zhou's four wins helped him end the season third overall.

And so, the door to F1 opened for 2022. With Alfa Romeo Racing deciding that the likely exposure on the giant Chinese market might do their sponsors some good, they signed him to race alongside experienced team leader Valtteri Bottas.

Zhou's first year in F1 produced a best result of eighth place in the Canadian GP, but there was disappointment as his car was inverted at the start of the following round at Silverstone and he only broke into the top 10 once after that, at Zandvoort to end the year ranked 18th.

TRACK NOTES

Nationality:	**CHINESE**
Born:	**30 MAY 1999,**
	SHANGHAI, CHINA
Teams:	**ALFA ROMEO 2022–24**

CAREER RECORD

First Grand Prix:	**2022 BAHRAIN GP**
Grand Prix starts:	**44**
Grand Prix wins:	**0**
	(best result: 8th
	2022 Canadian GP)
Poles:	**0**
Fastest laps:	**2**
Points:	**12**
Honours:	**2021 ASIAN F3 CHAMPION,**
	2015 ITALIAN F4 RUNNER-UP

A SECOND YEAR OF LEARNING

Two ninth-place finishes in the first half of the season, in Melbourne and then four races later in Spain, were the high points of a campaign in which Zhou largely occupied that all but invisible zone towards the tail of the field – not well-placed enough for the TV directors to pick him out as a challenger, or slow enough to be lapped frequently and thus picked out by the TV directors as the leaders went by. However, while Zhou's performances were steady rather than spectacular, usually trailing team-mate Valtteri Bottas, they were deemed enough for the Chinese driver to be told at the Singapore GP that he had gained another year's contract. This is largely because the team values stability as it attempts to turn itself into an outfit capable of scoring points on a more frequent basis. A third ninth place was recorded in Qatar and then he was set for points in Brazil before being instructed to park the car.

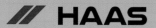

HAAS

This American team has kept on its drivers for 2024 and must provide a car that doesn't consume its tyres as badly as last year's if Nico Hulkenberg and Kevin Magnussen are going to have any chance of scoring on a regular basis.

Neither Nico Hulkenberg (above) nor Kevin Magnussen could do much about their Haas chassis' shortcomings in 2023 and deserve better.

It's safe to say that Haas F1's eight-year spell in Formula One has been one of mixed fortunes, with more downs than ups as it tries to take on the long-established and better-funded teams. However, now that the United States of America is being allocated three Grands Prix each season, the sport needs an American team and, for now, Haas F1 is that. In time, though, as more American fans are attracted to F1 by the Netflix *Drive to Survive* series, the newcomers will want more in the way of results – starting with points on a regular basis, then wins and then, perhaps unrealistically, world titles.

Gene Haas made his fortune by manufacturing machining tools. As a race fan, he thought that the best way to promote Haas CNC was to enter a team in NASCAR, the stock car series beloved of America's blue-collar workers. This proved a hit as the results began to flow and publicity soared. Joining forces with former champion Tony Stewart propelled the team to the front and brought it the title in 2011. Kevin Harvick drove Haas CNC to another championship in 2014.

Haas then began to investigate how he could make Haas CNC a global brand and picked F1. It was soon established that Haas F1 would need a base in Britain, where the majority of F1 expertise is located, as

2023 DRIVERS & RESULTS

Driver	Nationality	Races	Wins	Pts	Pos
Nico Hulkenberg	German	22	0	9	16th
Kevin Magnussen	Danish	22	0	3	19th

FOR THE RECORD

Team bases:	**Annapolis, USA & Banbury, England**
Active in Formula One:	**From 2016**
Grands Prix contested:	**166**
Wins:	**0**
Pole positions:	**1**
Fastest laps:	**3**
Constructors' titles:	**0**
Drivers' titles:	**0**

THE TEAM

Team owner:	**Gene Haas**
Team principal:	**Guenther Steiner**
Chief operating officer:	**Joe Custer**
Technical director:	**Simone Resta**
Head of engineering operations:	**Ben Agathangelou**
Director of engineering:	**Ayao Komatsu**
Aerodynamics team leader:	**Christian Cattaneo**
Chief designer:	**Andrea de Zordo**
Head of aerodynamics:	**Arron Melvin**
Operations manager:	**Peter Crolla**
Chassis:	**Haas VF-24**
Engine:	**Ferrari V6**
Tyres:	**Pirelli**

well as one alongside the NASCAR outfit's headquarters in North Carolina.

The sight of the celebrations after Romain Grosjean finished sixth on the team's debut in Melbourne in the opening race of 2016 will live on for the sheer surprise etched on his and Haas's faces as they celebrated. When Grosjean followed this up with fifth next time out, F1 insiders were bemused. It seems that the team's first car, designed for Haas F1 by Dallara, was a good one and its Ferrari customer engine worked well too; by season's end, the team was classified eighth ahead of Renault, Sauber and Manor.

Second generation F1 racer Kevin Magnussen joined from Renault for 2017 and stayed for four years and the team ranked eighth again, this time just behind Scuderia Toro Rosso.

The 2018 season was to be the team's best so far as Haas F1 ranked fifth, easily ahead of McLaren thanks to Magnussen claiming a couple of fifth places, one of which was one place behind Grosjean's peak of fourth in the Austrian GP.

When Magnussen kicked off 2019 with sixth at the Australian GP, it might have been thought that the team had found a new level, but it ended the year ranked ninth. There was then no progress in 2020 as the team finished ninth again, outscoring only Williams. There was a further downturn in 2021 as Haas F1 replaced its experienced drivers with rookies Mick Schumacher and Nikita Mazepin and not surprisingly the team finished last.

There was probably extra hope going into 2022 as F1 was being run to a new set of technical regulations, but Haas F1 advanced only as far as eighth ahead of AlphaTauri and Williams, largely helped by another astonishing opening round in which the returning Magnussen raced to fifth place at Sakhir in by far the season's best result.

Staying competitive in the World Championship only gets more difficult with every passing year, meaning that Haas F1 should be falling ever further behind the top teams, even with budget caps being observed. So achievements like Nico Hulkenberg starting last year's Canadian GP from fifth – having been second fastest but then hit with a grid penalty – and then Kevin Magnussen lining up sixth in Singapore have been most impressive. Alas, come race time the VF-23s would consume their tyres at a prodigious rate, making any top-ten finish a near miracle.

Team owner Gene Haas and Romain Grosjean had every reason to smile after the team's debut in 2016.

> "We've got a race team that is always ready to race, a team that just wants to do well, but we just need to get better with the performance of the car."
>
> Gunther Steiner

There were examples last year of the pace that this German F1 veteran can achieve, but only in qualifying, as the Haas VF-23 would fall back in races due to its appetite for tyres. If this year's car is better, regular points will be the target.

Nico knows that he will only succeed if this year's Haas can race as well as it qualifies.

It's a strange thing for a driver who set the junior single-seater scene alight to be employed chiefly for his experience, but this is what has befallen Nico, and it was his years of F1 knowledge that brought him back into F1 in 2023 with Haas for his first full-season ride since 2019.

Nico won the German kart title at both junior and then senior level. More powerful single-seaters held no fear for him as Nico duly won the German Formula BMW title at the first attempt. A less than generous budget for graduation to Formula 3 resulted in him using an unfashionable Ligier chassis against the predominant Dallaras, yet he was still good enough to rank fifth.

Nico's big break came when he was selected to race for the German team in the inter-nation A1GP series through the winter of 2006–07 and he waltzed to the title. This opened up drives with more competitive teams, and Nico was crowned European F3 champion after a dominant campaign in 2008. Then, ignoring the fact that rookies seldom do a great deal more than spend their first year of GP2 learning the ropes, he powered his way to the title at his first attempt.

This opened the door to F1, with Nico starting with Williams in 2010, even taking pole at Interlagos, but the team hired a different driver in 2011 and so he spent the year on the side lines before getting a ride with Force India for 2012.

Talk of Nico being signed by Ferrari for 2013 was scuppered as they thought that this tall German would be too heavy for the car and so put them at a disadvantage. So instead Nico spent a year at Sauber, then three more at Force India, during which time he finished fourth on three occasions. He was given a huge career boost in 2015 when he won the Le Mans 24 Hours for Porsche.

Nico then spent three years with Renault before dropping out of F1, called back only as a stand-in driver, with Racing Point in 2020 then Aston Martin in 2022.

TRACK NOTES

Nationality:	**GERMAN**
Born:	**19 AUGUST 1987, EMMERICH, GERMANY**
Teams:	**WILLIAMS 2010, FORCE INDIA 2012 & 2014–16, SAUBER 2013, RENAULT 2017–19, RACING POINT 2020, ASTON MARTIN 2022, HAAS 2023–4**

CAREER RECORD

First Grand Prix:	**2010 BAHRAIN GP**
Grand Prix starts:	**203**
Grand Prix wins:	**0 (best result: 4th, 2012 Belgian GP, 2013 Korean GP, 2016 Belgian GP)**
Poles:	**1**
Fastest laps:	**2**
Points:	**530**

Honours: **2015 LE MANS 24 HOURS WINNER, 2009 GP2 CHAMPION, 2008 EUROPEAN F3 CHAMPION, 2007 F3 MASTERS WINNER, 2006/07 A1GP CHAMPION, 2005 GERMAN FORMULA BMW ADAC CHAMPION, 2003 GERMAN KART CHAMPION, 2002 GERMAN JUNIOR KART CHAMPION**

HELD BACK BY A TYRE-HUNGRY CAR

Qualifying second in a rain-hit qualifying session at last year's Canadian GP, behind only Red Bull Racing's dominant star Max Verstappen, was a major highlight of Nico's 2023 campaign with Haas F1. Unfortunately, not only would he have to start three places further back due to a procedural error under a red flag, but he would then fall to 15th in the race as his Haas VF-23 did what it usually did and ate its tyres. Due to this voracious appetite for rubber, the team could seldom opt for a one-stop strategy adopted by its rivals and this was its Achilles' heel. There were other flashes of great speed from Nico in qualifying, but his best result of the season would be his run to seventh place in the third round, the Australian GP at Albert Park. In almost all circumstances and settings, the result would be a trip down the order between the end of qualifying and the end of the race. The team was aware that the car was to blame, not the drivers, so he and Kevin were kept on for 2024.

KEVIN MAGNUSSEN

Haas F1 gave Kevin a second vote of confidence when it re-signed him for a third year in his F1 comeback, knowing that it will be his years of experience that might help the team to develop a car that can race to points on a regular basis.

Kevin had three runs to point-scoring results last year and will press on for more in 2024.

Kevin's early car-racing career showed that his lack of regular kart racing hadn't held him back, as he won the Danish Formula Ford title in 2008 and then shone in Formula Renault the following year. Kevin then lined up in the German F3 Championship in 2010 and ranked third.

In 2011, he took a tilt at the British F3 crown that his father Jan had won in hugely dominant style 17 years before. Although he won seven races for Carlin, Kevin had to make do with the runner-up spot behind Felipe Nasr. However, he kept moving up the single-seater ladder to try Formula Renault 3.5. Adapting well to these more powerful cars, Kevin improved from seventh place overall with one win in 2012 to be champion for DAMS after winning five times in 2013. This was enough to impress McLaren, who gave him his F1 debut the following year alongside Jenson Button.

In the season-opening 2014 Australian GP at Melbourne's Albert Park, Kevin secured second place for McLaren behind Mercedes's Nico Rosberg after Daniel Ricciardo was disqualified – and this remains Kevin's best F1 finish. That this was on his F1 debut was more remarkable, but there haven't been many moments since to make F1 fans sit up and take notice. Indeed, he was without a ride for 2015 as Fernando Alonso joined Button, but he bounced back when he returned to F1 in 2016 with Renault to outscore team-mate Jolyon Palmer.

Looking for a change, Kevin moved to marginally higher-ranked Haas F1 for 2017 and so began a four-year stay with the American team until the end of 2020. Then, with Haas F1 electing to bring on rookies Nikita Mazepin and Mick Schumacher, with their healthy budgets being a major factor in the deal, Kevin found himself on the side lines, largely contesting the IMSA Sportscar series in the USA and impressing by being good enough to share victory in Detroit.

Then, seeing the error of its rookie-led selection, Haas F1 asked Kevin to re-join its F1 attack for 2022.

TRACK NOTES

Nationality:	**DANISH**
Born:	**5 OCTOBER 1992,**
	ROSKILDE, DENMARK
Teams:	**McLAREN 2014,**
	RENAULT 2016, HAAS 2017-20 &
	2022-24

CAREER RECORD

First Grand Prix:	**2014 AUSTRALIAN GP**
Grand Prix starts:	**163**
Grand Prix wins:	**0 (best result: 2nd,**
	2014 Australian GP)
Poles:	**1**
Fastest laps:	**2**
Points:	**186**
Honours:	**2013 FORMULA RENAULT**
	3.5 CHAMPION, 2011 BRITISH F3
	RUNNER-UP, 2009 NORTHERN EUROPE
	FORMULA RENAULT RUNNER-UP, 2008
	DANISH FORMULA FORD CHAMPION

SQUEEZING INTO THE POINTS ZONE

With points being hard to come by for mid-ranking teams in F1 – allocated only down to tenth place at the end of a Grand Prix and top eight in the occasional sprint races held on the Saturdays of Grand Prix meetings – Kevin knew that he faced a challenge in his sixth year with Haas F1. There was immediate pressure from the form in qualifying of new team-mate Nico Hulkenberg, and Kevin responded by qualifying an outstanding fourth for the Miami GP, but the Haas VF-23's appetite for tyres made good results in the races so much harder to come by. Yet, Kevin managed a trio of tenth-place finishes on the Jeddah Corniche Circuit, the temporary Miami International Autodrome and then on the streets of Singapore. This strong race form fell away a little in the second half of the season, his Singapore result aside, and the balance between Kevin and his team-mate swung largely in the German's favour. Being taken out at the start of the race in Brazil was a further frustration.

TALKING POINT:
THE ANDRETTI CLAN THROWS ITS HAT INTO THE RING

Andretti Global was granted the right last October by the FIA to file an entry for the World Championship in 2026 as F1's 11th team. This is welcome but it does raise the prospect of bringing America's greatest racing dynasty back to the sport in which father Mario became world champion while son Michael didn't last a season, so he has unfinished business.

Landing an entry to enter the World Championship used to be remarkably simple. All you needed in the 1970s was a chassis, a Ford Cosworth DFV engine, a small transporter, an engineer, a few mechanics and a driver. You didn't even have to commit to a full-season campaign, so many Grands Prix had a few extra entries for local heroes. These days, the requirements are considerably more stringent, and a full examination of a putative team's finances, technical capabilities and structure are analysed.

When it was announced that a place for an extra team (an 11th) was on offer from 2026 onwards, there were numerous applications. A couple were dismissed early in the bid process, including one headed by Craig Pollock, who brought BAR into F1 in 1999. Eventually, Andretti Formula Racing's bid was the only one from the four remaining candidates thought to be acceptable by the FIA, defeating the bids from Carlin Rodin, Hitech and Lucky Suns.

Although Andretti's plans had been accepted by the sport's governing body, Formula 1 itself said 'we note the FIA's conclusions in relation to the first and second phases of their process and will now conduct our own assessment of the merits of the remaining application.' There has been considerable opposition from the ten existing teams, all aware that an extra team would mean a smaller share of the prize money than if they remained as just ten, even with a £165m anti-dilution fee being provided by F1. Furthermore,

an 11th team might also reduce the value of their teams should they wish to sell. In fact, although probably half of the ten teams are in financial difficulty, the recent upswing in interest in F1 has certainly boosted their values, with Alpine's rising by as much as 50 per cent after leading sporting celebrities, including golfer Rory McIlroy and boxer Anthony Joshua, invested in them last year.

The F1 rights holders were naturally anxious to add an eleventh team if it felt that it would boost the appeal of the World Championship. Certainly, having the Andretti name in F1 could only add extra exposure in the burgeoning American F1 market, but only if its cars could prove competitive – far from guaranteed.

Michael became frustrated last November as F1 rivals continued to resist his push to enter the sport, saying that the teams appeared to think of them 'as a bunch of hillbillies' who would not be up to the job of running an F1 team. He disputed that and stressed that he believed that the team's arrival would add to the viewing audience and thus add value to all the teams.

Comparing the Andretti bid with how Haas F1 has operated since it arrived in F1 back in 2016, Michael outlined how he planned to build his cars in the USA, run with engines built in the USA and have an American driver, making a point about the way that Haas has relied on Italian expertise and engines and exclusively employed non-American drivers across the team's eight-year existence.

To that end, Andretti Formula Racing's bid is in association with Cadillac, bringing General Motors' luxury brand to a new market. This is something that certainly appeals to F1's owners Liberty Media, who are keen to have another premium brand in its stable. However, with no definite Cadillac F1 engine in the pipeline until 2028, it might have to be a rebranding job.

Cadillac has mostly stayed away from motorsport, largely leaving that to other GM marques like Chevrolet, Pontiac, Oldsmobile or Buick. The exceptions were a brief foray into sports-prototypes that began in 2000 and peaked with ninth place in the 2002 Le Mans 24 Hours and later a more successful spell when the North American-based IMSA Sportscar series adopted the Daytona Prototype class, taking three titles between 2017 and 2021. When it saw the move to hybrids being embraced by the World Endurance Championship, Cadillac entered a team both in that and the IMSA Sportscar series from 2023.

Whether Andretti's F1 bid will hit its target remains to be seen.

Opposite top left: Mario and Michael Andretti outline their F1 ambitions at the United States GP.

Opposite top right: Cadillac joined the World Endurance Championship because of its hybrid formula.

Opposite middle: Mario Andretti leads Lotus team-mate Ronnie Peterson in their 1978 campaign for Lotus.

Opposite bottom: Michael Andretti raced for McLaren in F1 in 1993 but was dropped.

TALKING POINT:
IT WAS HIT AND MISS AS LAS VEGAS JOINED THE F1 CIRCUS

Formula One's investment in Las Vegas is considerable and long term, yet its debut proved that life is always more complicated at a street venue. The problems were many but, fortunately, the racing proved to be excellent. So, can we expect more street venues in the World Championship's calendar in the future, or are they more trouble than they are worth?

The history of F1 using street circuits dates back to the Monaco GP in 1950, the World Championship's inaugural season, although Grand Prix racing had been held on street circuits since the dawn of racing, long before permanent circuits came into being. While the Monte Carlo circuit is still used today, not all the street venues have been roaring successes.

Last November's Las Vegas GP attracted considerable attention, both on and off the track, which is exactly what Formula One owner Liberty Media wanted, and exactly why it had invested such a fortune – £560 million – in making it happen. Las Vegas drew in the celebrities that Liberty hopes will convince fans of other sports in the USA that F1 is worthy of their support. A second big uptick was the setting in this casino city. It provided a spectacular backdrop when the cars ran after dark, blasting past the illuminated landmarks.

However, there were other problems that detracted from the spectacle. The most obvious was when Carlos Sainz's Ferrari was damaged extensively when it ran over an unsecured drain cover at 200 mph (320 kph). Ferrari team boss Frederic Vasseur was livid. Not only was that first practice session curtailed after nine minutes of track action, but the second was delayed for four hours. And then, just as it was about to begin, people were told to leave the grandstands because those officiating the event had reached the maximum number of hours that they were allowed to work under state law.

The drivers suggested that start times ought to be different this year. After all, the 22:00 start might have suited the casinos but not the majority of American fans, with those living on the East Coast having to stay up into the small hours of the morning.

Yet, the adage that there is no such thing as bad publicity when you have a product to promote seemed to reign, as it kept the event in the news, something that has seldom been the case since the USA first hosted a round of the World Championship at Sebring in 1959.

The history of street circuits being used in the World Championship includes more venues than most fans would realise, as some were used only a few times. Long-running street venues like Long Beach in California and the Adelaide street circuit that hosted the Australian GP from 1985 to 1995 were popular, but others were less inspiring. The first occasion the USA got a street circuit wrong was in Las Vegas in the early 1980s. The tight, twisty Caesars Palace circuit was laid out around a car park and two visits proved more than enough. Likewise, the Phoenix circuit used between 1989 and 1991 was a collection of 90-degree bends that offered no chance for the F1 cars to be shown at their best. Indeed, the event was dropped after a nearby ostrich race attracted a larger crowd…

But the strength and longevity of a street circuit and whether it remains in the F1 calendar is not just about attendance figures. Driver safety has long been a consideration, too. Drivers in the 1950s were disconcerted by the thought of their car ending up in the harbour in Monte Carlo and later the dangers inherent in the tramlines and cobbled surface at Oporto. Then Barcelona's undulating Montjuic Park circuit was proved to be simply too dangerous and unfortunately its barriers proved insufficient in 1975 when four spectators were killed when Rolf Stommelen crashed.

The USA's constant attempts to make F1 popular produced a one-off race in Dallas's Fair Park in 1984, where soaring temperatures led to the disintegration of the temporary track. At least the circuit used in downtown Detroit fared better from 1982 to 1988.

Modern-day F1 street circuits like the ones in Valencia, Singapore, Sochi and Baku were created to have fast corners as well as slow. This was taken to extremes when the Jeddah Corniche Circuit made its bow in 2021, with cars topping 200 mph (320 kph) in Saudi Arabia and Las Vegas too.

It's safe to assume that street circuits will continue to be a part of the World Championship, but lessons need to be learned, drain covers fixed in place and the scheduling sorted so that any delay doesn't have the fans being shut out again.

Opposite top left: Juan Manuel Fangio won the first World Championship round held in Monaco in 1950.

Opposite top right: Caesars Palace in 1982.

Opposite middle: Spanish ace Fernando Alonso made sure that he won when Valencia hosted a race in 2012.

Opposite bottom: Las Vegas provided a unique backdrop for the World Championship on F1's return in 2023.

TALKING POINT:
CAN F1 ACADEMY PRODUCE ANOTHER FEMALE F1 RACER?

There has been a glaring absence of female racers from F1's 74-year history, with Giovanna Amati being the most recent of only five when she failed to qualify in 1992. F1 Academy is the latest formula created to try to redress that by propelling a female star towards the top and it's now tied in with F1.

Maria-Teresa de Filippis became the first female F1 racer when she entered the World Championship with a Maserati 250F in 1958. This wasn't peculiar, as having the wherewithal to buy an F1 car, one of the key ingredients then, was no problem for the Italian heiress. Now, drivers must graduate via the ladder of junior single-seater series which is a far more exacting process and Formula Academy has been created to try to boost the number of female racers.

The number of female racers that have reached F1 since de Filippis has been meagre. Another Italian, Lella Lombardi, came next, running a full season with a works March in 1975, peaking with sixth in the Spanish GP. Former ski racer Divina Galica tried but failed to qualify in 1976. Then Desire Wilson also failed to qualify in 1980, but she was by far the best to try, having already won a round of the British F1 championship. A dozen years later, Giovanna Amati tried to qualify for Brabham. And that has been that.

There have been several attempts, most recently, the female-only W Series, but nothing has changed, with its best graduate Jamie Chadwick no closer to F1 despite having won all three W Series titles. The prize money wasn't enough to help her into F1's feeder formula, F2, or F3, and her 12th place in last year's IndyCar feeder series – INDY NXT – suggested that, although good, she isn't good enough for F1.

In fact, the most successful females in racing in 2023 were competing in sports car racing, with Sarah Bovy, Rahel Frey and Michelle Gatting becoming the first female

crew to take a class win in the World Endurance Championship at Sakhir in their Iron Dames Porsche.

To get to F1, you need to have a single-seater background and it was fortunate last year that the F1 Academy was established following the financial collapse of the W Series. Former racer Susie Wolff runs F1 Academy and she is clear about its remit and about how it will provide role models to boost the number of female racers: 'F1 Academy is all about progression and creating more opportunities for young women across motorsport.'

Many of the racers had come through karts and junior single-seater categories, like F4. Spanish racer Marta Garcia adapted best to the Tatuus chassis and 175bhp Autotechnica engine to land the inaugural title thanks to winning seven of the 21 races. Her prize is a fully-funded season in the Formula Regional European Championship. This is still three levels below F1, so there is still a long way to go and much more money needed to enable her to achieve the dream of racing in F1.

For 2024, the big news is that each of the ten F1 teams will be involved in the F1 Academy, entering one driver each, with that driver's car sporting the F1 race livery. 'I want to thank the F1 teams for their support and vision as we embark on this journey together,' says Wolff. As in 2023, the cars will be run by five teams – ART Grand Prix, Campos Racing, MP Motorsport, PREMA Racing and Rodin Carlin – with each fielding three cars.

TV coverage will be boosted

considerably. This year all seven triple-header rounds will be on F1 support programmes – at Jeddah, Miami, Barcelona, Zandvoort, Marina Bay, Losail and Yas Marina, an improvement from just the final round last year when the last three races were part of the US GP package.

A further change for this year is that the drivers' contribution to their budget has been reduced from 150,000 Euros to 100,000, which should make it accessible to more drivers.

F1 Academy is casting its net wide to identify the best young female racers and it has started the F1 Academy's Champions of the Future programme in karting, offering support for three girls in each of the categories in the mixed-gender series. That's to say in Minis (for eight to 11 years), Juniors (11 to 14) and Seniors (14 plus), with the top three Seniors to get a test in an F1 Academy car at season's end.

Time will tell whether F1 Academy will produce a talent that can go all the way to F1, but this is the most high-profile push yet.

Opposite top left: Maria-Teresa de Filippis was the first woman to race in F1 as long ago as 1958.

Opposite top right: Marta Garcia celebrates winning the 2023 F1 Academy Championship.

Opposite middle: Giovanna Amati tried but failed to qualify the uncompetitive Brabham in the first three races of 1992.

Opposite bottom left: Lella Lombardi in contemplative mood before racing to sixth place in the 1975 Spanish GP.

Opposite bottom right: Jessica Edgar leads the F1 Academy field away in their US GP support race at COTA.

// KNOW THE TRACKS 2024

There was a considerable effort from the organisers to make this year's F1 calendar more cohesive, to group races according to region to help reduce both travel time and the environmental impact by cutting down on constant criss-crossing of the planet. There are due to be 24 Grands Prix again, with Imola back on the calendar after flooding caused the cancellation of its visit last year.

Twenty-four Grands Prix held between the first weekend of March and the second weekend in December is fantastic news for F1 fans. However, it doesn't leave many weekends free for the teams and their personnel to take some well-earned rest across the season as F1 owner, Liberty Media, continues to push for more races per year. With 24 Grands Prix in place for 2024, the 1990s' average of 16 per year, with only a few of these held outside Europe, seems very tame indeed.

Make no mistake, F1 is almost constantly on the road in a flurry of logistics and jet lag. This constant activity is fabulous

for diehard race fans, but not so wonderful for the crews and their families, with burn-out a concern that the teams have tried to counter. Another problem with being on the road so much is how teams that have not got to grips with their new cars at the start of the season soon find themselves on the back foot and so it takes extra intellectual input to get them firing.

However, Liberty Media views global expansion as the best way to spread the word, alongside the propulsion given to F1 in recent years by Netflix's *Drive to Survive* series, which brought a whole new raft of fans to the sport. And these are fans, largely

American, who are more used to their favourite sports having races and matches every weekend, action whenever the fans want it. If it was a case of having a race in Georgia one weekend and South Carolina another, the logistics of putting on lots of races wouldn't be so tricky, but F1 tends to jump time zones rather than state lines.

So, how best to fit 24 Grands Prix into a season? The start of the campaign is sensible, with back-to-back races in the Middle East, starting with Bahrain and then Saudi Arabia. Following these with the race that traditionally was the season opener in Melbourne is logical and fits the format of the past few campaigns. However, the identity of the fourth round of the season represents the biggest change in years; bringing the Japanese GP at Suzuka forward from autumn to spring as the cars and equipment head back towards Europe means that it can be paired with the Chinese GP in nearby Shanghai, which is back on the F1 calendar since the COVID pandemic.

It might have made more sense for the next four Grands Prix to be run in the order of Miami, Montreal, Imola and Monaco, but the Canadian GP is actually the fourth of these. After that,

F1 returns to Europe for a seven-race spell that visits Barcelona-Catalunya, the Red Bull Ring, Silverstone, the Hungaroring and Spa-Francorchamps, before having a summer break and then rounding off this spell with Grands Prix at Zandvoort and Monza.

The next two races are held to the east of Europe, with each having its own distinctive setting. The first of these comes when F1 edges into Asia for the Azerbaijan GP in Baku and then travels further south and east to go deep into south-east Asia for the Singapore GP night race, with both of these races providing their own distinctive city backdrop. In the case of Singapore's Marina Bay Circuit, the city is illuminated in the dark and looks stunning.

From there, a quartet of races at the Circuit of the Americas, Mexico City, Interlagos and Las Vegas keep F1 in the Americas before a more sensible conclusion with the last two races being in the Middle East, first at Losail in Qatar and finally at Abu Dhabi's Yas Marina.

So, we're all set for another global extravaganza and the benefits of a little more streamlining of the calendar will make life slightly easier.

// SAKHIR

The first Middle Eastern country to host F1, Bahrain's race is now part of the furniture, its Sakhir circuit blessed with one of the best sets of esses visited all year.

Accelerate, plan the best route to the apex, guess where a rival might place their car and attack. This has always been the approach required at circuits designed by Hermann Tilke. The German circuit architect likes the first corner to be a tight one, to encourage overtaking, preferably approached down a lengthy straight.

Turn 1 at Sakhir was designed like an earlier Tilke circuit, Sepang, to feed almost immediately into a tight second corner, meaning that a degree of patience and luck is required for drivers to merge where they hoped to in the heat of battle.

Accelerating through a right kink, the drivers then leave the 'oasis' section of the track, with grass verges disappearing and the feel of being in the desert replacing it as the track climbs a gentle slope to the right-hand hairpin at turn 4.

Passing is possible here, but the most important consideration is a clean exit for the downhill stretch that follows, with a left/right/left esse a real challenge. A good run can set up a passing opportunity into the tight turn 8.

After a slight climb to turn 9 and a drop to turn 10, the track doubles back behind the paddock and another overtaking chance can occur into turn 11.

The track climbs again to turn 13 before the decline to turns 14 and 15, with a clean run through here essential for an attacking chance into turn 1. This requires great precision, though, as the cars arrive at 205mph (330kph), and drivers brake as late as they dare and drop down to second gear while also trying to make sure they don't outbrake themselves.

INSIDE TRACK

BAHRAIN GRAND PRIX

Date:	**2 March**
Circuit name:	**Bahrain International Circuit**
Circuit length:	**3.363 miles/5.412km**
Number of laps:	**57**

PREVIOUS WINNERS

2015	**Lewis Hamilton** MERCEDES
2016	**Nico Rosberg** MERCEDES
2017	**Sebastian Vettel** FERRARI
2018	**Sebastian Vettel** FERRARI
2019	**Lewis Hamilton** MERCEDES
2020	**Lewis Hamilton** MERCEDES
2020*	**Sergio Perez** RACING POINT
2021	**Lewis Hamilton** MERCEDES
2022	**Charles Leclerc** FERRARI
2023	**Max Verstappen** RED BULL

* As the Sakhir GP

How it started: When Bahrain became the first Middle Eastern country to host a Grand Prix, in 2004, it was seen as an oddity, a race of convenience chosen chiefly because of its location between the time zones of the F1 fanbases in Europe and the Far East. The fact that oil-rich Bahrain had the money to build a circuit from scratch was also seen as a benefit at a time when F1 was pushing to increase its global spread.

A notable Grand Prix: Sergio Perez's F1 career appeared to be coming to an end in 2020 when he was given every reason to love this venue. He won the Sakhir GP – the second of two races at Sakhir in a row in that COVID-affected year – for the Racing Point team and this earned him his ride with Red Bull Racing for 2021. Famously, the race was the one in which George Russell stood in for Lewis Hamilton and would have won on his Mercedes debut but for a blunder in the pits, followed by a later puncture which wrecked his chances.

Location: The Bahrain International Circuit is located at Sakhir, which is in gently rolling scrub-dotted hills to the south of Bahrain's capital city, Manama.

BAHRAIN INTERNATIONAL CIRCUIT

Speed
0   100   200   300
309km/h maximum   **START**

⏱1 Timing sector	▬ DRS	Gear
DRS detection	▲ Overtaking opportunity	

2023 POLE TIME: **VERSTAPPEN (RED BULL), 1M29.708S, 134.952MPH/217.185KPH**
2023 WINNER'S AVERAGE SPEED: **122.324MPH/196.861KPH**
2023 FASTEST LAP: **ZHOU (ALFA ROMEO), 1M33.996S, 128.795MPH/207.276KPH**
LAP RECORD: **DE LA ROSA (MCLAREN), 1M31.447, 132.392 MPH/213.018KPH, 2005**

JEDDAH

With Saudi Arabia gathering sports by the handful, Formula One is part of its portfolio. It showcases this by taking it to the people with its track near Jeddah.

INSIDE TRACK

SAUDI ARABIAN GRAND PRIX

Date:	9 March
Circuit name:	**Jeddah Corniche Circuit**
Circuit length:	**3.837 miles/6.174km**
Number of laps:	**50**

PREVIOUS WINNERS

2021	**Lewis Hamilton**	MERCEDES
2022	**Max Verstappen**	RED BULL
2023	**Sergio Perez**	RED BULL

The story of the lap is about the two sections that link the opposite ends of its long, thin layout, namely turn 13 and turn 27. The run between these two corners is the more high-speed leg, predominantly dotted with flat-outsweepers, while the opposite leg has more severe corners in its many twists. The number of corners, 27, is by far the highest of any circuit visited by the World Championship.

The start of the lap gives away little, as circuit architect Hermann Tilke designed it like so many other of his F1 designs, to be tight, with a hard left followed by a more open right. What follows is a gradual building of speed, with turns 4 to 11 taken in sixth gear, sometimes seventh. Drivers are seldom given much line of sight as the corners come at them thick and fast. They keep their throttle planted and take all of them at more than 150mph (240kph). From F1's first visit here in 2021, drivers have aired concerns that any cars that clash or spin won't be spotted until they are almost upon them. So, the short straight from turn 12 to the hairpin at turn 13 is a relief.

The return leg has just as many corners, but they are more open, with the drivers shifting to eighth gear after turn 19 and reaching the fastest point of the lap just before turn 22, hitting 205mph (330kph) before having to take a tighter left-hander.

Then two right-hand kinks feed into a more open arcing section around to turn 27, the second hairpin. From here, it's just a short dash to the start/finish line.

How it started: Saudi Arabia was a slow starter when F1 began to visit the Middle East. Despite its considerable oil wealth, it remained on the side lines until 2021 when it joined the circus with its remarkable, high-speed circuit near Jeddah.

Looking to the future: For 2027, the Saudi Arabian GP is expected to move to a new, purpose-built circuit near Qiddiya. This has been designed with the assistance of former F1 racer Alexander Wurz and will offer Saudi F1 fans a chance to watch Grand Prix cars in a different environment.

A notable Grand Prix: For Lewis Hamilton, the 2021 race was all about reducing Max Verstappen's points advantage ahead of the final round. Hamilton arrived here eight points down and, after a race in which he and the Dutchman clashed when Verstappen was told to hand the lead back after he'd edged past, Hamilton hung on to win and leave Saudi Arabia level on points, with just one race to go at Yas Marina.

Rising national star: There are currently no Saudi stars rising through the single-seater ranks, but Reema Juffali has been racing in GTs in assorted European series. Bandar Alesayi is competitive in Middle Eastern Porsche circles, but he's 47 years of age.

Location: The Red Sea port city of Jeddah, an ingress point for religious pilgrimages to Mecca, is undergoing much development. Its temporary F1 circuit is sited eight miles (13km) north of its centre on a narrow corniche above a lagoon.

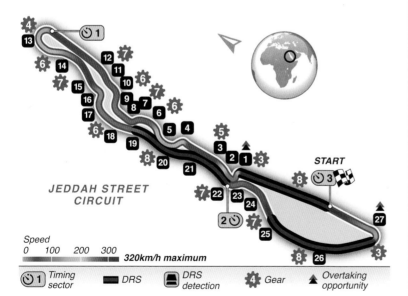

JEDDAH STREET CIRCUIT

Speed
0 100 200 300
320km/h maximum

🕐 1 Timing sector   ▬ DRS   ▭ DRS detection   ⚙ Gear   ▲ Overtaking opportunity

2023 POLE TIME: **PEREZ (RED BULL), 1M28.265S, 156.495MPH/251.855KPH**
2023 WINNER'S AVERAGE SPEED: **141.538MPH/227.783KPH**
2023 FASTEST LAP: **VERSTAPPEN (RED BULL), 1M31.906S, 150.271MPH/241.838KPH**
LAP RECORD: **HAMILTON (MERCEDES), 1M30.734S, 152.212MPH/244.962KPH, 2021**

// MELBOURNE

It still feels strange for an F1 season to begin anywhere other than Melbourne's Albert Park, but it continues to feel like the *real* start, with the first full-house crowd and genuine enthusiasm of the F1 calendar.

The magnificence of this long-standing Grand Prix venue is not the circuit itself, but its setting in a park in Melbourne's inner suburbs, just a few blocks from the Melbourne Bay beaches. This means ease of access thanks to a world-class public transport system while Australia's sports-mad populace guarantees a sell-out and a vociferous crowd.

The lap begins with a right/left combination that was given a better flow for last year's race. The first heavy braking is for the corner at the end of the short straight that leads from there. Wider than it used to be, its only real action comes on lap 1 when the field is still bunched.

The nature of the circuit at either end of the lake that it circumnavigates is the same, namely being very short straights between tights corners.

However, the biggest change to the stretch of the lap on the opposite side of the lake to the paddock is that its entry from turn 6 was made faster for 2023. The slow corners having been removed, it means that a top speed of up to 185mph (300kph) can now be achieved after the cars have blasted through a now more open esse by the sailing club.

Then, as with the west end of the lake, the return section around its eastern end is medium speed at best. Even with the final two corners having been made less acute, overtaking is incredibly hard to achieve. As with so many circuits, the best chance remains under braking for the first corner of the lap, although this has been added to by turn 11 now offering a little bit of an opening for the brave.

INSIDE TRACK

AUSTRALIAN GRAND PRIX

Date:	**24 March**
Circuit name:	**Albert Park**
Circuit length:	**3.280 miles/5.278km**
Number of laps:	**58**

PREVIOUS WINNERS

2012	**Jenson Button** McLAREN
2013	**Kimi Raikkonen** LOTUS
2014	**Nico Rosberg** MERCEDES
2015	**Lewis Hamilton** MERCEDES
2016	**Nico Rosberg** MERCEDES
2017	**Sebastian Vettel** FERRARI
2018	**Sebastian Vettel** FERRARI
2019	**Valtteri Bottas** MERCEDES
2022	**Charles Leclerc** FERRARI
2023	**Max Verstappen** RED BULL

How it started: There has been an Australian GP since 1928, but it didn't become a round of the World Championship until 1985. That was on a temporary circuit in the middle of Adelaide, but Melbourne wanted the race and took it over with its own temporary circuit in 1996 and has resisted challenges from Sydney ever since.

A notable Grand Prix: Every F1 fan likes an unexpected result and that was a likely prospect in 2012 when all of the teams struggled to get to grips with Pirelli's new tyres. A poor start from McLaren team-mate Lewis Hamilton let Jenson Button into the lead, but it was the way that Button used his tyre expertise that stood out as he was never caught.

Rising national star: Jack Brabham was Australia's first world champion, in 1959, but it is the son of another Australian world champion that is now knocking on F1's door. This is Jack Doohan, son of Mick, five-time world 500cc motorcycle champion, who won two F2 races last year.

Location: Albert Park is a municipal green space in the southern suburbs of Melbourne, and the circuit runs around a lake in the middle of that, all reachable by tram from the city centre.

MELBOURNE GRAND PRIX CIRCUIT

Lauda
Marina
Clark
Whiteford
Waite
Hill
Ascari
Senna
Prost
Pit lane
START

Speed
0 100 200 300
315km/h maximum

Symbol	Meaning
Timing sector	
DRS	
DRS detection	
Gear	
Overtaking opportunity	

2023 POLE TIME: **VERSTAPPEN (RED BULL)**, 1M16.732S, 153.867MPH/246.626KPH
2023 WINNER'S AVERAGE SPEED: **74.771MPH/120.332KPH**
2023 FASTEST LAP: **PEREZ (RED BULL)**, 1M20.235S, 147.149MPH/236.814KPH
LAP RECORD: **PEREZ (RED BULL)**, 1M20.235S, 147.149MPH/236.814KPH, 2023

SUZUKA

As the World Championship adds new venues, this gem's place on the calendar becomes all the more important, as it provides the drivers with a rare shot at a difficult circuit.

A circuit map shows its flow and the way the corners turn. However, to understand its challenge, the gradient of each of its sections is needed. Great tracks invariably have plenty of ups and downs, which is one of the many reasons why Suzuka remains a challenge.

The lap begins on a downward straight that narrows as it enters a gentle first corner. This is made more consequential by the fact that it feeds almost straight into tighter turn 2.

Then comes one of the best sequences used by F1: The Esses. With the incline increasing, the track jinks left, right, left, right and left again as the gradient levels out. Any deviation multiplies through the five corners and can lead to problems.

Accelerating through the final left, the drivers then hit the Degner Curves, with

the first taken in sixth before slowing for the second that feeds the track under a bridge that carries Suzuka's return leg.

The hairpin provides the second passing point, then drivers are flat-out until they turn into the dip down through Spoon Curve on to a long straight. The 130R kink is awesome and the drivers can hit 195mph (315kph) before having to prepare for braking into the Casio Triangle and perhaps make a pass into there. The track then starts dipping through one final corner.

Changing from its traditional date in early autumn to one in spring may bring different weather to the event, but the challenge will still be one of which the drivers are wary. Regardless of rain or shine, the Japanese fans are magnificent and bring a passion to brighten even the dullest of days.

INSIDE TRACK

JAPANESE GRAND PRIX

Date:	**7 April**
Circuit name:	**Suzuka International Racing Course**
Circuit length:	**3.609 miles/5.807km**
Number of laps:	**53**

PREVIOUS WINNERS

2012	**Sebastian Vettel** RED BULL
2013	**Sebastian Vettel** RED BULL
2014	**Lewis Hamilton** MERCEDES
2015	**Lewis Hamilton** MERCEDES
2016	**Nico Rosberg** MERCEDES
2017	**Lewis Hamilton** MERCEDES
2018	**Lewis Hamilton** MERCEDES
2019	**Valtteri Bottas** MERCEDES
2022	**Max Verstappen** RED BULL
2023	**Max Verstappen** RED BULL

How it started: Japan made its World Championship bow with a Grand Prix at Fuji in 1976, 14 years after the circuit opened. It returned there only once more, in 1977, when two marshals were killed. It was 10 more years before Suzuka first hosted the Japanese GP when Gerhard Berger won for Ferrari.

A notable Grand Prix: There have been so many great Japanese GPs, but one that stands out was in 2005 when Kimi Raikkonen chased and caught Giancarlo Fisichella's Renault – and somehow moved his McLaren ahead between the final corner and the finish line to lead going into the final lap.

A local hero: No Japanese driver has won in F1 yet, but Aguri Suzuki raced to third place at Suzuka for Larrousse in 1990, a result equalled by Takuma Sato for BAR in the 2004 United States GP at Indianapolis.

Rising national star: Former French F4 champion Ayumu Iwasa was a frequent winner in F2 last year, in his second year in F1's feeder category, so he is very much Japan's next in line behind Yuki Tsunoda.

Location: The circuit is woven into a sloping valley on a hillside some 30 miles (48km) south-west of Nagoya, which makes it over 90 miles (145km) east of Osaka.

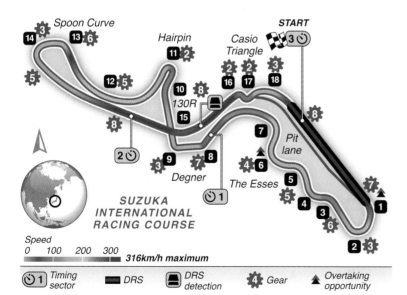

Spoon Curve · Hairpin · Casio Triangle · START · 130R · Pit lane · Degner · The Esses

SUZUKA INTERNATIONAL RACING COURSE

Speed
0   100   200   300
316km/h maximum

Symbol	Meaning
⏱ 1	Timing sector
▬	DRS
▣	DRS detection
⚙ 4	Gear
▲	Overtaking opportunity

2023 POLE TIME: VERSTAPPEN (RED BULL), 1M28.877S, 146.155MPH/235.214KPH
2023 WINNER'S AVERAGE SPEED: 126.005MPH/202.786KPH
2023 FASTEST LAP: VERSTAPPEN (RED BULL), 1M34.183S, 137.921MPH/221.963KPH
LAP RECORD: HAMILTON (MERCEDES), 1M30.983S, 142.772MPH/229.770KPH, 2019

// SHANGHAI

Back on the calendar for the first time since COVID, this venue, with its super-sized facilities, will remind F1 that its wide-open spaces offer plenty of scope for racing.

To gauge the size of the buildings along the main straight, you have to take the lift up to the eighth floor of the administration block at the entry of the pit lane and enter one of a pair of wing-shaped bridges that span the pit straight to connect it to the gargantuan grandstands. Looking down into the pits makes the crews look tiny.

Built to coax the World Championship to China, this Hermann Tilke-designed circuit is modelled on the shape of the Shang-letter of Shanghai. More importantly, he produced a brilliant first few corners, with turn 1 bucking up sharply to the right, continuing to turn right at turn 2 and feeding down into a sharp left at turn 3. Getting a passing manoeuvre wrong into 1 or 2 means that places can often change again into 3.

Then it's hard acceleration up to a broad hairpin at turn 6, another possible overtaking point.

The run back around the rear of the paddock is technical before a tight left and then more open turn 10 turns the track back in the opposite direction.

The far section is a copy of the first few corners, albeit without a gradient change, and the key is a clean exit to its final twist as it leads on to the lengthy back straight. The cars hit 205mph (330kph) before braking at the far end and this is where most of the overtaking is done, usually on the way into the hairpin but sometimes on the way out. The 90-degree left on to the start/finish straight can be tricky but is also crucial, as any mistake will allow a rival to catch a tow past the pits to challenge into turn 1.

INSIDE TRACK

CHINESE GRAND PRIX

Date:	**21 April**
Circuit name:	**Shanghai International Circuit**
Circuit length	**3.387 miles/5.451km**
Number of laps:	**56**

PREVIOUS WINNERS

2010	**Jenson Button** McLAREN
2011	**Lewis Hamilton** McLAREN
2012	**Nico Rosberg** MERCEDES
2013	**Fernando Alonso** FERRARI
2014	**Lewis Hamilton** MERCEDES
2015	**Lewis Hamilton** MERCEDES
2016	**Nico Rosberg** MERCEDES
2017	**Lewis Hamilton** MERCEDES
2018	**Daniel Ricciardo** RED BULL
2019	**Lewis Hamilton** MERCEDES

How it started: The first Chinese GP was held in 2004 and Rubens Barrichello arrived fresh from winning the Italian GP for Ferrari. Imbued with confidence, he resisted pressure from BAR's Jenson Button and McLaren's Kimi Raikkonen to win by one second.

A notable Grand Prix: For sheer drama, the 2007 Chinese GP stands out. This was the penultimate round and rookie Lewis Hamilton could have been crowned, but impending rain made everyone start on intermediate tyres. Most stayed on these after their first pit stop, but Ferrari's Kimi Raikkonen was catching Hamilton and went past. Then, with his tyres shot, Hamilton slid off at the pit entrance and beached his car in a gravel trap. With Raikkonen winning as Hamilton scored nothing, the Briton had one more chance, at Interlagos.

Rising national star: China took a long time to produce an F1 driver, having to wait until 2022 before Zhou Guanyu joined Alfa Romeo. Next in line is 19-year-old Cenyu Han, who raced in Eurocup 3 last year.

Location: Built on swampy countryside 20 miles (32km) north of the centre of Shanghai, the circuit no longer feels so far out as the city has expanded continuously towards it.

START ⏱ 3

SHANGHAI INTERNATIONAL CIRCUIT

Speed
0 100 200 300
348km/h maximum

⏱1	Timing sector		DRS		DRS detection	⚙️4	Gear	▲	Overtaking opportunity

2019 POLE TIME: **BOTTAS (MERCEDES)**, 1M31.547S, 133.193MPH/214.355KPH
2019 WINNER'S AVERAGE SPEED: **123.483MPH/198.727KPH**
2019 FASTEST LAP: **GASLY (RED BULL)**, 1M34.742S, 128.702MPH/207.126KPH
LAP RECORD: **M SCHUMACHER (FERRARI)**, 1M32.238S, 132.202MPH/212.759KPH, 2004

MIANI

This is one of the circuits to which commentator Martin Brundle comes to see if he can complete a grid walk without a minor celebrity snubbing him. The track itself, though, is acceptable.

There are many things that mark out this circuit, and its location in the car park of Miami's Hard Rock Stadium is the first of these. The second is that it is unusual in that its course is anti-clockwise, putting it very much in the minority of those visited by the World Championship.

The lap starts with a tight right where drivers weigh up the risks of trying to gain a place or two on the opening laps of the race, before feeding directly into an esse. Then, continuing to arc to the right, the drivers are able to accelerate into seventh gear before running through a left/right/esse sweep. Their pace is then slowed by third-gear turn 7, where the track changes direction and feeds into a high-speed run.

The fastest point of the lap comes on the approach to turn 11, The Beach South, where cars can even exceed 200mph

(320kph) after accelerating hard all the way from the exit of turn 7 and carrying as much momentum as possible through the sweeping twists in between.

Then the lap takes on a very different nature as it runs through a sequence of six low-speed corners, with the left/right chicane at turn 14 breaking the flow further.

Turn 16 is a 90-degree left-hander and it feeds the cars on to the lap's longest straight where they can get close to 200mph (320kph) and, like into turn 11, passing is a possibility into the hairpin at turn 17. The lap is then completed by a sweep through two open corners on to the short start/finish straight.

Like many a temporary circuit, the track surface can be bumpy and this has so far made finding a good set-up very tricky.

INSIDE TRACK

MIAMI GRAND PRIX

Date:	**5 May**
Circuit name:	**Miami International Autodrome**
Circuit length:	**3.364 miles/5.412km**
Number of laps:	**57**

PREVIOUS WINNERS

2022	**Max Verstappen**	RED BULL
2023	**Max Verstappen**	RED BULL

How it started: With its large Hispanic and thus F1-focused population, Miami was considered for years as being a sensible place for a Grand Prix to be held. Yet, despite temporary venues being created for sportscar racing in the 1980s, it took until 2022 for F1 to find a foothold. The site was perhaps further from the city centre than had been hoped, but the grounds of the Hard Rock Stadium offered sufficient space on which to build a temporary circuit.

A notable Grand Prix: From the two Grands Prix held on the Miami International Autodrome to date, both won by Max Verstappen for Red Bull Racing in 2022 and 2023, the latter stands out. The Dutchman had to battle his way forward from ninth to take the lead from pole-starting team-mate Sergio Perez with ten laps to go.

Rising national star: Jak Crawford was a race winner in F2 last year but the 18-year-old from North Carolina will clearly need another campaign in F1's feeder formula before a move to F1.

Location: This temporary circuit is located in the car parking lot of the Hard Rock Stadium in the suburb of Miami Gardens on the northern side of the sprawling metropolis.

The toughest corner: Getting turn 16 right is probably the most important point of the lap, as there is little distance in which to adjust line between the turn 14/15 chicane and this 90-degree left-hander on to the circuit's longest straight. Get it right and a driver's chance of catching a tow that might turn into a pass is improved.

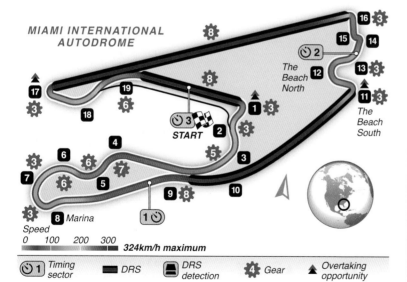

MIAMI INTERNATIONAL AUTODROME

The Beach North

The Beach South

START

Marina

Speed
0   100   200   300
324km/h maximum

⏱1	Timing sector	▬ DRS	▣ DRS detection	4 Gear	▲ Overtaking opportunity

2023 POLE TIME: **PEREZ (RED BULL), 1M26.841S, 139.382MPH/224.313KPH**
2023 WINNER'S AVERAGE SPEED: **131.166MPH/211.092KPH**
2023 FASTEST LAP: **VERSTAPPEN (RED BULL), 1M29.708S, 134.952MPH/217.184KPH**
LAP RECORD: **VERSTAPPEN (RED BULL), 1M29.708S, 134.952MPH/217.184KPH, 2023**

IMOLA

The sudden search for venues caused by global travel restrictions imposed because of COVID brought a few old favourites back onto the F1 calendar, including Imola, and the Italian circuit has kept its place since then.

Despite never being able to stake a claim to be Italy's premier circuit, Imola has managed to stage 30 Grands Prix, largely thanks to hosting the San Marino GP although it's not located in the principality.

The first feeling on arriving at this circuit at the foot of the rolling hills should be one of arriving in a springlike Eden, with orchards in its infield. The second, even with recent improvements to the infrastructure, is that of going back to its heyday in the 1990s when it hosted Italy's warm-up Grand Prix ahead of the real thing at Monza.

Because of the restrictive boundaries of the site, the circuit remains old school, as it doesn't have the space for modern day run-off areas. On the plus side, the racing footage looks more exciting with landscape so close at hand and it's made

better still by plenty of gradient change.

The lap starts with the Tamburello chicane followed by a second one, the Variante Villeneuve, then the original first corner of consequence, the hairpin at Tosa. It's uphill out of here, with the track rising behind a park before Piratella, a sharp left that feeds the cars down into Acque Minerale. This pair of right-handers, the second tighter than the first, has to be negotiated before the track rises sharply again for a run up to a chicane on the crest. This is not overtaking country: it's far too tight.

Dropping to the first Rivazza and then again to the second, the track levels out for the blast on to the start/finish straight down which cars can hit 205mph (330kph) in their attempts to line up an overtaking move into that first chicane.

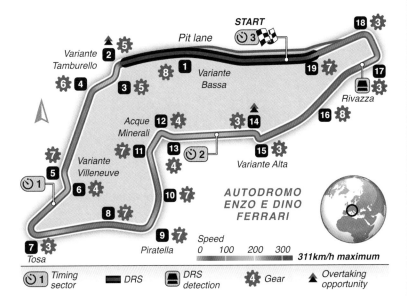

START

Pit lane

Variante Tamburello

Variante Bassa

Rivazza

Acque Minerali

Variante Villeneuve

Variante Alta

AUTODROMO ENZO E DINO FERRARI

Speed
0   100   200   300
311km/h maximum

Piratella

Tosa

⏱1 Timing sector — DRS 🎮 DRS detection ⚙ Gear ▲ Overtaking opportunity

2022 POLE TIME: VERSTAPPEN (RED BULL), 1M27.999S, 124.787MPH/200.825KPH
2022 WINNER'S AVERAGE SPEED: 125.058MPH/201.262KPH
2022 FASTEST LAP: VERSTAPPEN (RED BULL), 1M18.446S, 139.983MPH/225.281KPH
LAP RECORD: HAMILTON (MERCEDES), 1M15.484S, 145.476MPH/223.121KPH, 2020

INSIDE TRACK

EMILIA ROMAGNA GRAND PRIX

Date:	**19 May**
Circuit name:	**Autodromo Enzo e Dino Ferrari**
Circuit length:	**3.051 miles/4.909km**
Number of laps:	**63**

PREVIOUS WINNERS

2000*	**Michael Schumacher**	FERRARI
2001*	**Ralf Schumacher**	WILLIAMS
2002*	**Michael Schumacher**	FERRARI
2003*	**Michael Schumacher**	FERRARI
2004*	**Michael Schumacher**	FERRARI
2005*	**Fernando Alonso**	RENAULT
2006*	**Michael Schumacher**	FERRARI
2020**	**Lewis Hamilton**	MERCEDES
2021**	**Max Verstappen**	RED BULL
2022**	**Max Verstappen**	RED BULL

* Run as the San Marino GP
** Run as the Emilia Romagna GP

How it started: Built in 1952, the Autodromo Enzo e Dino Ferrari hosted a non-championship F1 race in 1963 and later the Italian GP in 1979 – Monza having been rested the year after Ronnie Peterson was killed there. Then, in 1981, its Grand Prix was given the title of the San Marino GP, meaning that Italy could hold two Grands Prix per year.

A notable Grand Prix: Bad blood surfaced between Ferrari drivers Didier Pironi and Gilles Villeneuve in 1982 when, from a grid depleted by ten of the teams boycotting it, the Ferrari duo fought over victory when the Renaults retired, and Pironi ignored team orders to win.

Its darkest day: Nothing will hopefully ever match the events of 1994 when Rubens Barrichello had a huge crash in practice; Roland Ratzenberger was killed in qualifying; JJ Lehto's Benetton was rear-ended on the grid; then Ayrton Senna crashed fatally.

The race that wasn't: There was due to be an Emilia Romagna GP in 2023, but this never happened due to the paddock being flooded.

Location: The circuit is on the southern edge of Imola, 20 miles (32km) south-east of Bologna.

MONACO

Monaco might not offer the drivers much space to play, but it's an essential part of the World Championship calendar, providing the colour and the history that new venues do not.

The streets of Monte Carlo have changed enormously since the 1950s, but there is a magic that F1 would be foolish to lose.

Certainly, space is limited for the teams' requirements, but the upside is that this is the one race that people outside the world of F1 know about. Monaco is glamorous, with the superyachts packing out the harbour and the castle and grand buildings draped over the hills that rise from there.

The circuit is never less than cramped, though. Even the start/finish straight isn't really straight, but it's the way that the circuit has to thread its way through the streets and around the buildings that gives it its distinctive nature.

The first corner, Ste Devote, is a hard right entered via a kink, then it's sharply uphill on the winding climb to Massenet, where the track turns hard left. Casino

Square follows, with the drivers skirting the park and diving down to Mirabeau, a sharp right into which the occasional passing move used to be attempted when the cars were smaller.

The slope continues down to the Grand Hotel hairpin and keeps falling through two rights to hit the level again before the drivers charge into the brightly-lit tunnel beneath the hotel. The fastest point comes on the slope down from the tunnel exit to the Nouvelle Chicane, with the fastest cars hitting 180mph (290kph) before the drivers brake heavily and drop down to second for the left/right/left flick.

Blasting along the harbourfront, it's now a quick flick through Tabac and a dazzling double esse around the swimming pool before two more rights and back on to the start/finish straight.

INSIDE TRACK

MONACO GRAND PRIX

Date:	**26 May**
Circuit name:	**Monte Carlo**
Circuit length:	**2.074 miles/3.337km**
Number of laps:	**78**

PREVIOUS WINNERS

2013	**Nico Rosberg**	MERCEDES
2014	**Nico Rosberg**	MERCEDES
2015	**Nico Rosberg**	MERCEDES
2016	**Lewis Hamilton**	MERCEDES
2017	**Sebastian Vettel**	FERRARI
2018	**Daniel Ricciardo**	RED BULL
2019	**Lewis Hamilton**	MERCEDES
2021	**Max Verstappen**	RED BULL
2022	**Sergio Perez**	RED BULL
2023	**Max Verstappen**	RED BULL

How it started: At the suggestion of cigarette manufacturer Antony Nogues, Monaco created a circuit around its streets in 1929 and its first Grand Prix was won by a Bugatti-driving Englishman who raced as 'W. Williams'.

A notable Grand Prix: In terms of dramatic finishes, the 1970 Monaco GP stands out as one of the best. Jackie Stewart had the lead in his Tyrrell-run March, but a misfire slowed him and Jack Brabham took over. However, Jochen Rindt began closing on him, exerting huge pressure with his Lotus. And it told, with Brabham sliding straight on into the straw bales at the final corner.

A local hero: Louis Chiron was the greatest driver from Monaco until Charles Leclerc burst onto the scene. Chiron's best result was third in his home Grand Prix in a works Maserati in 1950. Although a Grand Prix winner, Leclerc has yet to stand on his home race podium.

Rising national star: Charles Leclerc's younger brother Arthur managed a podium finish, for third place in Melbourne, in F2 last year.

Location: There isn't a Grand Prix closer to the heart of the country in which it is held than this one curled around the harbour and through the streets of capital Monte Carlo.

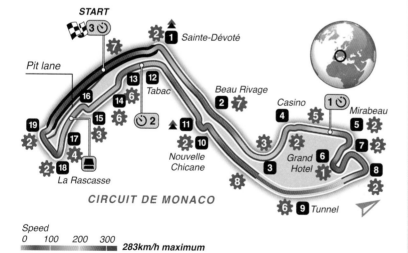

START

Pit lane

Sainte-Dévoté

Tabac

Beau Rivage

Casino

Mirabeau

Nouvelle Chicane

Grand Hotel

La Rascasse

Tunnel

CIRCUIT DE MONACO

Speed
0   100   200   300
283km/h maximum

Timing sector	DRS	DRS detection	Gear	Overtaking opportunity

2023 POLE TIME: VERSTAPPEN (RED BULL), 1M11.365S, 104.673MPH/168.455KPH
2023 WINNER'S AVERAGE SPEED: 89.184MPH/143.452KPH
2023 FASTEST LAP: HAMILTON (MERCEDES), 1M15.650S, 98.673MPH/158.799KPH
LAP RECORD: HAMILTON (MERCEDES), 1M12.909S, 102.383MPH/164.769KPH, 2021

// MONTREAL

This is a circuit that is made up mainly of medium-speed corners, but it has one long straight at the end of its lap that has offered plenty of slipstreaming action over the years.

INSIDE TRACK

CANADIAN GRAND PRIX

Date:	**9 June**
Circuit name:	**Circuit Gilles Villeneuve**
Circuit length:	**2.710 miles/4.361km**
Number of laps:	**70**

PREVIOUS WINNERS

2012	**Lewis Hamilton**	McLAREN
2013	**Sebastian Vettel**	RED BULL
2014	**Daniel Ricciardo**	RED BULL
2015	**Lewis Hamilton**	MERCEDES
2016	**Lewis Hamilton**	MERCEDES
2017	**Lewis Hamilton**	MERCEDES
2018	**Sebastian Vettel**	FERRARI
2019	**Lewis Hamilton**	MERCEDES
2022	**Max Verstappen**	RED BULL
2023	**Max Verstappen**	RED BULL

There are F1 circuits built in open spaces, like Silverstone, and others that are hemmed in by their surroundings, like Monaco or the home of the Canadian GP.

Built on an island across the St Lawrence River from Montreal, the plot is less than ideal, as there is so little space, with the 1976 Olympic Games rowing course narrowing the plot behind the pits yet further.

The approach to the first corner is through a right-hand kink, and there is often a concertina effect here on lap 1 that can catch out those behind. Running wide on the exit can put cars out of position for turn 2, Virage Senna, where the track doubles back to feed the cars on to an arcing run between woods and water that is interrupted by a chicane and later a sharp left.

The flow picks up again, with just a right/left esse before the drivers reach l'Epingle, the lap's tightest hairpin. It's the perfect place for a dive up the inside in front of the grandstands, but it's tight enough to make any move a gamble.

The track then runs alongside the rowing lake, hitting its fastest point where cars top 195mph (315kph). It looks as though they are heading directly ahead into the pits before having to brake hard for the lap's final corner, a right/left chicane that offers two things. The first is the most likely place for overtaking, but the second is the most likely point for collision, with either a rival or the wall on the exit. Drivers getting it wrong here have been frequent and it was once known as the Champions' Wall, as so many former champions clipped it.

How it started: When this circuit took over the Canadian GP from Mosport Park in 1978, it was both cold and wet. In short, conditions were miserable, but this tailor-made circuit in a display ground was blessed by local hero Gilles Villeneuve taking victory for Ferrari to earn it a second shot in 1979.

A notable Grand Prix: For sheer genius in changeable conditions, Jenson Button's win in 2011 takes the prize. He started seventh in his McLaren but gained ground as others spun in the rain, then fitted dry tyres and chased down Sebastian Vettel; he passed him when the Red Bull slid wide at turn 6 on the final lap. With all the rain delays, the race took more than four hours.

A local hero: No one has come close to the adoration afforded to Gilles Villeneuve when he thrilled fans with his flamboyant performances for Ferrari from 1978 until his death in 1982. Even his son Jacques, who won the 1997 F1 title, has had to play a secondary role.

Location: The circuit sits on the Île Notre-Dame on the opposite side of the St Lawrence River from Montreal, but it is reached easily by the city's metro which saves on the need for parking.

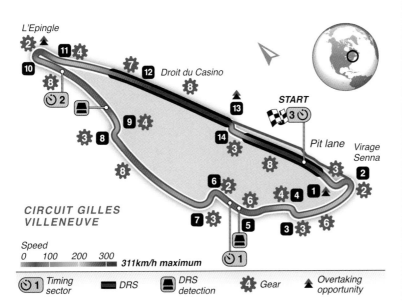

CIRCUIT GILLES VILLENEUVE

L'Epingle · Droit du Casino · START · Pit lane · Virage Senna

Speed
0 100 200 300 · 311km/h maximum

Timing sector · DRS · DRS detection · Gear · Overtaking opportunity

2023 POLE TIME: **VERSTAPPEN (RED BULL)**, 1M25.858S, 113.616MPH/182.848KPH
2023 WINNER'S AVERAGE SPEED: **121.111MPH/194.910KPH**
2023 FASTEST LAP: **PEREZ (RED BULL)**, 1M14.481S, 130.986MPH/210.803KPH
LAP RECORD: **BOTTAS (MERCEDES)**, 1M13.078S, 133.491MPH/214.833KPH, 2019

BARCELONA

As long as Spanish fans have Fernando Alonso and Carlos Sainz Jr in F1, this long-standing Spanish GP venue will have a lively feel, if not much in the way of overtaking.

In the 1970s, motorsport was hugely popular in Spain, but only as long as it was two-wheeled sport. Spanish racing drivers were harder to find, and it took until the arrival of Fernando Alonso at the start of the 21st century for the fans to love F1.

This circuit north of Barcelona was the scene of his arrival and suddenly this venue that had hosted the Spanish GP since 1991 was packed with fans with a united cause.

The track itself isn't that exciting, as it tends to offer close racing rather than overtaking. The first corner is the most likely passing place, as its approach is broad and the removal of the gravel trap between there and turn 2 means that those forced wide on lap 1 aren't beached.

Climbing into turn 3, which bends through 160 degrees then feeds into a 180-degree right at turn 4, the lap tightens up at turn 5. It then drops steeply, goes through a kink and brings the drivers to Wurth. This is a 90-degree left at the foot of a climb to Campsa, an open right at the crest. A good exit on to the infield straight is vital here if a driver is to have a passing shot into the reprofiled corner at its far end.

Then it's uphill to turn 12. This right-hander used to feed into a very weak and simplistic section of the circuit, but the removal last year of the chicane before the final corner was a major improvement. This allowed drivers to get a better flow onto the start/finish straight for the first time since 2006, offering them more of a chance of catching a tow at 200mph (320kph) down towards the first corner.

INSIDE TRACK

SPANISH GRAND PRIX

Date:	**23 June**
Circuit name:	**Circuit de Barcelona-Catalunya**
Circuit length:	**2.894 miles/4.657km**
Number of laps:	**66**

PREVIOUS WINNERS

2013	**Fernando Alonso** FERRARI
2014	**Lewis Hamilton** MERCEDES
2015	**Nico Rosberg** MERCEDES
2016	**Max Verstappen** RED BULL
2017	**Lewis Hamilton** MERCEDES
2018	**Lewis Hamilton** MERCEDES
2019	**Lewis Hamilton** MERCEDES
2020	**Lewis Hamilton** MERCEDES
2021	**Lewis Hamilton** MERCEDES
2022	**Max Verstappen** RED BULL
2023	**Max Verstappen** RED BULL

How it started: The Spanish GP found its way to this new circuit in 1991. It was an immediate success, as its facilities became popular with the teams for the then regular testing that they conducted back in the day.

A notable Grand Prix: Michael Schumacher's charge to victory for Ferrari in 1996 was notable but, for novelty value, Max Verstappen's triumph on his debut for Red Bull after being promoted from Scuderia Toro Rosso early in 2016 stands out. The 18-year-old grabbed the opportunity with both hands to advance from fourth, albeit helped by Mercedes' Lewis Hamilton and Nico Rosberg colliding. The Dutchman set off after team-mate Daniel Ricciardo and, when the team put the Australian on a poor strategy, Verstappen raced through.

A local hero: Fernando Alonso stands above all other Spanish racing drivers. This isn't just because he is a double world champion, crowned in 2005 and 2006 with Renault, but because his pace doesn't appear to have slowed in 23 years at the sport's top level.

Location: Just where the hills start to roll 15 miles (24km) north of Barcelona, the circuit is located on a hillside that was once in fields but is now surrounded by industrial estates.

CIRCUIT DE BARCELONA-CATALUNYA

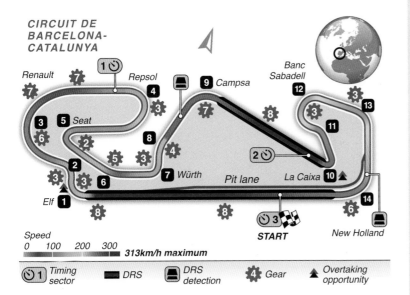

⏱1	Timing sector
▬	DRS
▣	DRS detection
⚙4	Gear
▲	Overtaking opportunity

Speed 0 100 200 300 — 313km/h maximum

2023 POLE TIME: VERSTAPPEN (RED BULL), 1M12.272S, 144.141MPH/231.974KPH
2023 WINNER'S AVERAGE SPEED: 130.214MPH/209.560KPH
2023 FASTEST LAP: VERSTAPPEN (RED BULL), 1M16.330S, 136.478MPH/219.641KPH
LAP RECORD: VERSTAPPEN (RED BULL), 1M16.330S, 136.478MPH/219.641KPH, 2023

The famous Orange Army of Dutch fans fill the grandstands at the Austrian Grand Prix.

// RED BULL RING

Uphill and down dale is the essence of this scenic circuit with a great passing place into turn 3. The racing can be close – often too close – and contact is not uncommon.

The climb from the grid to the first corner at the Red Bull Ring is unusually steep, the gradient enough to make your calves burn on a track walk. For the drivers, all they can see at this point is the sky as they climb and yet they know that they have to commit to the turn-in before they can set their eyes on the apex. Fortunately, there is plenty of run-off space on the exit of the corner as the climb flattens out.

The climb from there is more gradual but it angles upwards towards its conclusion at the turning point to turn 3, with cars topping 200mph (320kph) on the approach. Turn 3 is a really tight right-hander and many a driver has decided to be the hero and dive up the inside here, but it's a game of diminishing returns and few of these moves have resulted in happiness for all parties involved.

The track then crosses the foot of the hill before the next heavy braking point into turn 4, where it drops away sharply through this tight right.

The lap then changes its nature as it snakes down the slope towards the back of the paddock, before turning uphill again out of turn 7. A kink to the right follows at turn 8 before the track runs between the trees over a crest and drops into the final two corners.

Each of these right-handers fall from entry to exit and a tidy exit line out of the penultimate curve can set drivers up for the optimum course through turn 10. If they can gain a tow past the pits they might try and line up an overtaking manoeuvre into the first corner.

INSIDE TRACK

AUSTRIAN GRAND PRIX

Date:	**30 June**
Circuit name:	**Red Bull Ring**
Circuit length:	**2.684 miles/4.318km**
Number of laps:	**71**

PREVIOUS WINNERS

2016	**Lewis Hamilton** MERCEDES
2017	**Valtteri Bottas** MERCEDES
2018	**Max Verstappen** RED BULL
2019	**Max Verstappen** RED BULL
2020	**Valtteri Bottas** MERCEDES
2020*	**Lewis Hamilton** MERCEDES
2021	**Max Verstappen** RED BULL
2021*	**Max Verstappen** RED BULL
2022	**Charles Leclerc** FERRARI
2023	**Max Verstappen** RED BULL

*As the Styrian GP

How it started: The Osterreichring was opened as Austria's first purpose-built circuit in 1969 and hosted a round of the World Sports Car Championship. In 1970, it welcomed F1 and held the Austrian GP until 1987, after which it was chopped as it became the A1-Ring, later Red Bull Ring.

A notable Grand Prix: The 1975 Austrian GP stands out for the torrential rain that beset it and the fact that the generally accident-prone Vittorio Brambilla was the one who made the fewest mistakes. He was in front when it was stopped early as cars were aquaplaning, only to see the chequered flag, celebrate and crash his March into the barriers.

A local hero: Niki Lauda, who died in 2019, became Austria's second world champion after Jochen Rindt when he won the title for Ferrari in 1975. By bouncing straight back from a fiery accident in 1976 to be champion again in 1977 was phenomenal, and he then took a career break and came back again to become champion with McLaren in 1984.

Location: The circuit is in the Styrian Alps near the town of Knittelfeld, which is 45 miles (72km) north-west of the closest city, Graz.

START

RED BULL RING

Speed
0   100   200   300
312km/h maximum

Symbol	Meaning
⏱1	Timing sector
▬	DRS
🔲	DRS detection
⚙4	Gear
▲	Overtaking opportunity

2023 POLE TIME: **VERSTAPPEN (RED BULL), 1M04.391S, 150.284MPH/241.860KPH**
2023 WINNER'S AVERAGE SPEED: **133.534MPH/214.902KPH**
2023 FASTEST LAP: **VERSTAPPEN (RED BULL), 1M07.012S, 144.139MPH/231.970KPH**
LAP RECORD: **SAINZ JR (MCLAREN), 1M05.619S, 147.199MPH/236.894KPH, 2020**

SILVERSTONE

This British circuit continues to keep up with the passage of time, nipping here and tucking there to retain its relevance as F1 evolves, just as it has been doing since 1950.

Silverstone has changed its format numerous times since it opened for racing in 1948, yet it retains its essence as a fast and open blast across a largely level site.

Starting in front of the Wing pit building, it's a short dash to the first corner, Abbey. This is a quick flick that can catch people out, like Zhou Guanyu who was inverted there in 2022, his Alfa Romeo then digging into the gravel and being launched over the barriers. To prevent this happening again, the gravel trap was replaced by asphalt run-off.

The first braking point comes at Village, a right-hand hairpin where there is the inevitable jostling for position on the opening lap of the race. Another hairpin follows, before drivers are able to accelerate through the gears as they take the kink onto the Wellington Straight.

The next overtaking point comes at the far end of the straight, into Brooklands, right in front of the drivers and guests in the British Racing Drivers' Club. Balancing the car through the two rights that make up Luffield, the drivers then blast along the straight past the old pits. Then they come to the best few corners. First of these is Copse, a seventh gear right followed by Maggotts and then, best of all, the Becketts sweepers, where the drivers have to keep changing direction, their cars on tiptoes in sixth.

Hangar Straight comes next and the fastest point of the lap comes on the approach to Stowe at the far end, with cars touching 185mph (300kph). Then, exiting the right-hander, the cars drop into a slight dip called the Vale before entering the long, long right at Club that completes the lap.

INSIDE TRACK

BRITISH GRAND PRIX

Date:	**7 July**
Circuit name:	**Silverstone**
Circuit length:	**3.661 miles/5.891km**
Number of laps:	**52**

PREVIOUS WINNERS

2015	**Lewis Hamilton**	MERCEDES
2016	**Lewis Hamilton**	MERCEDES
2017	**Lewis Hamilton**	MERCEDES
2018	**Sebastian Vettel**	FERRARI
2019	**Lewis Hamilton**	MERCEDES
2020	**Lewis Hamilton**	MERCEDES
2020*	**Max Verstappen**	RED BULL
2021	**Lewis Hamilton**	MERCEDES
2022	**Carlos Sainz Jr**	FERRARI
2023	**Max Verstappen**	RED BULL

* 70th Anniversary GP

How it started: Britain was littered with airfields after World War II and a decision to create a circuit from its runways and perimeter roads in 1948 was such a success that it hosted the British GP that year. Two years later, it held the first round of the inaugural World Championship.

A notable Grand Prix: The 2020 British GP stands out for the way that tyre failures struck. Valtteri Bottas lost second with a blow-out two laps before the finish. Red Bull brought Max Verstappen in as a precaution and then leader Lewis Hamilton also suffered tyre failure on the final lap, but just managed to limp to the line ahead of Verstappen.

A local hero: Lewis Hamilton, with his seven F1 titles, is the favourite of the younger fans, but Nigel Mansell, world champion with Williams in 1992, is still the hero for many.

Rising national star: F2 race winner Ollie Bearman looks to be the next young Briton capable of making the step up to F1, but a second year in F2 might be wise.

Location: The circuit is to the south of the village of the same name which is a few miles west of Towcester, on the Northamptonshire/Buckinghamshire border.

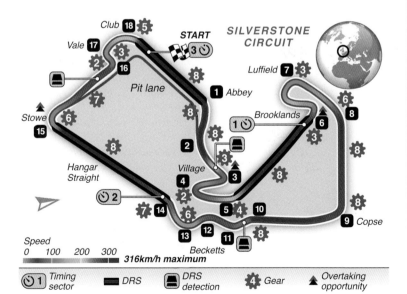

SILVERSTONE CIRCUIT

Speed
0 100 200 300
316km/h maximum

⏱1 Timing sector | DRS | DRS detection | 4 Gear | ▲ Overtaking opportunity

2023 POLE TIME: **VERSTAPPEN (RED BULL), 1M26.720S, 152.190MPH/244.926KPH**

2023 WINNER'S AVERAGE SPEED: **133.858MPH/215.424KPH**

2023 FASTEST LAP: **VERSTAPPEN (RED BULL), 1M30.275S, 145.973MPH/234.922KPH**

LAP RECORD: **VERSTAPPEN (RED BULL), 1M27.097S, 151.300MPH/243.494KPH, 2020**

// HUNGARORING

This circuit uses its gradient changes well as it runs to the far side of a valley and back, but its tight nature makes overtaking a hope rather than a likelihood.

INSIDE TRACK

HUNGARIAN GRAND PRIX

Date:	**21 July**
Circuit name:	**Hungaroring**
Circuit length:	**2.722 miles/4.381km**
Number of laps:	**70**

There is one element that the undulating Hungaroring circuit really lacks, and this is a straight of notable length. Instead, the lap is made up principally of medium-speed corners as it traverses a valley, runs along its far side and then returns. There is no point at which the full majesty of an F1 car is unleashed for long enough to show its full potential.

The dipping start/finish straight leads down to the first corner and on down through its exit, along the short run to turn 2, where the track drops again; it's already clear to the drivers that this is no Silverstone. It's only when they reach turn 3 down a short slope that they get to tackle a corner that isn't a hairpin. Instead, it's a right-hand kink opening on to another straight that takes the cars down to the lowest point of the outward leg of the lap. The track then rises up again as it climbs the far side of the valley.

Turn 4 is tricky as it has a blind entry over a crest, then the flow slows again through turn 5 as the cars are brought back onto the level, running through a series of twisting turns until dropping off this plateau at turn 11.

The track descends into another dip before running through a tight right and a hairpin behind the paddock and then another, still heading upwards, that brings the cars back onto the level of the start/finish straight. It's only when accelerating along here that the cars hit the fastest point of the lap, at 183mph (295kph), before having to brake again and perhaps seek an inside line for an overtaking move into turn 1.

PREVIOUS WINNERS

2014	**Daniel Ricciardo**	RED BULL
2015	**Sebastian Vettel**	FERRARI
2016	**Lewis Hamilton**	MERCEDES
2017	**Sebastian Vettel**	FERRARI
2018	**Lewis Hamilton**	MERCEDES
2019	**Lewis Hamilton**	MERCEDES
2020	**Lewis Hamilton**	MERCEDES
2021	**Esteban Ocon**	ALPINE
2022	**Max Verstappen**	RED BULL
2023	**Max Verstappen**	RED BULL

How it started: Precisely after the first Hungarian GP was held in a circuit laid out in capital Budapest's Nepliget Park, this purpose-built circuit opened for business and hosted the second in 1986. This was a surprise, as Hungary was still a communist country, but it proved a good decision as a crowd of 200,000 filled the spectator banking and grandstands to watch, with Nelson Piquet winning for Williams.

A notable Grand Prix: Overtaking has never been easy here, and this is why Jenson Button's win for Honda in 2006 stands out as he started 14th on the grid. But what made the chase all the more exciting was rain and who could master the changing conditions best. Rivals Fernando Alonso and Kimi Raikkonen respectively lost a wheel after a pit stop when leading and crashed out, to help Button's charge, and the Briton stayed calm and took his first win in 114 attempts. It was Honda's first since 1967.

A local hero: Hungary's only Grand Prix winner was Ferenc Szisz, who triumphed in the very first Grand Prix, held at Le Mans, in 1906.

Location: The circuit is set in rolling hills near the village of Mogyrod, which is a dozen miles (19km) to the north-east of Budapest.

HUNGARORING

START

Pit lane

Speed
0   100   200   300

308km/h maximum

(clock) 1 Timing sector	▬ DRS	(icon) DRS detection	⚙ Gear	▲ Overtaking opportunity

2023 POLE TIME: **HAMILTON (MERCEDES), 1M16.609S, 127.922MPH/205.871KPH**
2023 WINNER'S AVERAGE SPEED: **116.480MPH/187.457KPH**
2023 FASTEST LAP: **VERSTAPPEN (RED BULL), 1M20.504S, 121.733MPH/195.910KPH**
LAP RECORD: **HAMILTON (MERCEDES), 1M16.627S, 127.892MPH/205.823KPH, 2020**

SPA-FRANCORCHAMPS

Fans drawn to F1 for the first time by Netflix's *Drive to Survive* series find this Belgian classic the most jaw-dropping of F1's venues for its high-speed blasts through the forest.

A lap of Spa-Francorchamps starts with a short blast from the grid to the first corner, the right-hand hairpin at La Source, but from there the lap immediately bares its teeth after the steep descent past the old pits towards Eau Rouge.

This is the start of the legendarily difficult two-corner combination with a flick to the left and then to the right as the cars hit a compression and rise sharply towards Raidillon where they flick left, and the drivers pray that they have kept more momentum than any rival. If so, then all is good, as the ascending straight to Les Combes offers an eternity for them to make the most of the slipstream and mount an overtaking move.

Les Combes is a right/left esse and its entry offers the best passing place. The track then dips again through a right-hander where taking too much kerb on the exit can lead to a delaying trip through a gravel trap. Then the track keeps dropping through the tight right at Bruxelles and the more open left known as Speakers' Corner.

The drop continues through the Double Gauche, formerly known as Pouhon. Levelling out again, the drivers have to negotiate the Fagnes sweepers and get into a good position for the right at Campus, which is vital to set a car up for the best exit to Curve Paul Frère to start the high-speed return leg from there.

If the run out of there was good, it will help a driver all the way through the fearsome left at Blanchimont, taken in top gear at 193mph (310kph) and as deep into the final chicane as possible for braking for that final corner.

BELGIAN GRAND PRIX

Date:	**28 July**
Circuit name:	**Spa-Francorchamps**
Circuit length:	**4.352 miles/7.004km**
Number of laps:	**44**

PREVIOUS WINNERS

2014	**Daniel Ricciardo**	RED BULL
2015	**Lewis Hamilton**	MERCEDES
2016	**Nico Rosberg**	MERCEDES
2017	**Lewis Hamilton**	MERCEDES
2018	**Sebastian Vettel**	FERRARI
2019	**Charles Leclerc**	FERRARI
2020	**Lewis Hamilton**	MERCEDES
2021	**Max Verstappen**	RED BULL
2022	**Max Verstappen**	RED BULL
2023	**Max Verstappen**	RED BULL

How it started: Opened as a road course in 1924, the circuit was 9.236 miles (14.864km) long and ran into the next valley close to Malmedy and Stavelot before returning up the hill. It was one of six circuits in the inaugural World Championship in 1950, when Juan Manuel Fangio won for Alfa Romeo.

A notable Grand Prix: The 1998 Belgian GP was remarkable for many reasons – 13 drivers being involved in a first corner accident; Damon Hill taking the lead for Jordan; Mika Hakkinen being spun by Michael Schumacher and being collected by Johnny Herbert; Schumacher clattering into the rear of David Coulthard's McLaren in the spray; and, finally, Hill leading home team-mate Ralf Schumacher for Jordan's first win.

A local hero: With no true talent coming through the single-seater ranks, Belgian fans have to look to the past, to when Jacky Ickx came closest to landing a world title, in 1970, when he raced for Ferrari. He just failed to overhaul Jochen Rindt's tally before going on to win the Le Mans 24 Hours six times.

Location: The circuit is laid out on a sloping wooded site in the Ardennes, 10 miles (16km) south of Spa, just below the village of Francorchamps.

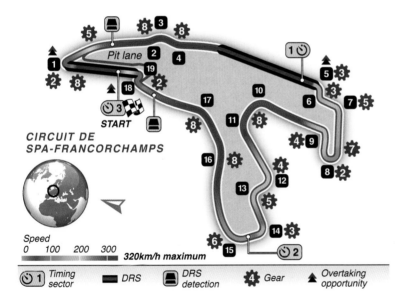

CIRCUIT DE SPA-FRANCORCHAMPS

Speed
0 100 200 300
320km/h maximum

⏱1 Timing sector   ▬ DRS   DRS detection   4 Gear   ▲ Overtaking opportunity

2023 POLE TIME: LECLERC (FERRARI), 1M46.988S, 146.441MPH/236.675KPH
2023 WINNER'S AVERAGE SPEED: 139.197MPH/224.017KPH
2023 FASTEST LAP: HAMILTON (MERCEDES), 1M47.305S, 146.008MPH/234.978KPH
LAP RECORD: BOTTAS (MERCEDES), 1M46.286S, 147.422MPH/237.290KPH, 2018

// ZANDVOORT

Even if there wasn't a Dutch driver to cheer to victory, this Dutch seaside circuit would be a special place both for its intimate atmosphere and its tortuous course over the dunes.

Despite recent modernisation, the nature of the Zandvoort circuit has its roots back in bygone decades. The pit buildings remain on a 1970s scale, the paddock is constricted and the proximity of the fans to the track still remarkably close.

On a spring or autumn day, the track can seem desolate, with the wind blowing in from the North Sea. However, in summer, the place comes alive, with the fans in the dunes able to show themselves and their orange banners rather than digging themselves into windproof burrows.

The lap starts with a run down to Tarzan, a slightly banked right-hander into which overtaking is usually an option. Then comes the run behind the paddock, with the left/right Gerlachbocht to be negotiated before the cars drop into the banked bowl at Hugenholtzbocht. A good exit is vital as the track climbs over the dunes through a high-speed sweep of corners that culminates at Scheivlak. This is a fearsome turn, because all the drivers can see as they power over the crest at its entrance is a giant dune ahead of them. They must keep their momentum flowing down and to the right in sixth gear.

Three tight corners in a row moderate the flow before a short infield straight brings the cars to the Audi S that was made more open in modifications made for F1's return.

The final two corners are contrasting. Drivers need to be precise through Kumhobocht so that they can get the best line into the banked final corner to be able to carry momentum on to the start/finish straight. If they do, they can hit 193mph (310kph) on the approach to Tarzan.

INSIDE TRACK

DUTCH GRAND PRIX

Date:	**25 August**
Circuit name:	**Zandvoort**
Circuit length:	**2.647 miles/4.259km**
Number of laps:	**72**

PREVIOUS WINNERS

1979	**Alan Jones** WILLIAMS
1980	**Nelson Piquet** BRABHAM
1981	**Alain Prost** RENAULT
1982	**Didier Pironi** FERRARI
1983	**Rene Arnoux** FERRARI
1984	**Alain Prost** McLAREN
1985	**Niki Lauda** McLAREN
2021	**Max Verstappen** RED BULL
2022	**Max Verstappen** RED BULL
2023	**Max Verstappen** RED BULL

How it started: The circuit was created after World War II, using access roads that had been laid out between German fortifications. It was an instant hit, landing its first World Championship round in 1952, won by Alberto Ascari for Ferrari, and has been the centre of a strong national racing scene ever since.

A notable Grand Prix: All things must come to an end, and the second part of Niki Lauda's F1 career ended in 1985, with his final visit to Zandvoort producing his last victory, which was all the more joyous, as his season had not been going well. He qualified only 10th but an inspired early pit stop for new tyres moved him to the front, where he was caught but never passed by McLaren team-mate Alain Prost. Prost would become go on to become champion and Lauda rank only 10th overall.

Rising national star: There will never be another Max Verstappen, but Richard Verschoor (a race winner in F2 last year) is proving that Dutch fans have a driver getting ready for stepping up to F1.

Location: Just 15 miles (24km) from the heart of Amsterdam, the circuit is built into the sand dunes on the northern edge of the coastal resort from which it takes its name.

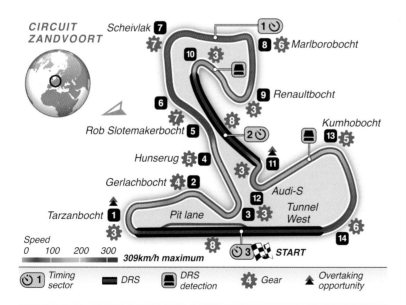

CIRCUIT ZANDVOORT

Scheivlak 7

Marlborobocht

Renaultbocht

Kumhobocht

Rob Slotemakerbocht

Hunserug

Gerlachbocht

Audi-S

Tunnel West

Tarzanbocht

Pit lane

Speed
0 100 200 300
309km/h maximum

START

| Timing sector | DRS | DRS detection | Gear | Overtaking opportunity |

2023 POLE TIME: **VERSTAPPEN (RED BULL), 1M10.567S, 135.008MPH/217.274KPH**
2023 WINNER'S AVERAGE SPEED: **79.340MPH/127.679KPH**
2023 FASTEST LAP: **ALONSO (ASTON MARTIN), 1M13.837S, 129.028MPH/207.651KPH**
LAP RECORD: **HAMILTON (MERCEDES), 1M11.097S, 134.001MPH/215.654KPH, 2021**

MONZA

The hope of the *tifosi* springs eternal at Monza. Their massed ranks waving Ferrari flags really add to the atmosphere at this temple of motorsport that oozes history from every pore.

It is said that a Ferrari qualifying on pole for the Italian GP adds immeasurably to national happiness. Converting that into victory, though, has been a task too far in recent decades, but this still doesn't stop the *tifosi* from praying for success.

Now more than a century old, Monza is still true to its roots as a temple of speed. Of course, the insertion of three chicanes stemmed its flow half a century ago, but the high-speed nature of the rest of the lap remains true.

The lap begins with a blast to the first chicane, where the track snaps right and then almost immediately, and more acutely, to the left. Many a driver has had to take evasive action up the escape road on the opening lap to avoid damage.

Then the drivers are hard on the throttle through the lengthy arc to the right that guides them up to the second chicane, the Variante della Loggia. This goes left then right and is more open in nature.

Lesmo I and Lesmo II are tricky right-handers and a clean exit from the second is vital for carrying speed on to the curved blast down to the Ascari chicane. The track runs through a wood and under a section of the original banked circuit. Drivers often end up in the gravel after leaving their braking just too late as the track rears up just before turn-in.

There is only one more corner, Parabolica, which is fast in and hopefully faster out so that drivers can catch a tow from a rival and drag past them after the pits. Then they need to haul their car down from 208mph (335kph) to second gear for the first chicane.

INSIDE TRACK

ITALIAN GRAND PRIX

Date:	**1 September**
Circuit name:	**Autodromo Nazionale Monza**
Circuit length:	**3.600 miles/5.793km**
Number of laps:	**53**

PREVIOUS WINNERS

2014	**Lewis Hamilton** MERCEDES
2015	**Lewis Hamilton** MERCEDES
2016	**Nico Rosberg** MERCEDES
2017	**Lewis Hamilton** MERCEDES
2018	**Lewis Hamilton** MERCEDES
2019	**Charles Leclerc** FERRARI
2020	**Pierre Gasly** ALPHATAURI
2021	**Daniel Ricciardo** McLAREN
2022	**Max Verstappen** RED BULL
2023	**Max Verstappen** RED BULL

How it started: One of the world's oldest permanent race circuits, Monza was opened for racing in 1922, with Pietro Bordino winning the second-ever Italian GP for Fiat. Later, it was one of the pack of six European circuits that hosted rounds of the inaugural World Championship in 1950, when Giuseppe Farina took victory for dominant Alfa Romeo.

A notable Grand Prix: For sheer feelgood factor, recent Italian GPs have been wonderful, especially with Pierre Gasly's surprise win in 2020 for midfield AlphaTauri. However, for an outburst of euphoria, McLaren's first win in nine years – 170 races – in 2021 was special. It was a race remembered for Max Verstappen's Red Bull ending up under Lewis Hamilton's Mercedes when the title protagonists clashed at the first chicane, but it was a victory earned on merit, with Daniel Ricciardo leading home team-mate Lando Norris by two seconds.

Rising national star: There were no young Italians in F2 last year but a couple of promising ones in the level below, F3, with Gabriele Mini and Leonardo Fornaroli showing pace-setting talent.

Location: The circuit is built within a wall-lined park on the outskirts of the town of Monza, 10 miles (16km) to the north-west of Milan.

AUTODROMO NAZIONALE MONZA

Curva di Lesmo · Curva del Serraglio · Variante della Roggia · Variante Ascari · Curva Biassono · Curva Parabolica · Pit lane · START

Speed
0   100   200   300
327km/h maximum

🕐1 Timing sector	DRS	DRS detection
Gear		Overtaking opportunity

2023 POLE TIME: **SAINZ JR (FERRARI), 1M20.294S, 161.388MPH/259.730KPH**
2023 WINNER'S AVERAGE SPEED: **149.326MPH/240.318KPH**
2023 FASTEST LAP: **PIASTRI (McLAREN), 1M25.072S, 152.324MPH/245.142KPH**
LAP RECORD: **BARRICHELLO (FERRARI), 1M21.046S, 159.909MPH/257.349KPH, 2004**

BAKU

Moving the date of this incident-filled race further back in the championship year ought to add excitement, as the path to the world title will be better formed.

INSIDE TRACK

AZERBAIJAN GRAND PRIX

Date: **15 September**
Circuit name: **Baku City Circuit**
Circuit length: **3.731 miles/6.003km**
Number of laps: **51**

PREVIOUS WINNERS

2016	**Nico Rosberg** MERCEDES
2017	**Daniel Ricciardo** RED BULL
2018	**Lewis Hamilton** MERCEDES
2019	**Valtteri Bottas** MERCEDES
2021	**Sergio Perez** RED BULL
2022	**Max Verstappen** RED BULL
2023	**Sergio Perez** RED BULL

Even F1 insiders didn't know what to expect when the World Championship announced that it would be heading to Azerbaijan in 2016. Many even had to locate it on the map. However, they all know where it is now, and the street circuit through its capital Baku provides a refreshingly different backdrop as well as a difficult and surprisingly high-speed track layout.

Starting on a broad straight alongside a park that lines the coastline to the Caspian Sea, the track feeds quickly into a pair of 90-degree left-handers. A short straight follows, but there is little chance of overtaking into turn 3, as that is another 90-degree left, again hemmed in by walls.

Turn 4 is a right-hander, followed by a chicane and a right at turn 7. Then the nature of the circuit changes entirely, as the spacious blocks of the new town are followed by a narrowing of the track as it turns left and runs uphill past the walls of the citadel.

At turn 10, the track bursts back into a wider area and then begins to open out after turn 12, with tight corners followed by more open ones. Open kinks to the left at turns 13 and 14 are taken in eighth gear, then a tighter one at turn 15.

Continuing past the city's grandest buildings the drivers are presented with a sudden drop out of turn 16, the cars plunged over the edge and running flat-out through four kinks before being fed back onto the start/finish straight. There they continue to accelerate on to 200mph (320kph) before having to think about braking heavily and perhaps trying to make a passing move into turn 1.

How it started: Oil-rich Azerbaijan was welcomed into the World Championship in 2016 because it had the funds to build the temporary infrastructure required for a street race and the added appeal to F1 of being on the western edge of Asia, thus in a useful time zone for the brand's global market. Its first race was won by Nico Rosberg for Mercedes.

A notable Grand Prix: Daniel Ricciardo probably sometimes has to remind people that he won here in 2017, as most people recall the race more for a ridiculous collision that occurred between race leader Lewis Hamilton and Sebastian Vettel. The German didn't think the Mercedes driver was going fast enough when the safety car withdrew and clipped Hamilton's tail. Then, inexplicably, he drove his Ferrari alongside and swerved into him. Hamilton was delayed when his headrest came loose and Ricciardo took over for Red Bull.

Toughest corner: Turn 16 is difficult as drivers have to drop to third, turn in over a brow and be sure that they are on the best line for the lap's longest run of acceleration all the way to the braking point for turn 1.

Location: The circuit straddles the modern part of capital city Baku along the shore of the Caspian Sea, then enters the citadel as it runs up the hill to the heart of the city.

BAKU CITY CIRCUIT

START

Speed
0   100   200   300

322km/h maximum

⏱1 Timing sector	▬ DRS	DRS detection	⚙4 Gear	▲ Overtaking opportunity

2023 POLE TIME: LECLERC (FERRARI), 1M40.203S, 134.044MPH/215.677KPH
2023 WINNER'S AVERAGE SPEED: 123.077MPH/198.074KPH
2023 FASTEST LAP: RUSSELL (MERCEDES), 1M43.370S, 129.905MPH/209.062KPH
LAP RECORD: LECLERC (FERRARI), 1M43.009S, 130.360MPH/209.795KPH, 2019

MARINA BAY

Holding a Grand Prix in Singapore had long been an ambition for the World Championship and its evening-into-night races have been a huge success since its debut in 2008.

Heat and humidity are guaranteed in this equatorial metropolis, so running its race after dark does at least make matters marginally more comfortable for the drivers and crews. With the circuit running past Singapore's central business district, it's a spectacular backdrop too, something that many of the circuits that opened since 2000 fail to match.

The lap begins with a tricky first corner combination of a flick to the left that arcs immediately to the right, then directly into a left-hand hairpin. It's rare that the entire field negotiates these three turns without contact on the opening lap.

A short straight feeding into a tight right, and then on to another straight, sets the tone for most of what follows, something that is hardly surprising as the track is laid out on a city grid. The run to turn 7 is a long one, though, and occasionally just long enough for a driver to consider attempting a passing move after powering through the lap's fastest point at 185mph (300kph). However, the fact that turn 7 is another 90-degree bend means that a driver has to be convinced that they can complete the move before turn-in as space is restricted.

Racing around three sides of the Singapore Cricket Ground, the track then powers past the famous Raffles Hotel before having an unusual feature to negotiate as it crosses the Anderson Bridge before turn 13, an acute left-hander. A good exit can be beneficial, as there is a rare straight of length up to turn 14 before the track snakes through seven more turns. It then opens out for a sweep past the giant Ferris wheel on to the start/finish straight.

INSIDE TRACK

SINGAPORE GRAND PRIX

Date:	**22 September**
Circuit name:	**Marina Bay Circuit**
Circuit length:	**3.070 miles/4.940km**
Number of laps:	**62**

PREVIOUS WINNERS

2012	**Sebastian Vettel**	RED BULL
2013	**Sebastian Vettel**	RED BULL
2014	**Lewis Hamilton**	MERCEDES
2015	**Sebastian Vettel**	FERRARI
2016	**Nico Rosberg**	MERCEDES
2017	**Lewis Hamilton**	MERCEDES
2018	**Lewis Hamilton**	MERCEDES
2019	**Sebastian Vettel**	FERRARI
2022	**Sergio Perez**	RED BULL
2023	**Carlos Sainz Jr**	FERRARI

How it started: The circuit and its temporary facilities impressed the F1 teams when they arrived here for the first time in 2008, as well as how magnificent the city backdrop looked in F1's first night race.

A notable Grand Prix: The fans at that inaugural Grand Prix were amazed by a surprise result. Fernando Alonso appeared to have been incredibly lucky with the timing of a safety car period just after he had pitted, with several rivals earning penalties as they were so low on fuel that they had to come in when the pit lane was closed. It was only in 2009 that the story broke that Renault had helped him to complete his climb from 15th on the grid to victory. It was revealed that the team had asked rookie team-mate Nelson Piquet Jr to spin off to trigger the safety car deployment and that led to two of the team's top management being banned from F1.

Toughest corner: Turn 1 is certainly the most difficult corner of the lap, as it's so easy for contact on lap 1 to wreck a driver's race.

Location: The circuit is laid out, on a temporary arrangement, using public roads that link Singapore's central business district, historic Raffles Avenue and Marina Bay.

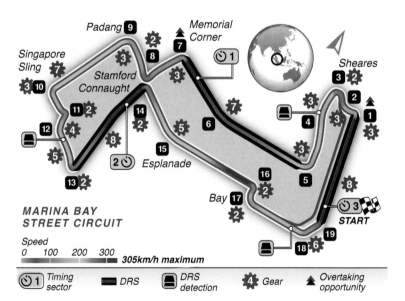

MARINA BAY STREET CIRCUIT

Speed
0   100   200   300
305km/h maximum

⏱1 Timing sector   ▬ DRS   ▣ DRS detection   ⚙4 Gear   ▲ Overtaking opportunity

2023 POLE TIME: **SAINZ JR (FERRARI), 1M30.984S, 121.454MPH/195.462KPH**
2023 WINNER'S AVERAGE SPEED: **107.046MPH/172.274KPH**
2023 FASTEST LAP: **HAMILTON (MERCEDES), 1M35.867S, 115.268MPH/185.507KPH**
LAP RECORD: **HAMILTON (MERCEDES), 1M35.867S, 115.268MPH/185.507KPH, 2023**

CIRCUIT OF THE AMERICAS

While the USA has opened temporary circuits in first Miami then Las Vegas, this Texan gem is the best place for America's new Formula One fans to see F1 cars put through their paces.

UNITED STATES GRAND PRIX

Date:	**20 October**
Circuit name:	**Circuit of the Americas**
Circuit length:	**3.426 miles/5.513km**
Number of laps:	**56**

PREVIOUS WINNERS

2013	**Sebastian Vettel** RED BULL
2014	**Lewis Hamilton** MERCEDES
2015	**Lewis Hamilton** MERCEDES
2016	**Lewis Hamilton** MERCEDES
2017	**Lewis Hamilton** MERCEDES
2018	**Kimi Raikkonen** FERRARI
2019	**Valtteri Bottas** MERCEDES
2021	**Max Verstappen** RED BULL
2022	**Max Verstappen** RED BULL
2023	**Max Verstappen** RED BULL

When the Circuit of the Americas (COTA) was designed, its aim was to use its plot in the rolling hills outside Austin to create a circuit made up of imitations of some of the best corners used at the best circuits in the world. And this is precisely what it achieved.

Drivers on the starting grid looking up to the left-hand hairpin will think of the steep climb to the first corner at the Red Bull Ring. It's a wide entry, affording plenty of possible lines. However, the exit from this highest point of the lap, which is 130 feet (40m) higher than its lowest point, is precipitous, with hard acceleration down and through turn 2.

Still accelerating, the drivers then enter COTA's equivalent of Silverstone's Becketts esses. Turn 7 is tighter and 8 and 9 tighter still, but then the drivers can run flat-out through a left kink towards the furthest point of the circuit, the turn 11 hairpin.

The straight out of here is the longest of the lap and, even though the cars start it in second gear, the fastest cars hit 193mph (310kph) at the lap's fastest point before braking heavily to take the tight left at its conclusion.

There is a notable change of flow from here. A trio of twisters take the cars to turn 15, out of which the corners become more open as the track runs around the foot of the giant observation tower, rising on approach and falling away on exit.

This just leaves a fourth gear corner before the tight, second gear, final corner out of which strong acceleration is vital for that run up to lofty turn 1.

How it started: It took years in planning, but the Circuit of the Americas was built specifically to provide the United States GP with a long-term home. From its debut in 2012, COTA has been a hit, with Lewis Hamilton the first driver to be given the race winner's Stetson when he triumphed for McLaren.

A notable Grand Prix: The 2022 United States GP was packed with incident, from the moment that polesitter Carlos Sainz Jr had his Ferrari spun around at turn 1. This allowed Max Verstappen into the lead. Then Valtteri Bottas spun out of third as he pressed Lewis Hamilton, then Lance Stroll launched Fernando Alonso's Alpine. Verstappen lost his lead with a slow pit stop and had to fight back past Hamilton and Charles Leclerc.

A local hero: The greatest racing driver from Texas is four-time Indianapolis 500 winner A.J. Foyt. The top Texan in F1 remains Jim Hall, who finished fifth in the 1963 German GP in a British Racing Partnership Lotus before establishing the Chaparral sportscar concern and running a very successful IndyCar team.

Location: COTA is ten miles (16km) to the south-east of Austin, just as the hills begin to rise as you leave the Texas state capital.

CIRCUIT OF THE AMERICAS

START

Pit lane

Speed
0   100   200   300
315km/h maximum

🕐1 Timing sector   ▬ DRS   DRS detection   ⚙4 Gear   ▲ Overtaking opportunity

2023 POLE TIME: **LECLERC (FERRARI), 1M34.723S, 130.192MPH/209.524KPH**
2023 WINNER'S AVERAGE SPEED: **120.579MPH/194.054KPH**
2023 FASTEST LAP: **TSUNODA (ALPHATAURI), 1M38.139S, 125.660MPH/202.231KPH**
LAP RECORD: **LECLERC (FERRARI), 1M36.169S, 128.235MPH/206.374KPH, 2019**

MEXICO CITY

This is a track at which the fans really add to the occasion, whether overlooking the first corner or sitting in the giant grandstands where the cars pass through a baseball stadium.

Built in the early 1960s, this circuit in the suburbs of capital Mexico City has changed remarkably little over the intervening decades and so it still retains a welcome old school vibe.

The run from the starting grid to the first corner is an unusually lengthy one and it is also wonderfully wide as the drivers flash through the parkland setting. Then comes a three-corner opening complex that has the cars turn to their right after heavy braking, then immediately left and finally right again. For many drivers on the opening lap, their ambition and progress can be markedly different things, as a driver's entry line into turn 1 might be good, but rivals might then squeeze them, push them wide or collide with them.

The straight that follows comes as a relief. Then this is followed by a left/right twin-set and a short blast to the point of the lap furthest from the pits. This is turn 6, a right-hand hairpin. The most dynamic section of the lap comes next, with a five-corner 'S' and then a short straight.

Heavy braking into the turn 12 right-hander then leads the cars into the middle of what is usually a baseball stadium, with its vertiginous stands affording a great view down to a hairpin at turn 13. There are then two more quick changes of direction before the cars dive through a gap and arrive halfway around what was once the lap's most challenging corner: the Peraltada. This is a slightly banked right-hander that brings the cars back to the start/finish straight, and strong acceleration out of here combined with a tow can help the cars hit 202mph (325kph) on their run down to Turn 1.

INSIDE TRACK

MEXICO CITY GRAND PRIX

Date:	**27 October**
Circuit name:	**Autodromo Hermanos Rodriguez**
Circuit length:	**2.675 miles/4.304km**
Number of laps:	**71**

PREVIOUS WINNERS

1991	**Riccardo Patrese**	WILLIAMS
1992	**Nigel Mansell**	WILLIAMS
2015	**Nico Rosberg**	MERCEDES
2016	**Lewis Hamilton**	MERCEDES
2017	**Max Verstappen**	RED BULL
2018	**Max Verstappen**	RED BULL
2019	**Lewis Hamilton**	MERCEDES
2021	**Max Verstappen**	RED BULL
2022	**Max Verstappen**	RED BULL
2023	**Max Verstappen**	RED BULL

How it started: Mexico was known in the 1950s for its Carrera Panamericana road race. However, it had huge talents in Pedro and Ricardo Rodriguez, so it was timely that the circuit opened as they reached the world stage. Its first Grand Prix was a non-championship race in 1962 in which Ricardo crashed fatally in qualifying before it made its World Championship bow the following year.

A notable Grand Prix: The 2016 title battle was shaping up between Mercedes team-mates Nico Rosberg and Lewis Hamilton. Hamilton locked up into the first corner, Max Verstappen thumped Rosberg and Hamilton cut the corner without penalty to reclaim the lead. He then drove off to win, but second for Rosberg meant he had a 19-point advantage with two races to go.

Rising national star: Patricio O'Ward is focused on IndyCar, winning races since 2021, but the 24-year-old has strong connections with McLaren so may still be Mexico's next F1 hopeful.

Out of breath: Mexico City's altitude of 7,350 feet (2,240m) makes drivers and their cars' engines work hard.

Location: Mexico City, population 22 million, is one of the world's most sprawling metropolises, with the circuit located in a park to its east.

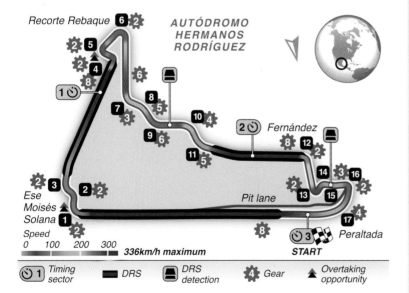

AUTÓDROMO HERMANOS RODRÍGUEZ

Recorte Rebaque

Ese Moisés Solana

Fernández

Pit lane

Peraltada

START

Speed
0 100 200 300
336km/h maximum

Timing sector · DRS · DRS detection · Gear · Overtaking opportunity

2023 POLE TIME: **LECLERC (FERRARI), 1M17.166S, 124.767MPH/200.793KPH**

2023 WINNER'S AVERAGE SPEED: **92.922MPH/149.544KPH**

2023 FASTEST LAP: **HAMILTON (MERCEDES), 1M21.334S, 118.436MPH/190.503KPH**

LAP RECORD: **BOTTAS (MERCEDES), 1M17.774S, 123.791MPH/199.223KPH, 2021**

// INTERLAGOS

When you combine a track that uses the rises and falls of its hillside setting with grandstands full of fans roaring with excitement, you have a proper F1 venue.

Acting as part of a double-header with the Mexico City circuit, this Brazilian gem gives the closing rounds of the World Championship a more organic and intimate feel, because they are most certainly not modern autodromes. Instead, they are tight and challenging, with the grandstands close to the action.

The first corner is a tricky one with which to start the lap. The track turns sharp left and down as it passes the end of the pit wall and the exit is unseen on arrival. Many a driver pushed onto the outside line on lap 1 will lose places by the handful as they recover.

The next two corners, the Senna S, push the cars into a compression and spit them out again onto an appreciable straight down the slope to the Descida do Lago left-handers. These are approached at 193mph (310kph) and entered at 100mph (160kph) in fourth gear, with a good balance essential to carry as much of that momentum as possible into the left-hander that starts the climb to the back of the paddock.

Ferradura turns the drivers left before tighter Laranja drops them back down again. Pinheirinho redirects them up again to Cotovelo, out of which there's a wonderful downhill sweep to Juncao.

From third gear Juncao, it's then a flat-out run through two kinks onto the start/finish straight where the cars hit 196mph (315kph), hemmed in by concrete walls on either side. The drivers then have to brake heavily to get their cars down to 65mph (105kph) in third gear for turn 1. Overtaking is a definite possibility here, but it's far from a given that it will work.

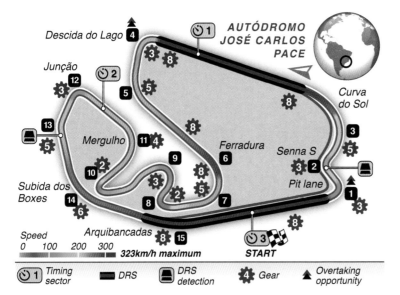

2023 POLE TIME: VERSTAPPEN (RED BULL), 1M10.727S, 136.283MPH/219.327KPH
2023 WINNER'S AVERAGE SPEED: 97.623MPH/157.109KPH
2023 FASTEST LAP: NORRIS (MCLAREN), 1M12.486S, 132.976MPH/214.005KPH
LAP RECORD: BOTTAS (MERCEDES), 1M10.540S, 136.645MPH/219.909KPH, 2018

INSIDE TRACK

SAO PAULO GRAND PRIX

Date:	**3 November**
Circuit name:	**Autodromo Jose Carlos Pace**
Circuit length:	**2.678 miles/4.309km**
Number of laps:	**71**

PREVIOUS WINNERS

2013	**Sebastian Vettel**	RED BULL
2014	**Nico Rosberg**	MERCEDES
2015	**Nico Rosberg**	MERCEDES
2016	**Lewis Hamilton**	MERCEDES
2017	**Sebastian Vettel**	FERRARI
2018	**Lewis Hamilton**	MERCEDES
2019	**Max Verstappen**	RED BULL
2021	**Lewis Hamilton**	MERCEDES
2022	**George Russell**	MERCEDES
2023	**Max Verstappen**	RED BULL

How it started: Opened in 1940, Interlagos was a magnificent circuit with a lap length of almost five miles (8km) as it ran back and forth across a lake-dotted hillside. However, F1 took until 1972 to visit Brazil, starting with a non-championship Grand Prix won by Carlos Reutemann for Brabham before local hero Emerson Fittipaldi gave Lotus victory in its first World Championship event in 1973.

A notable Grand Prix: George Russell fans will always remember the race here in 2022, run under the title of the Sao Paulo GP, as this was his first F1 win. It was built on winning the sprint race and then leading away from pole in his Mercedes while Max Verstappen hit Lewis Hamilton on a restart and came off worse. Then, with Ferrari unable to match them, Russell headed home a Mercedes one-two.

Rising national star: If Brazil's best-placed driver in F2 last year has a name that seems familiar, that's because it's Fittipaldi. Indeed, Enzo is grandson of Emerson, world champion in 1972 and 1974. Enzo came on strong through the year to become a winner and rank 7th.

Location: Interlagos is in the southern suburbs of sprawling Sao Paulo, nine miles (14km) from the city centre.

LAS VEGAS

The casino city's flamboyant architecture was always going to provide a spectacular setting for F1's second attempt at wowing Las Vegas, and the popularity of *Drive to Survive* helped to fill the grandstands.

If at first you don't succeed, try again. This is definitely the case with taking F1 to this centre of nightclubs and gambling in Nevada. The lessons from the two races held in Las Vegas in 1981 and 1982 have been learnt, most notably not to tuck the track into a car park. Instead, for last year, F1 was put in the heart of the city.

The temporary circuit wasn't put where it is just to be staged in a more public setting but also to show F1 cars doing what they do best, in stretching their legs rather than snaking around that first F1 circuit at an average speed of just over 100mph (160kph). Sports fans, especially ones new to a sport, like big figures, so the 21st century's second attempt was designed with far longer straights than the Caesars Palace circuit had.

The lap starts with a very short blast to a left-hand hairpin before a more open turn 3 moves the cars o to a short straight down to turn 5 at Caesars Forum. This is a definite passing place, as it's a 90-degree corner.

Then the track runs through a wide parabola and two sweepers before reaching its next tight corner, turn 9, by The Palazzo.

This is the point at which the pace changes, with a long, kinked straight (Las Vegas Boulevard) that sees the cars reach 212mph (342kph) at the lap's fastest point before they have to brake hard for a tight corner that feeds directly into a chicane.

There is then another straight that allows the drivers back up towards full speed before they try to line up a possible pass into turn 1.

INSIDE TRACK

LAS VEGAS GRAND PRIX

Date:	**23 November**
Circuit name:	Las Vegas Strip Circuit
Circuit length:	3.853 miles/6.201km
Number of laps:	50

PREVIOUS WINNERS

1981*	**Alan Jones**	WILLIAMS
1982*	**Michele Alboreto**	TYRRELL
2023	**Max Verstappen**	RED BULL

* Held at the Caesars Palace circuit

How it started: The World Championship had two American races each year at the start of the 1980s, with its long-standing home at Watkins Glen in upstate New York and a street race at Long Beach in California. Yet, it wanted more to help win over American racing fans and so it was decided that a race in Las Vegas would be a good thing. It's safe to say, though, that the twisting, low-speed circuit laid out around the car park of the Caesars Palace casino didn't show F1 at its best. Alan Jones won the first of the races there for Williams in 1981.

A notable Grand Prix: The 1981 Caesars Palace GP remains one of the mysteries of F1. Or, more to the point, how Carlos Reutemann lost his mojo and blew his only opportunity to take a tilt at the world title. The Williams driver arrived with a one-point advantage over Brabham's Nelson Piquet, with Ligier's Jacques Laffite a further five points down. Alan Jones led every lap to win for Williams, but Reutemann made an awful start from pole and fell to fifth by the end of lap 1. It was also bad for Piquet, who was losing places. Yet Reutemann kept fading and dropped to eighth, meaning that Piquet was heading to the title in fifth. The Brazilian's neck was tired, and two rivals lined up to pass him on the last lap, which would have given the crown to Reutemann, but somehow Piquet held on.

Location: Las Vegas's second temporary F1 circuit is located right in the heart of the city, running along Las Vegas Boulevard.

LAS VEGAS STREET CIRCUIT

START

Caesars Forum

Palazzo

Treasure Island

Caesars Palace

Bellagio

Planet Hollywood

Las Vegas Boulevard

Speed
342km/h maximum

⏱1	Timing sector		DRS		DRS detection		Gear	Speed

2023 POLE TIME: **LECLERC (FERRARI), 1M32.726S, 149.594MPH/240.748KPH**
2023 WINNER'S AVERAGE SPEED: **129.640MPH/208.636KPH**
2023 FASTEST LAP: **PIASTRI (MCLAREN), 1M35.490S, 145.263MPH/233.779KPH**
LAP RECORD: **PIASTRI (MCLAREN), 1M35.490S, 145.263MPH/233.779KPH, 2023**

// LOSAIL

Back for a third time, Qatar's Losail International Circuit certainly looks spectacular with its buildings illuminated at night and powerful floodlights, and it's surprisingly popular with the drivers.

Bahrain struck first in the battle to introduce the World Championship to the Middle East; then Dubai built an F1-standard circuit but never landed a Grand Prix; and Abu Dhabi followed along in 2009 to top them all. Qatar looked on enviously. Although it turned itself into a global transport hub and assembled an art collection of great importance, it took until it hosted the 2022 Football World Cup for its brand to be global. With eyes on the future, it also made its F1 World Championship bow in 2021.

The circuit used for this wasn't another new facility but one that had been in use for over a decade, yet the drivers liked it all the more because of that; it wasn't like more recent circuit layouts.

The lap starts a little like it does at Sakhir, except that the corners are slightly more open. Hard acceleration out of turn 2 takes the cars to the 90-degree right-hander at turn 4, with a similar corner at turn 5. The drivers need to have a car that handles well after this point as the middle section of the lap's 16 corners is twist after middle-speed twist, with the occasional hairpin thrown in for good measure. Fortunately, it opens out from turn 10.

Then, powering out of turn 16 and on past the pits, the drivers reach the fastest point of the lap, using their DRS to harness any tow they can from a rival to try to line up an overtaking move into the first corner of the following lap.

The circuit is on borrowed time, though, as the Qatari authorities plan to build a newer, more spectacular circuit for the years ahead.

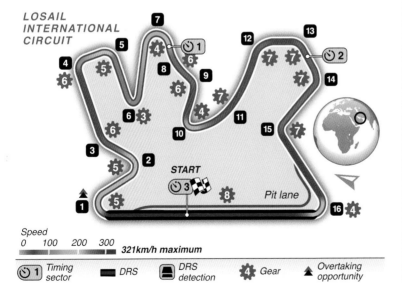

LOSAIL INTERNATIONAL CIRCUIT

START

Pit lane

Speed
0   100   200   300
321km/h maximum

⏱1 Timing sector   DRS   DRS detection   ⚙4 Gear   ▲ Overtaking opportunity

2023 POLE TIME: **VERSTAPPEN (RED BULL), 1M23.778S, 144.691MPH/232.858KPH**
2023 WINNER'S AVERAGE SPEED: **131.264MPH/211.250KPH**
2023 FASTEST LAP: **VERSTAPPEN (RED BULL), 1M24.319S, 143.763MPH/231.364KPH**
LAP RECORD: **VERSTAPPEN (RED BULL), 1M23.196S, 144.654KPH/232.799KPH, 2021**

INSIDE TRACK

QATAR GRAND PRIX

Date:	**1 December**
Circuit name:	**Losail International Circuit**
Circuit length:	**3.368 miles/5.419km**
Number of laps:	**57**

PREVIOUS WINNERS

2021	**Lewis Hamilton** MERCEDES
2023	**Max Verstappen** RED BULL

How it started: The Losail International Circuit opened for racing in 2004 and landed a Moto GP to launch its reputation and gradually attracted four-wheeled motorsport as well. Then, in 2021, the rejigging of the World Championship calendar – because of regular venues being prevented from holding their Grands Prix by travel restrictions put in place during the COVID pandemic – gave it a chance to leap in with a Grand Prix won for Mercedes by Lewis Hamilton.

A notable Grand Prix: The inaugural Qatar GP in 2021 was one in which Lewis Hamilton was desperate for victory so that he could close down Max Verstappen's 14-point advantage. He qualified on pole, with Verstappen starting seventh after being hit with a five-place grid penalty for not respecting waved yellow flags, even though Red Bull team principal Christian Horner claimed that the flag might have been waved by a 'rogue' marshal. The Dutchman went on the charge, gaining three places on the opening lap and moved his Red Bull up to second to reduce the damage to his points lead with two races to run.

Toughest corner: Turn 10 is among the most difficult to get right. It is a left-hander that is tight on entry but then opens out past the apex as it turns through 130 degrees. Getting a good exit is vital, as the next five corners are largely open in format, allowing drivers to build momentum all the way down to the braking zone for the final corner, turn 16.

Location: The circuit is on the east coast of the Qatar peninsula, just north of capital city Doha.

YAS MARINA

Built with no expense spared, this circuit provided a spectacular backdrop as day turned to night, but the racing was dull, so it was tweaked to provide more scope for overtaking.

Designed by circuit architect Hermann Tilke very much with overtaking in mind, this is a circuit that should have worked a treat from its World Championship debut in 2009. After all, two long straights into tight corners ought to make passing possible yet, somehow, it didn't and this led to tweaks for F1's visit in 2022.

The start of the lap remained untouched as a 90-degree left with plenty of run-off on its exit, then a left/right/left sweep as the cars built up pace. There was then a left/right chicane before the drivers reached the turn 7 hairpin. However, this tended to break up the field and so it was a good thing when the chicane was removed, allowing more of a chance for outbraking into what has become turn 5. This modification has created greater opportunity for the field to

be scrambled on its exit to enter the lap's longest straight. Any inability to get the power down early multiplies all the way up to 196mph (315kph) down the run to the tight left at turn 6, and this is what makes passing there more likely.

A second slightly curved straight follows, but the corner at its far end has had a chicane removed from its approach and is now more of a broad sweep, providing another challenge.

A change of scenery follows, as the next stretch of the lap runs through two kinks and two tighter corners around the yachts in the marina. Then, bizarrely, it runs under the span of a spectacular hotel before drivers accelerate out of turn 14, keep their throttle planted and finally brake for the fourth gear final corner onto the start/finish straight.

ABU DHABI GRAND PRIX

Date:	**8 December**
Circuit name:	**Yas Marina Circuit**
Circuit length:	**3.282 miles/5.281km**
Number of laps:	**58**

PREVIOUS WINNERS

2014	**Lewis Hamilton**	MERCEDES
2015	**Nico Rosberg**	MERCEDES
2016	**Lewis Hamilton**	MERCEDES
2017	**Valtteri Bottas**	MERCEDES
2018	**Lewis Hamilton**	MERCEDES
2019	**Lewis Hamilton**	MERCEDES
2020	**Max Verstappen**	RED BULL
2021	**Max Verstappen**	RED BULL
2022	**Max Verstappen**	RED BULL
2023	**Max Verstappen**	RED BULL

How it started: Building a world-leading sports complex to attract tourism at Yas Marina – complete with a marina, Ferrari World and a golf course – was a no-expense-spared project, and the facilities the teams found when they arrived in 2009 put all others in the shade. That first race was won by Sebastian Vettel for Red Bull Racing after early leader Lewis Hamilton retired his McLaren with brake failure.

A notable Grand Prix: Abu Dhabi's second race, in 2010, was extraordinary as it was a four-driver title shoot-out, that ended with Sebastian Vettel taking both victory and the title for Red Bull Racing. Meanwhile Ferrari's Fernando Alonso, championship leader by eight points when they'd arrived, was left frustrated by being trapped behind Vitaly Petrov's Renault and ending up sixth on the track and second in the standings.

Rising national star: At last, the fruits of a strong United Arab Emirates karting scene are beginning to show themselves, with the teenagers Keanu Al Azhari and Federico Al Rifai gaining valuable experience in the local Formula 4 series.

Location: The Yas Marina sports resort facility, around which this circuit spreads itself, is on Yas Island, which is to the east of the capital.

YAS MARINA CIRCUIT

Speed
0 100 200 300
320km/h maximum

| ⏱1 | Timing sector | ▬ DRS | DRS detection | ⚙4 Gear | ▲ Overtaking opportunity |

2023 POLE TIME: VERSTAPPEN (RED BULL), 1M23.445S, 141.569MPH/227.833KPH

2023 WINNER'S AVERAGE SPEED:131.143MPH/211.054KPH

2023 FASTEST LAP: VERSTAPPEN (RED BULL), 1M26.993S, 135.780MPH/218.541KPH

LAP RECORD: VERSTAPPEN (RED BULL), 1M26.103S, 137.198MPH/220.800KPH, 2021

// REVIEW OF THE 2023 SEASON

Last year really was all about Red Bull Racing. More than that, it was all about Max Verstappen, who was truly superb in delivering the team 19 victories. No other team was able to mount a full-season challenge, with Aston Martin starting well then fading, Ferrari and Mercedes suffering fluctuating form and McLaren solidly second fastest by season's end.

Max Verstappen was nigh on peerless in 2023, not just compared to his rivals but compared to the very greatest of world champions across the sport's seven decades. Undoubtedly, the Red Bull RB19 was a highly effective piece of machinery, but the skills of the Dutch ace left his team-mate Sergio Perez trailing in his wake. In fact, he was so fast and so relentless that it really didn't matter where on the grid he started, as the wins just kept on coming.

Being made to look second best by a margin got the better of Perez and he faded after winning two of the first four races;

he spent most of the mid-season failing to get into the final qualifying shoot-out, putting his seat in jeopardy.

If their loss of relative form in 2022, the first year of new technical regulations, was a shock for previously dominant Mercedes, then their failure to make up ground was also surprising at the start of 2023. Eventually, its no-sidepod approach was scrapped and although Lewis Hamilton qualified on pole in Hungary, there were to be no wins for him or for George Russell.

Ferrari also experienced patchy form through 2023, sometimes good, like for Charles Leclerc's pole in Baku, but often less than

convincing and sometimes as weak in the tactics chosen as they had been in 2022. As summer turned to autumn, though, Ferrari hit its stride and the regular miracle of Monza produced pole for Carlos Sainz Jr, who then raced hard before being passed by the Red Bulls. Next time out, in Singapore, the Spaniard turned pole into victory, thus becoming the only driver to beat Red Bull in 2023.

With the likely challengers not performing in the early-season races, it was Aston Martin that plugged the gap, with the evergreen Fernando Alonso collecting five podium results in the first six rounds. A mid-season dip in form was replaced with a glorious third place after a fabulous scrap with Perez in Brazil, where an often out of sorts Lance Stroll raced to fifth place.

By the late stages of the year, McLaren was on the up, but that certainly wasn't the story back in spring when neither Lando Norris nor rookie Oscar Piastri could predict what their cars were going to do. A corner was finally turned at the British GP when Norris finished second and Piastri fourth before a lull in form that was rectified by the Singapore GP. After Marina Bay, Piastri won the sprint race in Qatar and Norris began a run of second places that helped the team overhaul Aston Martin.

Alpine appeared to be in meltdown, with the top management criticising all and sundry in a demotivating fashion. Yet the team rebounded, and Esteban Ocon finished third in Monaco and Pierre Gasly matched that feat at the Dutch GP.

Williams was heading in the right direction again in 2023 after its recent change of ownership, largely thanks to Alex Albon, who is acknowledged in F1 circles for his extraordinary ability to preserve tyres. He did this sufficiently well to break into the top 10, peaking with seventh at Monza. Rookie Logan Sargeant let the pressure get to him, but he then settled back into the groove.

AlphaTauri picked up the minor points on occasion, albeit with Nyck de Vries being dropped and Yuki Tsunoda leading the way. Daniel Ricciardo made his return, was substituted by impressive rookie Liam Lawson, then came seventh in Mexico.

Alfa Romeo started well, with Valtteri Bottas eighth at the opening race, but that was to remain the best result that he or Zhou Guanyu had all year.

Haas ended up bottom, two places down on 2022, with Nico Hulkenberg shining in qualifying, then he and Kevin Magnussen finding that there was little that they could do over a race distance.

BAHRAIN GP

The Ferraris were quick, but the Red Bulls shocked by being quicker still despite their reduced amount of wind tunnel time, so Max Verstappen started where he'd left off in 2022. Fernando Alonso shone in his first race for Aston Martin, as the team advanced to outpace Mercedes.

The close season offers fans a chance to hope their team will have got on top of the technical regulations better than their rivals.

Qualifying proved that Red Bull Racing was still in charge, which was a surprise considering the sanctioned ten per cent reduction of its aerodynamic testing allowance for exceeding the cost cap. Ferrari was next, ahead of Mercedes.

Verstappen simply got the job done, only ceding the lead to team-mate Sergio Perez when he pitted. The Mexican scrapped with Charles Leclerc but got ahead for a Red Bull one-two. Leclerc came away with nothing as he retired, leaving the way clear for Fernando Alonso to prove that age is no impediment; the 41-year-old Spaniard fighting back from a poor first lap that left him seventh – after being clipped by team-mate Lance Stroll – to claim third. Carlos Sainz couldn't hold on to a podium finish as his Ferrari's tyres faded. Lewis Hamilton would have winced when Alonso passed him, showing how Mercedes was facing a second year of no longer being the most competitive team.

When Stroll injured his wrists, it was thought that he would have to miss the race, but he came through to finish sixth, splitting Mercedes's drivers.

The Alpine drivers had mixed fortunes. Pierre Gasly qualified last after assorted problems, but tigered through to ninth, while Esteban Ocon's trials were limited to the race, when he was hit with three time penalties for three different driving infringements and eventually was withdrawn from the race.

While Ferrari and Mercedes were worried about not being able to match Red Bull, McLaren was at sea, as Lando Norris's car had continual problems and rookie Oscar Piastri's car didn't go the distance.

SAKHIR ROUND 1   DATE: **5 MARCH 2023**

Laps: **57** · Distance: **191.530 miles/308.238km** · Weather: **Hot & dry**

Pos	Driver	Team	Result	Stops	Qualifying Time	Grid
1	Max Verstappen	Red Bull	1h33m56.736s	2	1m29.708s	1
2	Sergio Perez	Red Bull	1h34m08.723s	2	1m29.846s	2
3	Fernando Alonso	Aston Martin	1h34m35.373s	2	1m30.366s	5
4	Carlos Sainz Jr	Ferrari	1h34m44.788s	2	1m30.154s	4
5	Lewis Hamilton	Mercedes	1h34m47.713s	2	1m30.384s	7
6	Lance Stroll	Aston Martin	1h34m51.238s	2	1m30.836s	8
7	George Russell	Mercedes	1h34m52.609s	2	1m30.340s	6
8	Valtteri Bottas	Alfa Romeo	1h35m09.383s	2	1m31.443s	12
9	Pierre Gasly	Alpine	1h35m10.489s	3	1m32.181s	20
10	Alex Albon	Williams	1h35m26.510s	3	no time	15
11	Yuki Tsunoda	AlphaTauri	1h35m27.606s	3	1m32.510s	14
12	Logan Sargeant	Williams	56 laps	3	1m31.652s	16
13	Kevin Magnussen	Haas	56 laps	3	1m31.892s	17
14	Nyck de Vries	AlphaTauri	56 laps	2	1m32.121s	19
15	Nico Hulkenberg	Haas	56 laps	3	1m31.055s	10
16	Zhou Guanyu	Alfa Romeo	56 laps	3	1m31.473s	13
17	Lando Norris	McLaren	55 laps	6	1m31.381s	11
R	Esteban Ocon	Alpine	41 laps/withdrew	3	1m30.984s	9
R	Charles Leclerc	Ferrari	39 laps/power unit	2	1m30.000s	3
R	Oscar Piastri	McLaren	13 laps/electronics	1	1m32.101s	18

FASTEST LAP: ZHOU, 1M33.996S, 128.795MPH/207.276KPH ON LAP 56 · RACE LEADERS: VERSTAPPEN 1-14 & 18-57, PEREZ 15-17

Max Verstappen is centre stage for the start-of-the-year group photo, with Perez next to him.

SAUDI ARABIAN GP

The outcome of this race was decided when Max Verstappen's Red Bull failed in qualifying. The Dutchman picked off his rivals to rise from 15th to second, but didn't have quite enough in store to pass his pole-starting team-mate Sergio Perez.

Verstappen would have expected to follow up his win in Bahrain with another, particularly as Red Bull's closest rivals were some way adrift. However, a driveshaft problem in second qualifying meant that he would start 15th. So it was going to be team-mate Sergio Perez's race to lose, especially as next fastest qualifier, Charles Leclerc, was hit with a ten-place grid penalty for his Ferrari having had to be fitted with an additional power unit element.

Fernando Alonso started from the outside of the front row and made the most of it, propelling his Aston Martin past Perez into the lead. The Mexican was eager to make the most of starting with Verstappen so far back and moved back into the lead on lap 4. Then came news that Alonso had lined his Aston Martin up wide of his grid markings and thus wide of the jump-start sensors. For this, he was hit with a five-second penalty.

While Verstappen moved up the order effortlessly, Perez controlled things from the front, but then the field was bunched by a safety car deployment when Verstappen had just passed Leclerc for fourth. This left just George Russell and Alonso between him and Perez, and he was up for the challenge.

Russell was deposed, then Alonso when he brought his Aston Martin in to serve his penalty. However, the gap to Perez settled at four seconds, much to Perez's relief as the Mexican cruised on to take his fifth F1 win.

The podium ceremony had only just been completed when news broke that Alonso had been given another five-second penalty for his car being worked on as he served his original penalty. So third place would be Russell's, but this decision was eventually overturned and Alonso had made it two podiums from two.

Red Bull's Sergio Perez leads Fernando Alonso's Aston Martin through Turn 2 at the start.

JEDDAH ROUND 2 — DATE: **19 MARCH 2023**
Laps: **50** · Distance: **191.662 miles/308.450km** · Weather: **Very hot**

Pos	Driver	Team	Result	Stops	Qualifying Time	Grid
1	**Sergio Perez**	Red Bull	1h21m14.894s	1	1m28.265s	1
2	**Max Verstappen**	Red Bull	1h21m20.249s	1	1m49.953s	15
3	**Fernando Alonso ****	Aston Martin	1h21m35.622s	1	1m28.730s	2
4	**George Russell**	Mercedes	1h21m40.760s	1	1m28.857s	3
5	**Lewis Hamilton**	Mercedes	1h21m45.959s	1	1m29.223s	7
6	**Carlos Sainz Jr**	Ferrari	1h21m50.770s	1	1m28.931s	4
7	**Charles Leclerc ***	Ferrari	1h21m58.056s	1	1m28.420s	12
8	**Esteban Ocon**	Alpine	1h22m07.726s	1	1m29.078s	6
9	**Pierre Gasly**	Alpine	1h22m09.641s	1	1m29.357s	9
10	**Kevin Magnussen**	Haas	1h22m19.720s	1	1m29.634s	13
11	**Yuki Tsunoda**	AlphaTauri	1h22m22.388s	1	1m29.939s	16
12	**Nico Hulkenberg**	Haas	1h22m25.482s	1	1m29.451s	10
13	**Zhou Guanyu**	Alfa Romeo	1h22m30.954s	2	1m29.461s	11
14	**Nyck de Vries**	AlphaTauri	1h22m32.372s	1	1m30.244s	18
15	**Oscar Piastri**	McLaren	1h22m39.915s	1	1m29.243s	8
16	**Logan Sargeant**	Williams	1h22m41.187s	1	2m08.510s	20
17	**Lando Norris**	McLaren	1h22m41.339s	2	1m30.447s	19
18	**Valtteri Bottas**	Alfa Romeo	49 laps	3	1m29.668s	14
R	**Alex Albon**	Williams	27 laps/brakes	1	1m29.994s	17
R	**Lance Stroll**	Aston Martin	16 laps/power unit	1	1m28.945s	5

FASTEST LAP: VERSTAPPEN, 1M31.906S, 150.271MPH/241.838KPH ON LAP 50 · RACE LEADERS: ALONSO 1-3, PEREZ 4-50
* 10-PLACE GRID PENALTY FOR USING ADDITIONAL POWER UNIT ELEMENT · ** 10S PENALTY FOR SERVING A PENALTY INCORRECTLY

// AUSTRALIAN GP

Max Verstappen had the pace to win, even though he was jumped by the Mercedes duo at the start, but this race will be remembered for the rash of red flags waved in a manner that the drivers thought unnecessary, leaving fans confused and F1 looking limp.

After two poor races, the mood was gloomy at Mercedes, but then came cooler conditions and George Russell qualified slower only than Verstappen, with Lewis Hamilton third. Both were helped by Sergio Perez spinning and failing to set a time, thus putting his car at the tail of the grid.

When Verstappen was jumped by Russell at the start, then pushed back to third by Hamilton, it seemed that he could be beaten. However, Alex Albon crashed at turn 7 on lap 7. Russell dived into the pits, but then was infuriated when the race was red flagged, feeling that a yellow flag would have been enough. The stoppage meant that Russell would take the restart from seventh.

Hamilton controlled the restart, but Verstappen passed him and powered away, his car in a class of its own. Hamilton then focused more on keeping Fernando Alonso back in third.

There would be no recovery drive for Russell, as his engine caught fire. The one who was tearing up the order, though, was Perez, and he would reach sixth place. However, there would be more race-shaping events before then, as Kevin Magnussen clipped the wall on the way out of turn 2 on lap 54 and left debris across the track. There were only two laps to go, but the race was stopped again.

Verstappen controlled the restart, but almost immediately there was trouble as Carlos Sainz's Ferrari spun Alonso out of third, then the Alpines clashed. Out came the red flag again and a decision was made that the fourth start would be behind the safety car, for the remaining lap of the race. Finally, Sainz was hit with a five-second penalty for his contact with Alonso and so fell from fourth to 12th, elevating Yuki Tsunoda to the final point-paying position.

Mercedes's George Russell gets alongside Max Verstappen's Red Bull after making a better start.

MELBOURNE ROUND 3
DATE: 2 APRIL 2023
Laps: **58** • Distance: **190.216 miles/306.124km** • Weather: **Warm & dry**

Pos	Driver	Team	Result	Stops	Qualifying Time	Grid
1	**Max Verstappen**	Red Bull	2h32m38.371s	3	1m16.732s	1
2	**Lewis Hamilton**	Mercedes	2h32m38.550s	3	1m17.104s	3
3	**Fernando Alonso**	Aston Martin	2h32m39.140s	3	1m17.139s	4
4	**Lance Stroll**	Aston Martin	2h32m41.453s	3	1m17.308s	6
5	**Sergio Perez !**	Red Bull	2h32m41.691s	5	no time	20
6	**Lando Norris**	McLaren	2h32m42.072s	3	1m18.119s	13
7	**Nico Hulkenberg**	Haas	2h32m43.210s	3	1m17.735s	10
8	**Oscar Piastri**	McLaren	2h32m43.753s	4	1m18.517s	16
9	**Zhou Guanyu**	Alfa Romeo	2h32m44.084s	5	1m18.540s	17
10	**Yuki Tsunoda**	AlphaTauri	2h32m44.423s	4	1m18.099s	12
11	**Valtteri Bottas !**	Alfa Romeo	2h32m44.884s	6	1m18.714s	19
12	**Carlos Sainz Jr ***	Ferrari	2h32m44.965s	4	1m17.270s	5
13	**Pierre Gasly**	Alpine	56 laps	2	1m17.675s	9
14	**Esteban Ocon**	Alpine	56 laps	3	1m17.768s	11
15	**Nyck de Vries**	AlphaTauri	56 laps	4	1m18.335s	15
16	**Logan Sargeant**	Williams	56 laps	6	1m18.557s	18
17	**Kevin Magnussen**	Haas	52 laps/accident	2	1m18.129s	14
R	**George Russell**	Mercedes	17 laps/engine	2	1m16.968s	2
R	**Alex Albon**	Williams	6 laps/spun off	0	1m17.609s	8
R	**Charles Leclerc**	Ferrari	0 laps/collision	0	1m17.369s	7

FASTEST LAP: PEREZ, 1M20.235S, 147.149MPH/236.814KPH ON LAP 53 • RACE LEADERS: RUSSELL 1-6, HAMILTON 7-11, VERSTAPPEN 12-58 ! MADE TO START FROM PIT LANE AS CAR MODIFIED UNDER PARC FERME CONDITIONS • * 5S PENALTY FOR CAUSING A COLLISION

AZERBAIJAN GP

Sergio Perez passed Charles Leclerc to win the sprint race and passed him again in the Grand Prix. He then read a safety car deployment well to usurp Red Bull Racing team-mate Max Verstappen and claim a second win in three years on the streets of Baku.

Charles Leclerc led away, but he was overhauled by Max Verstappen and then by Sergio Perez. Then a yellow flag was shown after Nyck de Vries crashed his AlphaTauri and the Dutchman pitted his Red Bull. Perez waited to come in after the safety car was deployed and this was enough for him to come out of the pits ahead.

With Verstappen also being passed by Leclerc in a similar manner, he had to attack to get by the Ferrari driver for second. However, such was Perez's lead that he could never be hauled in by his team leader, and so landed his fifth F1 victory.

Fernando Alonso moved his Aston Martin onto the tail of Leclerc's Ferrari but wasn't able to relieve him of the final place on the podium as he continued to shine.

It wasn't a great race for Carlos Sainz Jr, as he finished another 23 seconds back in fifth, pushed to the finish by Lewis Hamilton's Mercedes, with Lance Stroll ensuring a double points score for Aston Martin.

George Russell, who had angered Verstappen when they came into contact in the sprint race, had to make do with eighth place. With a large gap back to the next car, he was able to take on a fresh set of tyres without losing a position and clawed back an extra point for setting the race's fastest lap.

Both Esteban Ocon and Nico Hulkenberg gambled on running a long first stint on hard tyres as a way of making up ground after both had to start the race from the pit lane and elected to stay out. Running in the top ten late on, they were praying for another safety car period that never came and so dropped out of the points as Lando Norris and Yuki Tsunoda completed the top ten.

BAKU ROUND 4   DATE: **30 APRIL 2023**

Laps: **51** • Distance: **190.170 miles/306.049km** • Weather: **Hot & sunny**

Pos	Driver	Team	Result	Stops	Grid	Sprint
1	**Sergio Perez**	Red Bull	1h32m42.436s	1	3	1
2	**Max Verstappen**	Red Bull	1h32m44.573s	1	2	3
3	**Charles Leclerc**	Ferrari	1h33m03.653s	1	1	2
4	**Fernando Alonso**	Aston Martin	1h33m04.460s	1	6	6
5	**Carlos Sainz Jr**	Ferrari	1h33m27.927s	1	4	5
6	**Lewis Hamilton**	Mercedes	1h33m28.581s	1	5	7
7	**Lance Stroll**	Aston Martin	1h33m34.053s	1	9	8
8	**George Russell**	Mercedes	1h33m56.676s	2	11	4
9	**Lando Norris**	McLaren	1h34m02.812s	1	7	17
10	**Yuki Tsunoda**	AlphaTauri	1h34m06.298s	1	8	R
11	**Oscar Piastri**	McLaren	1h34m08.937s	1	10	10
12	**Alex Albon**	Williams	1h34m11.059s	1	12	9
13	**Kevin Magnussen**	Haas	1h34m12.165s	1	16	11
14	**Pierre Gasly**	Alpine	1h34m13.768s	2	17	13
15	**Esteban Ocon ***	Alpine	1h34m20.230s	1	19	18
16	**Logan Sargeant**	Williams	1h34m23.379s	1	14	W
17	**Nico Hulkenberg ***	Haas	50 laps	1	20	15
18	**Valtteri Bottas**	Alfa Romeo	50 laps	3	13	16
R	**Zhou Guanyu**	Alfa Romeo	36 laps/overheating	1	15	12
R	**Nyck de Vries**	AlphaTauri	9 laps/accident	0	18	14

FASTEST LAP: RUSSELL, 1M43.370S, 129.905MPH/209.062KPH ON LAP 51 • RACE LEADERS: LECLERC 1-2, VERSTAPPEN 3-9, PEREZ 10-51
* MADE TO START FROM PITLANE AS CAR MODIFIED IN PARC FERME

Sergio Perez celebrates his second win from four starts, flanked by Leclerc and Verstappen.

Max Verstappen re-established himself as Red Bull Racing's lead driver by usurping pole-starting team-mate Sergio Perez, powering his way forward from ninth on the grid to catch, pass, beat and demoralise the Mexican. The advantage was worth more than the seven-point swing.

When Charles Leclerc crashed his Ferrari in the final qualifying session, it interrupted Verstappen's second run after he had made a mistake on his first. With no chance to make amends, he would line up ninth on F1's second visit to the temporary circuit laid out around the car park of the Hard Rock Stadium. Sergio Perez would start from pole ahead of Fernando Alonso.

Perez knew that his team-mate would mount a mighty charge, and so he did, picking off the drivers between them, one by one. Closing in after their pit stops, Verstappen hit the front on lap 48 of 57 and stayed there. To be beaten when a driver started one place behind you is one thing, but to be beaten when your team-mate and chief rival had started eight places back is quite another. And this race in Miami was really the moment at which the 2023 title race pivoted in Verstappen's favour.

Dispirited he may have been, but Red Bull Racing's performance advantage was still large enough for Perez to finish in a comfortable second place, with Alonso's Aston Martin another 11 seconds back. Meanwhile Mercedes's George Russell was the best of the rest, helped first by team-mate Lewis Hamilton moving out of his way as he was running a different race strategy, and then given breathing space when the chasing Carlos Sainz Jr was hit with a five-second penalty for speeding in the pit lane.

After a terrible performance in the Azerbaijan GP, for which both Alpine drivers were criticised by their own team, Pierre Gasly and Esteban Ocon bounced back to scoop the points for eighth and ninth. Meanwhile Kevin Magnussen gave Haas F1 a rare moment to savour, as he claimed the final point by finishing tenth in a race when McLaren notably got its tyre choice wrong.

MIAMI ROUND 5

DATE: 7 MAY 2023

Laps: **57** · Distance: **191.585 miles/308.326km** · Weather: **Hot but overcast**

Pos	Driver	Team	Result	Stops	Qualifying Time	Grid
1	**Max Verstappen**	Red Bull	1h27m38.241s	1	No time	9
2	**Sergio Perez**	Red Bull	1h27m43.625s	1	1m26.841s	1
3	**Fernando Alonso**	Aston Martin	1h28m04.546s	1	1m27.202s	2
4	**George Russell**	Mercedes	1h28m11.470s	1	1m27.804s	6
5	**Carlos Sainz Jr ***	Ferrari	1h28m20.752s	1	1m27.349s	3
6	**Lewis Hamilton**	Mercedes	1h28m29.490s	1	1m27.975s	13
7	**Charles Leclerc**	Ferrari	1h28m31.229s	1	1m27.861s	7
8	**Pierre Gasly**	Alpine	1h28m33.911s	1	1m27.786s	5
9	**Esteban Ocon**	Alpine	1h28m36.364s	1	1m27.935s	8
10	**Kevin Magnussen**	Haas	1h28m41.186s	1	1m27.767s	4
11	**Yuki Tsunoda**	AlphaTauri	1h28m42.550s	1	1m28.429s	17
12	**Lance Stroll**	Aston Martin	1h28m42.995s	1	1m28.476s	18
13	**Valtteri Bottas**	Alfa Romeo	1h28m49.878s	1	No time	10
14	**Alex Albon**	Williams	1h28m51.102s	1	1m27.795s	11
15	**Nico Hulkenberg**	Haas	1h28m53.191s	1	1m27.903s	12
16	**Zhou Guanyu**	Alfa Romeo	1h28m56.681s	1	1m28.091s	14
17	**Lando Norris**	McLaren	1h29m05.958s	1	1m28.394s	16
18	**Nyck de Vries**	AlphaTauri	1h29m07.190s	1	1m28.395s	15
19	**Oscar Piastri**	McLaren	56 laps	1	1m28.484s	19
20	**Logan Sargeant**	Williams	56 laps	1	1m28.577s	20

FASTEST LAP: **VERSTAPPEN, 1M29.708S, 134.952MPH/217.184KPH ON LAP 56** · RACE LEADERS: **PEREZ 1-19 & 46-47, VERSTAPPEN 20-45 & 48-57** · *** 5S PENALTY FOR SPEEDING IN PIT LANE**

Max Verstappen completes his chase by overtaking Red Bull team-mate Sergio Perez to win.

MONACO GP

This was a race that Max Verstappen controlled from the start, his Red Bull the class of the field. Having to start last meant that team-mate Sergio Perez had no chance to follow him home, although Fernando Alonso might have won but for being put onto the wrong tyres.

The first step to any possible win on the streets of Monte Carlo is to bag pole position. Once Max Verstappen had done that, albeit by just 0.084 seconds from Fernando Alonso, he would have felt confident. With Perez stumbling and being eliminated in first qualifying, leaving him to start in last position and thus out of the running for a useful helping of points, Verstappen's hopes were greater still.

However, Alonso had other ideas and kept his Aston Martin on Verstappen's tail in the early stages of the race. The arrival of rain after mid-distance led both to a spin at the Fairmont Hairpin caused by Lance Stroll in the second Aston Martin that put the Canadian out of the race. At almost the same time, the team from Silverstone could have put the Spaniard into a winning position. Unfortunately for Aston Martin, their change to slick tyres was premature and a subsequent change to intermediate tyres on the following lap cost Alonso his chance of a first victory since he won the 2013 Spanish GP for Ferrari.

Having watched this stumble, Red Bull called Verstappen in a lap later, fitted intermediates and off he went with 23 laps to race on to an easy victory by 28 seconds.

Alpine's Esteban Ocon started third and finished third for Alpine after resisting first Carlos Sainz Jr and later Lewis Hamilton, with the Spaniard losing further places with a slip up. For Alpine, this was the first sign that a season that it thought was going nowhere might be turned around.

George Russell also ought to have finished and was furious with himself after a loss of concentration that led to him spinning at Mirabeau. However, the Mercedes driver was still able to finish fifth ahead of local hero Charles Leclerc, who was the better-placed Ferrari driver.

Three happy drivers, with Verstappen joined by Fernando Alonso and Alpine's Esteban Ocon.

MONTE CARLO ROUND 6

DATE: **28 MAY 2023**

Laps: **78** · Distance: **161.734 miles/260.286km** · Weather: **Warm & dry, then wet**

Pos	Driver	Team	Result	Stops	Qualifying Time	Grid
1	**Max Verstappen**	Red Bull	1h48m51.980s	1	1m11.365s	1
2	**Fernando Alonso**	Aston Martin	1h49m19.901s	2	1m11.449s	2
3	**Esteban Ocon**	Alpine	1h49m28.970s	2	1m11.553s	3
4	**Lewis Hamilton**	Mercedes	1h49m31.042s	2	1m11.725s	5
5	**George Russell ***	Mercedes	1h49m48.264s	1	1m11.964s	8
6	**Charles Leclerc !**	Ferrari	1h49m53.870s	2	1m11.471s	6
7	**Pierre Gasly**	Alpine	1h49m54.342s	2	1m11.933S	7
8	**Carlos Sainz Jr**	Ferrari	1h49m55.371s	2	1m11.630s	4
9	**Lando Norris**	McLaren	77 laps	2	1m12.254s	10
10	**Oscar Piastri**	McLaren	77 laps	1	1m12.395s	11
11	**Valtteri Bottas**	Alfa Romeo	77 laps	1	1m12.625s	15
12	**Nyck de Vries**	AlphaTauri	77 laps	1	1m12.428s	12
13	**Zhou Guanyu**	Alfa Romeo	77 laps	2	1m13.523s	19
14	**Alex Albon**	Williams	77 laps	2	1m12.527s	13
15	**Yuki Tsunoda**	AlphaTauri	76 laps	1	1m12.082s	9
16	**Sergio Perez**	Red Bull	76 laps	5	1m13.850s	20
17	**Nico Hulkenberg ****	Haas	76 laps	3	1m13.279s	18
18	**Logan Sargeant ***	Williams	76 laps	3	1m13.113s	16
19	**Kevin Magnussen**	Haas	70 laps/withdrew	1	1m13.270s	17
R	**Lance Stroll**	Aston Martin	53 laps/accident	1	1m12.623s	14

FASTEST LAP: HAMILTON, 1M15.650S, 98.673MPH/158.799KPH ON LAP 33 · RACE LEADERS:VERSTAPPEN 1-78
! 3-PLACE GRID PENALTY FOR IMPEDING · * 5S PENALTY · ** 10S PENALTY

Max Verstappen delivers another blistering performance at the Canadian Grand Prix, leading from lights to flag.

When Charles Leclerc retired before halfway, this race was put on a plate for Max Verstappen and he made the most of it, although possibly the best drive was Lewis Hamilton's recovery to fifth after a first-lap tangle with Kevin Magnussen.

The only moment in which a rival driver was able to threaten Verstappen's dominance was right at the start of the race when Carlos Sainz Jr looked to go around the outside at the first corner. However, anxious for points, the Spaniard elected not to risk it all on his opening lap move and tucked back in behind the Dutchman's Red Bull.

Such was the pace of the Red Bulls that Verstappen and team-mate Sergio Perez were able to decide after they were switched from medium compound tyres to hards for the second stint whether they would cruise in on those or stop again. What a luxury. So far was he ahead, Verstappen ignored team advice and pitted again for mediums so that he could gun for the points for fastest lap, successfully as it happens. This was Max's 40th F1 win.

It wasn't all smiles at Red Bull, as Perez wasn't able to climb from 11th on the grid after a poor qualifying run to reach the podium, ending up fourth, behind the Mercedes duo after George Russell resisted every attack that the Mexican mounted.

Lewis Hamilton was delighted that Mercedes's latest developments offered him a car good enough to finish second, a result made even more pleasing as he chased, caught and passed Sainz Jr, as did both Russell and Perez. The second Ferrari, Charles Leclerc's, had to start from the pit lane and the Monegasque driver, not seemingly helped by an intelligent race strategy, failed to break into the points as his season continued to disappoint.

The Aston Martins finished sixth and seventh, with Fernando Alonso catching team-mate Lance Stroll before electing not to overtake the team boss's son. Behind them, Yuki Tsunoda lost a point-scoring drive when a penalty dropped him from ninth to 12th.

BARCELONA ROUND 7
DATE: 4 JUNE 2023

Laps: **66** • Distance: **190.907 miles/307.236km** • Weather: **Overcast but warm**

Pos	Driver	Team	Result	Stops	Qualifying Time	Grid
1	**Max Verstappen**	Red Bull	1h27m57.940s	2	1m12.272s	1
2	**Lewis Hamilton**	Mercedes	1h28m22.030s	2	1m12.818s	4
3	**George Russell**	Mercedes	1h28m30.329s	2	1m13.447s	12
4	**Sergio Perez**	Red Bull	1h28m33.752s	2	1m13.334s	11
5	**Carlos Sainz Jr**	Ferrari	1h28m43.638s	2	1m12.734s	2
6	**Lance Stroll**	Aston Martin	1h29m01.260s	2	1m12.994s	5
7	**Fernando Alonso**	Aston Martin	1h29m02.067s	2	1m13.507s	8
8	**Esteban Ocon**	Alpine	1h29m07.182s	2	1m13.083s	6
9	**Zhou Guanyu**	Alfa Romeo	1h29m09.818s	2	1m13.521s	13
10	**Pierre Gasly** !	Alpine	1h29m11.420s	2	1m12.816s	10
11	**Charles Leclerc** !!	Ferrari	1h29m12.359s	2	1m14.079s	20
12	**Yuki Tsunoda** *	AlphaTauri	1h29m13.356s	2	1m14.477s	15
13	**Oscar Piastri**	McLaren	65 laps	2	1m13.682s	9
14	**Nyck de Vries**	AlphaTauri	65 laps	2	1m14.083s	14
15	**Nico Hulkenberg**	Haas	65 laps	3	1m13.229s	7
16	**Alex Albon**	Williams	65 laps	2	1m14.063s	18
17	**Lando Norris**	McLaren	65 laps	3	1m12.792s	3
18	**Kevin Magnussen**	Haas	65 laps	3	1m14.042s	17
19	**Valtteri Bottas**	Alfa Romeo	65 laps	2	1m13.977s	16
20	**Logan Sargeant** !!!	Williams	65 laps	2	1m14.699s	19

FASTEST LAP: VERSTAPPEN, 1M16.330S, 136.478MPH/219.641KPH ON LAP 61 • RACE LEADERS: VERSTAPPEN 1-66
* 5S PENALTY FOR FORCING A RIVAL OFF THE TRACK • ! 2X 3-PLACE GRID PENALTY FOR IMPEDING, • !! 15-PLACE GRID PENALTY FOR USING AN ADDITIONAL POWER UNIT • !!! MADE TO START FROM PIT LANE AS CAR MODIFIED IN PARC FERME

Lewis Hamilton drove an excellent race to second, acknowledged by his pit crew's applause.

CANADIAN GP

This was Max Verstappen's 41st Grand Prix victory, and so he moved level with the late, great Ayrton Senna, equal fifth in the all-time charts. The Dutchman won with ease, with former world champions Fernando Alonso and Lewis Hamilton enjoying a good scrap over second.

Rain made qualifying more exciting, but the third session was red flagged when Oscar Piastri crashed, leaving three minutes to run after the track was cleared. At this point, Verstappen was fastest by fully 1.2 seconds from a remarkable Nico Hulkenberg lap. Many prayed that this surprise result for the Haas driver wouldn't be overhauled, and this was ensured when more rain swept in as the drivers ventured back out. However, the German was then penalised three grid positions for lapping too slowly during a red flag period.

Race day was dry, though, and Verstappen did what he has become accustomed to doing, namely pulling ever further clear of the pack, leaving all others in his wake.

Fellow front-row starter Fernando Alonso's Aston Martin was passed immediately by Lewis Hamilton and their scrap for second certainly helped Verstappen make his escape as the Spaniard tried several times to regain position into the final chicane.

George Russell's Mercedes clouted the wall at turn 9 and left debris that needed to be cleared, and this put Alonso back on to Hamilton's tail and he finally regained second on lap 23. Russell pitted for repairs but would be called in to retire later in the race.

This meant that Ferrari's Charles Leclerc and Carlos Sainz Jr were able to advance from poor grid positions to finish fourth and fifth, while Sergio Perez had even more ground to make up after failing to qualify in the top ten for a third race in a row, something that is disastrous for someone driving for the team with the most competitive car. He made it up from 12th to sixth and, knowing that he was too far back to attack the Ferraris, settled for pitting for fresh rubber and claiming the point for fastest lap.

Max Verstappen leads Lewis Hamilton and Fernando Alonso into the first corner at the start.

MONTREAL ROUND 8 — DATE: 18 JUNE 2023

Laps: 70 · Distance: 189.686 miles/305.270km · Weather: Warm & overcast

Pos	Driver	Team	Result	Stops	Qualifying Time	Grid
1	Max Verstappen	Red Bull	1h33m58.348s	2	1m25.858s	1
2	Fernando Alonso	Aston Martin	1h34m07.918s	2	1m27.286s	2
3	Lewis Hamilton	Mercedes	1h34m12.516s	2	1m27.627s	3
4	Charles Leclerc	Ferrari	1h34m16.996s	1	1m20.615s	10
5	Carlos Sainz Jr !	Ferrari	1h34m19.888s	1	1m29.294s	11
6	Sergio Perez	Red Bull	1h34m49.376s	2	1m20.959s	12
7	Alex Albon	Williams	1h34m59.161s	1	No time	9
8	Esteban Ocon	Alpine	1h35m00.040s	2	1m27.945s	6
9	Lance Stroll !	Aston Martin	1h35m02.750s	2	1m21.484s	16
10	Valtteri Bottas	Alfa Romeo	1h35m02.780s	1	1m21.821s	14
11	Oscar Piastri	McLaren	1h35m03.449s	2	1m31.349s	8
12	Pierre Gasly	Alpine	1h35m03.597s	2	1m22.886s	15
13	Lando Norris *	McLaren	1h35m06.711s	2	1m28.046s	7
14	Yuki Tsunoda !	AlphaTauri	1h35m11.771s	2	1m22.746s	19
15	Nico Hulkenberg !!	Haas	69 laps	2	1m27.102s	5
16	Zhou Guanyou	Alfa Romeo	69 laps	2	1m23.342s	20
17	Kevin Magnussen	Haas	69 laps	2	1m21.678s	13
18	Nyck de Vries	AlphaTauri	69 laps	2	1m23.137s	17
R	George Russell	Mercedes	53 laps/brakes	1	1m27.893s	4
R	Logan Sargeant	Williams	6 laps/oil leak	0	1m23.337s	18

FASTEST LAP: **PEREZ, 1M14.481S, 130.976MPH/210.786KPH ON LAP 70** · RACE LEADERS: **VERSTAPPEN 1-70**
* 5S PENALTY FOR UNSPORTSMANLIKE BEHAVIOUR · ! 3-PLACE GRID PENALTY FOR IMPEDING ANOTHER DRIVER · !! 3-PLACE GRID PENALTY FOR RED FLAG INFRINGEMENT

AUSTRIAN GP

Perhaps refreshed after two weekends off, the teams headed to the Red Bull Ring hoping that their latest modifications might have brought them closer to Red Bull Racing's pace, but pole position, fastest lap and yet another Max Verstappen win squashed their hopes.

If the other nine teams wanted to see at least some hope for their efforts, Ferrari for once got things right. It didn't end in a life-affirming win, but for Charles Leclerc to finish just five seconds down on Verstappen was a definite step forward.

Verstappen won a wet/dry sprint race from Sergio Perez, with the Mexican second and Ferrari's Carlos Sainz Jr third.

The Dutchman was never likely to be toppled in the Grand Prix, though, and he led away with the Ferraris behind. However, the safety car had to be deployed as Yuki Tsunoda's AlphaTauri was beached after hitting Esteban Ocon's Alpine.

At the second time of asking, Verstappen pulled clear again. Leclerc had no answer to his pace, but team-mate Carlos Sainz Jr thought that he did, although Ferrari ignored this. Then the Spaniard had a slow pit stop and, instead of pushing for a podium position, he ended up behind the consistently advancing Perez as well as Lando Norris and Fernando Alonso. The pit stop went better for Leclerc, though, as he emerged ahead of Verstappen and stayed there for nine laps before Verstappen simply motored by.

Any hopes of a good cluster of points came to nothing when Nico Hulkenberg's power unit began to smoke. For other drivers, their disappointment came from exceeding track limits, chiefly at the final two corners, and having to accept the time penalties that came with that. Sainz Jr dropped from fourth place at flag-fall to sixth because of a ten-second penalty and Lewis Hamilton fell behind team-mate George Russell to end up eighth on another mediocre day for Mercedes. Worst affected was Alpine's Esteban Ocon who collected a handful of time penalties, and his 30-second punishment dropped him from 12th to 14th.

Charles Leclerc found some pace on a better day for Ferrari and finished in second place.

RED BULL RING ROUND 9

DATE: **2 JULY 2023**

Laps: **71** · Distance: **190.420 miles/306.452km** · Weather: **Warm but overcast**

Pos	Driver	Team	Result	Stops	Grid	Sprint
1	**Max Verstappen**	Red Bull	1h25m33.607s	4	1	1
2	**Charles Leclerc**	Ferrari	1h25m38.762s	3	2	12
3	**Sergio Perez**	Red Bull	1h25m50.795s	3	15	2
4	**Lando Norris**	McLaren	1h25m59.934s	3	4	9
5	**Fernando Alonso**	Aston Martin	1h26m03.924s	3	7	5
6	**Carlos Sainz Jr** !!	Ferrari	1h26m04.984s	3	3	3
7	**George Russell**	Mercedes	1h26m22.010s	3	11	8
8	**Lewis Hamilton** !!	Mercedes	1h26m22.803s	3	5	10
9	**Lance Stroll**	Aston Martin	1h26m32.650s	4	6	4
10	**Pierre Gasly** !!	Alpine	1h26m41.274s	3	9	15
11	**Alex Albon** !!	Williams	1h26m53.374s	3	10	13
12	**Zhou Guanyu**	Alfa Romeo	70 laps	3	17	19
13	**Logan Sargeant** !!!	Williams	70 laps	3	18	18
14	**Esteban Ocon** !!!!!	Alpine	70 laps	3	12	7
15	**Valtteri Bottas**	Alfa Romeo	70 laps	3	14	20
16	**Oscar Piastri**	McLaren	70 laps	4	13	11
17	**Nyck de Vries** !!!!, *	Alpha Tauri	70 laps	3	20	17
18	**Kevin Magnussen** !, *	Haas	70 laps	3	19	14
19	**Yuki Tsunoda** !!!	AlphaTauri	70 laps	4	16	16
R	**Nico Hulkenberg**	Haas	12 laps/power unit	2	8	6

FASTEST LAP: VERSTAPPEN, 1M07.012S, 144.139MPH/231.970KPH ON LAP 71 · RACE LEADERS: VERSTAPPEN 1-24 & 35-71, LECLERC 25-34
* REQUIRED TO START FROM PITLANE AS CAR MODIFIED IN PARC FERME · ! 5S PENALTY FOR EXCEEDING TRACK LIMITS · !! 10S PENAL-TY FOR EXCEEDING TRACK LIMITS · !!! 15S PENALTY FOR EXCEEDING TRACK LIMITS · !!!! 20S PENALTY FOR EXCEEDING TRACK LIMITS · !!!!! 30S PENALTY FOR EXCEEDING TRACK LIMITS

BRITISH GP

Max Verstappen made it six wins in a row, but this was one that he had to work for, as McLaren hit form. Lando Norris led before having to settle for second, with team-mate Oscar Piastri denied a first top-three finish by the timing of a safety car period.

There was much change in this British GP. Obviously, with Max Verstappen continuing his winning streak and Red Bull Racing equalling McLaren's record of 11 wins in a row, the change wasn't right at the front. It came from McLaren finding form thanks to a new front wing.

While the Dutch ace bagged another pole, it was tight, and he only grabbed it right at the end of the third session from a buoyant Norris, with Piastri setting the third fastest time. On the other side of the Red Bull garage, however, Mexican team-mate Sergio Perez was again despondent after yet another weak performance in the best car in the field, as he ended up 15th.

Norris grabbed the lead at the start and stayed there for four laps before Verstappen found a way by. Although he stayed in touch, his 3.8 second deficit at race's end was down to the safety car being deployed after the power unit on Kevin Magnussen's Haas caught fire.

Rookie Piastri might have made his first podium but pitting under the safety car enabled Lewis Hamilton to get ahead and set off after Norris. Behind them, George Russell drove defensively to prevent Perez getting past. A few seconds further back, Fernando Alonso finished seventh, which showed how Aston Martin's form was fading. Impressively, the Williams of Alex Albon came through to eighth, with team-mate Logan Sargeant finishing 11th to suggest that this once great team was making progress. He actually finished 12th, but Lance Stroll was given a five-second penalty for causing a collision with Pierre Gasly and that dropped him to 14th.

Between the Williams duo came the Ferraris, which came away with just three points. This was a disappointment as its drivers had qualified fourth and fifth, with a weak strategy again affecting Charles Leclerc's chances.

SILVERSTONE ROUND 10

DATE: **9 JULY 2023**

Laps: **52** · Distance: **190.262 miles/306.198km** · Weather: **Warm & sunny**

Pos	Driver	Team	Result	Stops	Qualifying Time	Grid
1	**Max Verstappen**	Red Bull	1h25m16.938s	1	1m26.720s	1
2	**Lando Norris**	McLaren	1h25m20.736s	1	1m26.961s	2
3	**Lewis Hamilton**	Mercedes	1h25m23.721s	1	1m27.211s	7
4	**Oscar Piastri**	McLaren	1h25m24.714s	1	1m27.092s	3
5	**George Russell**	Mercedes	1h25m28.144s	1	1m27.155s	6
6	**Sergio Perez**	Red Bull	1h25m29.820s	1	1m26.968s	15
7	**Fernando Alonso**	Aston Martin	1h25m34.131s	1	1m27.659s	9
8	**Alex Albon**	Williams	1h25m34.816s	1	1m27.530s	8
9	**Charles Leclerc**	Ferrari	1h25m35.627s	2	1m27.136s	4
10	**Carlos Sainz Jr**	Ferrari	1h25m36.386s	1	1m27.148s	5
11	**Logan Sargeant**	Williams	1h25m40.570s	1	1m29.031s	14
12	**Valtteri Bottas**	Alfa Romeo	1h25m42.768s	1	no time	20
13	**Nico Hulkenberg**	Haas	1h25m43.601s	2	1m28.696s	11
14	**Lance Stroll ***	Aston Martin	1h25m44.421s	1	1m28.935s	12
15	**Zhou Guanyu**	Alfa Romeo	1h25m46.758s	3	1m30.123s	17
16	**Yuki Tsunoda**	AlphaTauri	1h25m48.163s	2	1m30.025s	16
17	**Nyck de Vries**	AlphaTauri	1h25m50.066s	2	1m30.513s	18
R	**Pierre Gasly**	Alpine	46 laps/crash damage	1	1m27.689s	10
R	**Kevin Magnussen**	Haas	31 laps/fire	0	1m32.378s	19
R	**Esteban Ocon**	Alpine	9 laps/hydraulics	0	1m28.956s	13

FASTEST LAP: **VERSTAPPEN, 1M30.275S, 145.973MPH/234.922KPH ON LAP 42** · RACE LEADERS: **NORRIS 1-4, VERSTAPPEN 5-52**
· * 5S PENALTY FOR CAUSING A COLLISION

Delighted McLaren CEO Zak Brown greets Lando Norris after his season-turning second place.

Lewis Hamilton was delighted to snatch a surprise pole by a tiny margin from Max Verstappen, but made a poor start and Verstappen simply took over. The Dutchman won by over half a minute, with performance to spare, from a resurgent Lando Norris.

It wasn't much of an exaggeration to say that Mercedes was all at sea in the middle part of 2023. Red Bull's RB19s set the pace at every circuit and modifications made to Mercedes's F1 W14 never seemed to get them any closer to the front. So, when Lewis Hamilton was only 16th on Friday and describing the car as 'being at its worst', he can't have expected what followed a day later when he produced a lap that would take pole, by 0.003 seconds from Verstappen. Hamilton was as delighted as he has been seen at any point in recent years. Keeping things balanced for Mercedes, George Russell was obstructed in Q1 and would start 18th…

Maybe his senses had been dulled by a year and a half of low expectations, but Hamilton blew his golden opportunity on one of the circuits easiest to defend a lead: he made a woeful start and Verstappen didn't need a second invitation.

Worse still for Hamilton was the fact that as he tried to repel Verstappen, both McLarens went past, dropping him to fourth, and this would be his finishing position.

As Verstappen set sail, Lando Norris moved ahead of team-mate Oscar Piastri for second at the first round of pit stops.

Sergio Perez qualified poorly again, ninth, but he advanced thanks to a clever strategy to pressure Norris, yet had to settle for third.

The Alfa Romeos qualified fifth and seventh, but their expected slide down the order came to pass, with Russell one of the beneficiaries as he climbed to sixth, also thanks to a five-second penalty for Charles Leclerc and a fumbled pit stop for Carlos Sainz Jr.

A most bizarre event occurred on the podium, when Norris banged to make his champagne erupt and this caused the winner's trophy to topple and smash.

HUNGARORING ROUND 11 · DATE: 23 JULY 2023

Laps: **70** · Distance: **190.531 miles/306.630km** · Weather: **Very hot & bright**

Pos	Driver	Team	Result	Stops	Qualifying Time	Grid
1	**Max Verstappen**	Red Bull	1h38m08.634s	2	1m16.612s	2
2	**Lando Norris**	McLaren	1h38m42.365s	2	1m16.694s	3
3	**Sergio Perez**	Red Bull	1h38m46.237s	2	1m17.045s	9
4	**Lewis Hamilton**	Mercedes	1h38m47.768s	2	1m16.609s	1
5	**Oscar Piastri**	McLaren	1h39m11.206s	2	1m16.905s	4
6	**George Russell**	Mercedes	1h39m14.459s	2	1m19.027s	18
7	**Charles Leclerc ***	Ferrari	1h39m18.951s	2	1m16.992s	6
8	**Carlos Sainz Jr**	Ferrari	1h39m19.707s	2	1m17.703s	11
9	**Fernando Alonso**	Aston Martin	1h29m24.343s	2	1m17.035s	8
10	**Lance Stroll**	Aston Martin	69 laps	2	1m18.144s	14
11	**Alex Albon**	Williams	69 laps	2	1m18.917s	16
12	**Valtteri Bottas**	Alfa Romeo	69 laps	2	1m17.034s	7
13	**Daniel Ricciardo**	AlphaTauri	69 laps	2	1m18.002s	13
14	**Nico Hulkenberg**	Haas	69 laps	2	1m17.186s	10
15	**Yuki Tsunoda**	AlphaTauri	69 laps	2	1m18.919s	17
16	**Zhou Guanyu**	Alfa Romeo	69 laps	2	1m16.971s	5
17	**Kevin Magnussen**	Haas	69 laps	2	1m19.206s	19
R	**Logan Sargeant**	Williams	67 laps/spin	2	1m19.248s	20
R	**Esteban Ocon**	Alpine	2 laps/collision damage	0	1m17.841s	12
R	**Pierre Gasly**	Alpine	1 lap/collision damage	0	1m18.217s	15

FASTEST LAP: **VERSTAPPEN, 1M20.504S, 121.733MPH/195.910KPH ON LAP 53** · RACE LEADERS: RACE LEADERS: VERSTAPPEN 1-70
* 5S PENALTY FOR SPEEDING IN PIT LANE

Max Verstappen dives boldly inside Lewis Hamilton's Mercedes to seize the initiative.

BELGIAN GP

Despite having to be patient after he had been put back to sixth on the grid, Max Verstappen moved to the front and made an eighth victory in a row look simple, with team-mate Sergio Perez following him home ten seconds clear of Ferrari's Charles Leclerc.

The last race before the World Championship's much-needed summer break resulted in a record 13th win in a row for Red Bull Racing and yet another huge points haul for runaway leader Max Verstappen. He was, though, denied the extra one for fastest lap, as Lewis Hamilton was confident enough to pit from fourth place and go out and get it on the final lap of the race.

Verstappen had qualified on pole by some considerable margin on a drying track, but a gearbox change meant a five-place grid penalty and so Charles Leclerc would line up on pole for Ferrari in his place. And yet this golden opportunity for the Monegasque driver was to end up with only third place at flag-fall.

Verstappen was wary of what might happen at the first corner, so took a cautious approach. Unfortunately for McLaren's fast-learning Oscar Piastri, the Australian elected to dive up the inside of Carlos Sainz Jr into La Source and the damage would put him out of the race. Sergio Perez made a better job of overtaking, wresting the lead from Leclerc on their first run up the Kemmel Straight.

The first corner contact helped Verstappen climb to fourth and he then calmly advanced past Hamilton and then Leclerc, then briefly took the lead when team-mate Perez made his first pit stop. He eventually eased away to win by 22 seconds.

In fact, little changed in his wake, other than a few drivers opting for intermediate tyres when there was a brief shower, but this was the wrong choice and they lost places.

Aware that he couldn't catch Leclerc for third, Hamilton came in late for fresh rubber and achieved his aim by setting fastest lap and was still able to finish ahead of Aston Martin's Fernando Alonso.

Ferrari's Carlos Sainz Jr rounds La Source hairpin with Fernando Alonso right on his tail.

SPA-FRANCORCHAMPS ROUND 12 DATE: **30 JULY 2023**
Laps: **44** · Distance: **191.414 miles/308.052km** · Weather: **Hot & sunny**

Pos	Driver	Team	Result	Stops	Grid	Sprint
1	**Max Verstappen** !!	Red Bull	1h22m30.450s	2	6	1
2	**Sergio Perez**	Red Bull	1h22m52.755s	2	2	9
3	**Charles Leclerc**	Ferrari	1h23m02.709s	2	1	5
4	**Lewis Hamilton**	Mercedes	1h23m20.121s	3	3	7
5	**Fernando Alonso**	Aston Martin	1h23m26.634s	2	9	20
6	**George Russell**	Mercedes	1h23m33.551s	1	8	8
7	**Lando Norris**	McLaren	1h23m44.169s	2	7	6
8	**Esteban Ocon**	Alpine	1h23m45.169s	2	14	9
9	**Lance Stroll**	Aston Martin	1h23m49.790s	1	10	11
10	**Yuki Tsunoda**	AlphaTauri	1h23m50.671s	2	11	18
11	**Pierre Gasly**	Alpine	1h23m53.534s	1	12	3
12	**Valtteri Bottas**	Alfa Romeo	1h23m55.641s	2	13	13
13	**Zhou Guanyu**	Alfa Romeo	1h24m05.891s	2	17	15
14	**Alex Albon**	Williams	1h24m06.634s	3	15	12
15	**Kevin Magnussen** !	Haas	1h24m12.204s	2	16	14
16	**Daniel Ricciardo**	AlphaTauri	1h24m13.521s	2	19	10
17	**Logan Sargeant**	Williams	1h24m14.926s	3	18	16
18	**Nico Hulkenberg** *	Haas	1h24m20.900s	2	20	17
R	**Carlos Sainz Jr**	Ferrari	23 laps/crash damage	1	4	4
R	**Oscar Piastri**	McLaren	0 laps/crash damage	0	5	2

FASTEST LAP: HAMILTON, 1M47.305S, 146.008MPH/234.978KPH ON LAP 44 • RACE LEADERS: PEREZ 1-22 & 15-16, VERSTAPPEN 13-14 & 17-44 • ! 3-PLACE GRID PENALTY FOR IMPEDING LECLERC • !! 5-PLACE GRID PENALTY FOR REPLACING GEARBOX • * MADE TO START FROM PIT LANE AS CAR MODIFIED IN PARC FERME

DUTCH GP

Max Verstappen drove peerlessly to secure his ninth win in a row in a race in which both Ferrari and Mercedes got their tactics wrong as conditions changed. Fernando Alonso drove a brilliant race to come home second for Aston Martin, while Pierre Gasly delighted Alpine with third.

Verstappen got away cleanly on a track made greasy by a shower just before the start, but the rain soon turned heavy and the drivers pitted to change to intermediate tyres. Not all teams reacted well, though, and when Charles Leclerc pitted, his Ferrari pit crew wasn't ready. This was when Sergio Perez hit the front. He then led from lap 3 to 12 before Verstappen went in front after a second pit stop. But later in the race, the Mexican blotted his copybook by spinning at Tarzan, just after changing to intermediates, letting Alonso through to second.

After a disastrous qualifying, Lewis Hamilton started the race on medium tyres to claw back places. Unfathomably, Mercedes left him out on the track after Verstappen and Alonso pitted on lap 2 and he fell to last, just as the rain stopped.

The race was halted with eight laps to go after Zhou Guanyu aquaplaned off at Tarzan. There was then a long delay, during which fans questioned why the Pirelli rain tyre was not up to operating in full wet conditions.

Although Alonso got close to Verstappen after the restart, he couldn't challenge. Then Perez began to attack and Alonso was cautious in defence, even after he heard that Perez had been given a five-second penalty. This gave Pierre Gasly extra reason to push and he claimed the third step on the podium once Perez's penalty was included. Behind them, Carlos Sainz Jr held off a challenge from Hamilton to secure fifth, while George Russell suffered a puncture and dropped to last as he limped back to the pits.

Liam Lawson was brought in by AlphaTauri to make his F1 debut after Daniel Ricciardo broke a hand in practice. Having started last, the New Zealander impressed as he advanced to 13th, two places ahead of team-mate Yuki Tsunoda.

ZANDVOORT ROUND 13

DATE: 27 AUGUST 2023

Laps: **72** · Distance: **190.504 miles/306.587km** · Weather: **Dry, damp then wet**

Pos	Driver	Team	Result	Stops	Qualifying Time	Grid
1	**Max Verstappen**	Red Bull	2h24m04.411s	6	1m10.567s	1
2	**Fernando Alonso**	Aston Martin	2h24m08.155s	5	1m11.506s	5
3	**Pierre Gasly**	Alpine	2h24m11.469s	5	1m20.128s	12
4	**Sergio Perez !**	Red Bull	2h24m14.479s	6	1m11.880s	7
5	**Carlos Sainz Jr**	Ferrari	2h24m16.952s	5	1m11.754s	6
6	**Lewis Hamilton**	Mercedes	2h24m17.620s	5	1m20.151s	13
7	**Lando Norris**	McLaren	2h24m17.643s	6	1m11.104s	2
8	**Alex Albon**	Williams	2h24m19.566s	4	1m11.419s	4
9	**Oscar Piastri**	McLaren	2h24m20.991s	5	1m11.938s	8
10	**Esteban Ocon**	Alpine	2h24m22.757s	6	1m22.110s	16
11	**Lance Stroll**	Aston Martin	2h24m24.498s	7	1m20.121s	11
12	**Nico Hulkenberg**	Haas	2h24m25.251s	5	1m20.250s	14
13	**Liam Lawson**	AlphaTauri	2h24m30.558s	7	1m23.420s	19
14	**Valtteri Bottas**	Alfa Romeo	2h24m31.799s	5	1m22.260s	18
15	**Yuki Tsunoda !!, ***	AlphaTauri	2h24m34.304s	5	1m20.230s	17
16	**Kevin Magnussen !!!, ****	Haas	2h24m35.821s	6	1m22.192s	20
17	**George Russell**	Mercedes	2h25m00.165s	7	1m11.294s	3
R	**Zhou Guanyu**	Alfa Romeo	62 laps/accident	4	1m22.067s	15
R	**Logan Sargeant**	Williams	14 laps/accident	2	1m16.748s	10
R	**Charles Leclerc**	Ferrari	41 laps/crash damage	0	1m12.665s	9

FASTEST LAP: ALONSO, 1M13.837S, 129.028MPH/207.651KPH ON LAP 56 · RACE LEADERS: VERSTAPPEN 1 & 13-72, NORRIS 2, PEREZ 3-12
* 3-PLACE GRID PENALTY FOR IMPEDING HAMILTON · ** HAD TO START FROM PITS AS CAR MODIFIED IN PARC FERME · ! 5S PENALTY FOR SPEEDING IN PIT LANE · !! 5S PENALTY FOR CAUSING COLLISION WITH RUSSELL · !!! 5S PENALTY FOR FALLING 10 CAR LENGTHS BEHIND SAFETY CAR

The crowd in the grandstand goes wild as Max Verstappen begins his victory celebrations.

ITALIAN GP

Ferrari fans dared to dream that Carlos Sainz Jr might turn his pole position into a race win to stop the Red Bull Racing juggernaut, but the Spaniard had to settle for third place as he was passed by both Max Verstappen and Sergio Perez.

Although Carlos Sainz Jr got a cracking getaway and was able to turn pole position into the lead at the start of the race by keeping Max Verstappen behind him, it always seemed to be a case of when, not if, the Dutchman would pass him. Impressively, the Spanish driver resisted the attacks for 14 laps, but then locked up into the first chicane and Verstappen was able to move alongside him before the second chicane and go through.

The pressure hardly eased on Sainz as his Ferrari team-mate Charles Leclerc then moved on to his tail. After a pit stop made by all the leading runners, Sergio Perez caught Sainz and tussled with him. Sainz was initially robust in defence but then, with nine laps to go, Perez went past and took second place. That was as far as Perez could advance; Verstappen was peerless as he secured a record tenth win in succession.

Sainz and Leclerc came third and fourth. Their battle for the final podium position was intense and seemed at times that it might end up with Ferrari leaving Monza with nothing. Next up was George Russell, who was fifth for Mercedes, even though he was given a five-second penalty for gaining an advantage by exceeding track limits when he jinked off the track to pass Esteban Ocon's Alpine as he left the pits. However, Russell was far enough clear of team-mate Lewis Hamilton for it to make no difference. Hamilton was also hit with a five-second penalty, in his case for clashing with Oscar Piastri's McLaren. Hamilton was on a charge on medium tyres late in the race as he ran a reverse tactic from his rivals who started on mediums. Piastri was not so lucky, as he had to pit for repairs and this left him 12th.

Carlos Sainz Jr emerges from the first chicane still in the lead, but it wasn't to last.

MONZA ROUND 14   DATE: **3 SEPTEMBER 2023**
Laps: **51** · Distance: **183.387 miles/295.134km** · Weather: **Hot & sunny**

Pos	Driver	Team	Result	Stops	Qualifying Time	Grid
1	**Max Verstappen**	Red Bull	1h13m41.143s	1	1m20.307s	2
2	**Sergio Perez**	Red Bull	1h13m47.207s	1	1m20.688s	5
3	**Carlos Sainz Jr**	Ferrari	1h13m52.336s	1	1m20.294s	1
4	**Charles Leclerc**	Ferrari	1h13m52.520s	1	1m20.361s	3
5	**George Russell ***	Mercedes	1h14m04.171s	1	1m20.671s	4
6	**Lewis Hamilton ****	Mercedes	1h14m23.822s	1	1m20.820s	8
7	**Alex Albon**	Williams	1h14m26.249s	1	1m20.760s	6
8	**Lando Norris**	McLaren	1h14m26.592s	1	1m20.979s	9
9	**Fernando Alonso**	Aston Martin	1h14m27.437s	1	1m21.417s	10
10	**Valtteri Bottas**	Alfa Romeo	1h14m45.199s	1	1m21.940s	14
11	**Liam Lawson**	AlphaTauri	1h14m51.781s	2	1m21.758s	12
12	**Oscar Piastri ***	McLaren	1h14m54.217s	2	1m20.785s	7
13	**Logan Sargeant ****	Williams	1h14m59.700s	1	1m21.944s	15
14	**Zhou Guanyu**	Alfa Romeo	1h15m01.307s	2	1m22.390s	16
15	**Pierre Gasly**	Alpine	1h15m03.653s	2	1m22.545s	17
16	**Lance Stroll**	Aston Martin	1h15m08.409s	1	1m22.860s	20
17	**Nico Hulkenberg**	Haas	50 laps	2	1m21.776s	13
18	**Kevin Magnussen**	Haas	50 laps	2	1m22.592s	19
R	**Esteban Ocon**	Alpine	39 laps/steering wheel	2	1m22.548s	18
NS	**Yuki Tsunoda**	AlphaTauri	0 laps/power unit	-	1m21.594s	11

FASTEST LAP: PIASTRI, 1M25.072S, 152.324MPH/245.142KPH ON LAP 43 · RACE LEADERS: SAINZ JR 1-14, VERSTAPPEN 15-20 & 25-51, PEREZ 21, PIASTRI 22, HAMILTON 23-24 · * 5S PENALTY FOR GAINING AN ADVANTAGE BY EXCEEDING TRACK LIMITS · ** 5S PENALTY FOR CAUSING A COLLISION

// SINGAPORE GP

Carlos Sainz Jr became the driver to end Red Bull Racing's 2023 victory streak in the 15th round. The Spanish Ferrari driver did it by leading away from pole, then holding position and being protected by Lando Norris from a Mercedes charge that ended with George Russell crashing into the wall.

The Marina Bay circuit for last year's Grand Prix was different from the 2022 iteration; it had four corners removed while a city improvement project was carried out. Carlos Sainz Jr mastered the revised layout the best. Fast in practice, he was also fastest in qualifying, giving the Spaniard pole, with George Russell second for Mercedes, then Charles Leclerc third and McLaren's Lando Norris fourth.

The *tifosi* were delighted to have their red cars at the sharp end of the grid, and doubly so as Red Bull's cars didn't even get out of Q2, perhaps something to do with updated technical direction from the FIA regarding flexible wings and floors. Certainly, Max Verstappen was angry to qualify 11th, with Sergio Perez 13th.

A clean start ensured that Sainz led away, while Russell was passed by Leclerc. A lap later, Lewis Hamilton also passed Russell, but had to give the place back for gaining an advantage by leaving the track. Norris moved back to fourth on lap 4.

Verstappen remained stuck in eighth behind Esteban Ocon's Alpine for many laps until he vaulted to second as most of his rivals pitted at around 20 laps.

Such was Sainz's advantage that he was able to pit and remain in the lead. When Verstappen finally made his one planned stop, on lap 40, he had been passed by four rivals on fresher rubber, with Russell and Norris trying to match Sainz's pace.

Mercedes opted for a second set of fresh tyres, bringing both of its drivers in again on lap 44. Coming back out in fourth and fifth, they had a challenge. Russell was now 17 seconds behind Sainz and it took him nine laps to pick off Leclerc, with Hamilton doing the same a lap later. The next target was Norris, but he resisted well. Then, making a final push, Russell clipped the wall and was out, heartbroken, leaving Hamilton to finish third.

Team principal Frederic Vasseur joins a jubilant Carlos Sainz Jr after Ferrari's breakthrough.

MARINA BAY ROUND 15   DATE: **17 SEPTEMBER 2023**

Laps: **62** • Distance: **190.228 miles/306.143km** • Weather: **Very hot & humid**

Pos	Driver	Team	Result	Stops	Qualifying Time	Grid
1	**Carlos Sainz Jr**	Ferrari	1h46m37.418s	1	1m30.984s	1
2	**Lando Norris**	McLaren	1h46m38.230s	1	1m31.270s	4
3	**Lewis Hamilton**	Mercedes	1h46m38.687s	2	1m31.485s	5
4	**Charles Leclerc**	Ferrari	1h46m58.595s	1	1m31.063s	3
5	**Max Verstappen**	Red Bull	1h46m58.859s	1	1m32.173s	11
6	**Pierre Gasly**	Alpine	1h47m15.859s	1	1m32.274s	12
7	**Oscar Piastri**	McLaren	1h47m18.897s	1	1m32.902s	17
8	**Sergio Perez ***	Red Bull	1h47m36.952s	1	1m32.310s	13
9	**Liam Lawson**	AlphaTauri	1h47m43.336s	1	1m32.268s	10
10	**Kevin Magnussen**	Haas	1h47m49.534s	2	1m31.575s	6
11	**Alex Albon**	Williams	1h47m50.835s	2	1m323.719s	14
12	**Zhou Guanyu !**	Alfa Romeo	1h48m01.067s	2	1m33.258s	19
13	**Nico Hulkenberg**	Haas	1h48m03.619s	1	1m31.808s	9
14	**Logan Sargeant**	Williams	1h48m04.307s	2	1m33.252s	18
15	**Fernando Alonso**	Aston Martin	1h48m05.021s	2	1m31.615s	7
16	**George Russell**	Mercedes	61 laps/accident	2	1m31.056s	2
R	**Valtteri Bottas**	Alfa Romeo	51 laps/hydraulics	1	1m32.809s	16
R	**Esteban Ocon**	Alpine	42 laps/gearbox	1	1m31.673s	8
R	**Yuki Tsunoda**	AlphaTauri	0 laps/crash damage	0	No time	15
W	**Lance Stroll**	Aston Martin	0 laps/driver injury	-	1m33.397s	20

FASTEST LAP: **HAMILTON, 1M35.867S, 115.268MPH/185.507KPH ON LAP 47** • RACE LEADERS: SAINZ JR 1-62
* 5S PENALTY FOR CAUSING A COLLISION WITH ALBON • ! MADE TO START FROM PIT LANE AS CAR MODIFIED IN PARC FERME

JAPANESE GP

Max Verstappen romped to his 13th win of the season to help Red Bull Racing wrap up the constructors' title with six rounds to spare. McLaren's Lando Norris and Oscar Piastri completed the podium, while, further down the grid, the Mercedes drivers entertained with a fierce battle.

The only blemish on Verstappen's run to victory at Suzuka was on the dash to the first corner when, in blocking Piastri, he left a gap for Norris to nip through. Moments later, though, he was back in front.

Unfortunately, there was contact between Sergio Perez and Lewis Hamilton as they ran four-abreast with the Ferraris on the way to turn 1. Behind them, Valtteri Bottas thumped into Alex Albon's Williams and the safety car was deployed. It led to frenetic scenes at Alfa Romeo, as not only did Bottas limp in with a puncture, but Zhou Guanyu arrived for a new nose. Albon reckoned that he had a damaged floor but continued.

A lap later, Perez pitted for a new front wing and his day would soon get worse when, first he was penalised for a safety car infringement and, second, he spun Kevin Magnussen and would need another front wing. Before he was hit with another penalty, he parked up and retired.

When the safety car withdrew, Verstappen blasted clear of the McLaren challenge as Norris went around the outside into second. The Mercedes duo was also busy trying to swap places as George Russell got ahead of Hamilton, who immediately struck back. Then Mercedes told Hamilton to pit on lap 17. Russell stayed out for another seven laps and would rise to second.

None of this affected Verstappen, though, as he pulled away from the McLarens to safety and victory, while Norris asked permission to pass Piastri for second. The frontrunners then all made their second pit stops, but Russell was on a different strategy which ultimately dropped him from third to seventh. He fought hard, but couldn't keep Piastri from the podium, then Leclerc picked him off; with four laps to go, he was asked to cede to Hamilton, with Sainz going through too.

SUZUKA ROUND 16

DATE: 24 SEPTEMBER 2023

Laps: **53** · Distance: **191.053 miles/307.471km** · Weather: **Hot & bright**

Pos	Driver	Team	Result	Stops	Qualifying Time	Grid
1	Max Verstappen	Red Bull	1h30m58.421s	2	1m28.877s	1
2	Lando Norris	McLaren	1h31m17.808s	2	1m29.493s	3
3	Oscar Piastri	McLaren	1h31m34.915s	2	1m29.458s	2
4	Charles Leclerc	Ferrari	1h31m42.419s	2	1m29.542s	4
5	Lewis Hamilton	Mercedes	1h31m47.797s	2	1m29.908s	7
6	Carlos Sainz Jr	Ferrari	1h31m48.642s	2	1m29.850s	6
7	George Russell	Mercedes	1h31m56.080s	1	1m30.219s	8
8	Fernando Alonso	Aston Martin	1h32m13.146s	2	1m30.560s	10
9	Esteban Ocon	Alpine	1h32m18.099s	2	1m30.586s	14
10	Pierre Gasly	Alpine	1h32m21.576s	2	1m30.509s	12
11	Liam Lawson	AlphaTauri	52 laps	2	1m30.508s	11
12	Yuki Tsunoda	AlphaTauri	52 laps	2	1m30.303s	9
13	Zhou Guanyu	Alfa Romeo	52 laps	3	1m31.398s	19
14	Nico Hulkenberg	Haas	52 laps	3	1m31.299s	18
15	Kevin Magnussen	Haas	52 laps	2	1m30.665s	15
R	Alex Albon	Williams	26 laps/floor damage	3	1m30.537s	13
R	Logan Sargeant *	Williams	22 laps/floor damage	3	No time	20
R	Lance Stroll	Aston Martin	20 laps/rear wing	1	1m31.181s	17
R	Sergio Perez	Red Bull	15 laps/withdrew	4	1m29.650s	5
R	Valtteri Bottas	Alfa Romeo	7 laps/crash damage	2	1m31.049s	16

FASTEST LAP: VERSTAPPEN, 1M34.183S, 137.921MPH/221.963KPH ON LAP 39 · RACE LEADERS: VERSTAPPEN 1-16 & 19-53, NORRIS 17, SAINZ JR 18 · * REQUIRED TO START FROM REAR OF GRID AS CAR MODIFIED IN PARC FERME

Sergio Perez puts Lewis Hamilton on the grass, with further trouble at the back of the pack.

QATAR GP

Max Verstappen wrapped up his third drivers' title, but the main talking points on F1's second visit to Qatar was how the soaring temperatures left drivers in discomfort and near to fainting and how Pirelli had to mandate a maximum stint length as its tyres weren't lasting.

For a driver to wrap up a World Championship in a sprint race seems wrong, lacking in the deserved fanfare, yet this is what happened when Max Verstappen came home third behind the McLarens on the Saturday at Losail. His 2023 season had been phenomenal, but to have landed that third title in a row with another Grand Prix win would have been preferable.

When Verstappen started from pole on Sunday he, like all the other drivers, knew that race strategy was already compromised; Pirelli insisted that due to fear for tyre life in the soaring heat, no stint should exceed 18 laps. That meant a minimum of three pit stops each and removed any scope for trying to find an advantage by adopting a different strategy.

Tyre life didn't remain a concern of Lewis Hamilton's for very long. He moved across on George Russell on the approach to the first corner and, with Verstappen right next to him, his Mercedes team-mate had nowhere to go. The contact spun Hamilton into retirement and forced a livid Russell to pit for a new nose, dropping him to last place.

Verstappen was able to control this race from the front, as he had throughout the year. With Mercedes's demise, a golden opportunity presented itself to McLaren to continue its late-season run of form – sprint race winner Oscar Piastri was able to close to just under five seconds behind Verstappen. Afterwards, the Australian showed the effects of cockpit temperatures of more than 50 degrees; he had to lie down to recover before going out onto the podium.

Team-mate Lando Norris made it a doubly good day for McLaren by advancing from tenth on the grid, a result of losing his best time for exceeding track limits, to be one second off Piastri's tail.

LOSAIL ROUND 17 DATE: **8 OCTOBER 2023**

Laps: **57** · Distance: **191.762 miles/308.611km** · Weather: **Extremely hot**

Pos	Driver	Team	Result	Stops	Grid	Sprint
1	**Max Verstappen**	Red Bull	1h27m39.168s	3	1	3
2	**Oscar Piastri**	McLaren	1h27m44.001s	3	6	1
3	**Lando Norris**	McLaren	1h27m45.137s	3	10	2
4	**George Russell**	Mercedes	1h28m13.287s	4	2	4
5	**Charles Leclerc**	Ferrari	1h28m18.144s	3	5	6
6	**Fernando Alonso**	Aston Martin	1h28m28.200s	3	4	9
7	**Esteban Ocon**	Alpine	1h28m41.558s	3	8	10
8	**Valtteri Bottas**	Alfa Romeo	1h28m45.731s	3	9	13
9	**Zhou Guanyu**	Alfa Romeo	1h28m55.295s	3	20	15
10	**Sergio Perez** *, !	Red Bull	1h28m59.349s	3	13	8
11	**Lance Stroll** **	Aston Martin	1h29m00.820s	3	17	16
12	**Pierre Gasly** **	Alpine	1h29m01.468s	3	7	11
13	**Alex Albon** **	Williams	1h29m10.182s	3	14	17
14	**Kevin Magnussen**	Haas	56 laps	3	19	19
15	**Yuki Tsunoda**	AlphaTauri	56 laps	3	11	18
16	**Nico Hulkenberg**	Haas	56 laps	3	15	7
17	**Liam Lawson**	AlphaTauri	56 laps	3	18	14
R	**Logan Sargeant**	Williams	40 laps/driver unwell	3	16	20
R	**Lewis Hamilton**	Mercedes	0 laps/accident	0	3	12
NS	**Carlos Sainz Jr**	Ferrari	fuel leak	-	12	5

FASTEST LAP: **VERSTAPPEN, 1M24.319S, 143.763MPH/231.364KPH ON LAP 56** · RACE LEADERS: **VERSTAPPEN 1-57**
! REQUIRED TO START FROM PIT LANE AS EXTRA POWER UNIT ELEMENTS FITTED · *5S PENALTY FOR EXCEEDING TRACK LIMITS
** 10S PENALTY FOR EXCEEDING TRACK LIMITS

It might have been a sprint race, but the points gathered gave Max Verstappen the title.

UNITED STATES GP

Max Verstappen chalked up his 50th Grand Prix win, but he was chased to the finish by a charging Lewis Hamilton, only for the Mercedes driver, along with Ferrari's Charles Leclerc, to be disqualified for excessive skid block wear, promoting Lando Norris to second.

Having his final run in qualifying annulled for exceeding track limits meant that Max Verstappen started from sixth, but he soon advanced from there.

Charles Leclerc was amazed to have taken pole, but it didn't result in the lead as he was beaten away by Lando Norris, whose McLaren was in front before they turned in to turn 1. Lewis Hamilton dropped back to fourth behind Carlos Sainz Jr, while Verstappen moved past George Russell into fifth.

While Norris tried to make a break in the opening laps, Hamilton chose his moments and passed both Ferraris to climb to second, his form showing how the new floor sported by the Mercedes F1 W14s was a step forward.

Then came the first of the two pit stops planned by most teams and the main change was that Verstappen got the jump on Hamilton to occupy second place. The Dutchman then set off after Norris, reeled him in and went into the lead without a fight.

After the second round of pit stops, the order was still Verstappen then Norris then Hamilton and it became clear that Hamilton had the pace to catch Norris and the skill to pass him on the exit of turn 1. He then homed in on Verstappen, showing how much progress Mercedes had made.

Verstappen was tense as his car was carrying a braking issue, but Hamilton only managed to take three seconds out of what had been a five-second gap once he'd passed Norris. Then, post-race disqualification meant that Hamilton would score no points, with Leclerc suffering a similar fate, as both their cars were found to have worn their skid blocks down beyond the maximum amount of wear. Their disqualification elevated Norris and Sainz Jr to second and third.

Lewis Hamilton and Lando Norris fight over second, but Hamilton was to be disqualified.

CIRCUIT OF THE AMERICAS ROUND 18 DATE: 22 OCTOBER 2023
Laps: **56** • Distance: **191.634 miles/308.405km** • Weather: **Hot & bright**

Pos	Driver	Team	Result	Stops	Grid	Sprint
1	**Max Verstappen**	Red Bull	1h35m21.362s	2	6	1
D	**Lewis Hamilton** !	Mercedes	1h35m23.587s	2	3	3
2	**Lando Norris**	McLaren	1h35m32.092s	2	2	4
3	**Carlos Sainz Jr**	Ferrari	1h35m36.496s	2	4	6
4	**Sergio Perez**	Red Bull	1h35m39.822s	2	9	7
D	**Charles Leclerc** !	Ferrari	1h35m46.024s	1	1	2
5	**George Russell**	Mercedes	1h35m46.361s	2	5	8
6	**Pierre Gasly**	Alpine	1h36m09.358s	2	7	10
7	**Lance Stroll** *	Aston Martin	1h36m10.058s	2	20	14
8	**Yuki Tsunoda**	AlphaTauri	1h36m35.747s	3	11	19
9	**Alex Albon** !!	Williams	1h36m48.076s	2	15	9
10	**Logan Sargeant**	Williams	1h36m49.360s	2	16	20
11	**Nico Hulkenberg** *	Haas	1h36m51.266s	2	18	16
12	**Valtteri Bottas**	Alfa Romeo	1h36m59.963s	2	13	18
13	**Zhou Guanyu**	Alfa Romeo	55 laps	2	12	15
14	**Kevin Magnussen** *	Haas	55 laps	2	17	17
15	**Daniel Ricciardo**	AlphaTauri	55 laps	2	14	11
R	**Fernando Alonso** *	Aston Martin	49 laps/floor	3	19	12
R	**Oscar Piastri**	McLaren	10 laps/crash damage	1	10	5
R	**Esteban Ocon**	Alpine	6 laps/crash damage	1	8	13

FASTEST LAP: **TSUNODA, 1M38.139S, 125.727MPH/202.23KPH ON LAP 56** • RACE LEADERS: **NORRIS 1-17 & 24-27, HAMILTON 18-20 & 36-38, LECLERC 21-23, VERSTAPPEN 28-35 & 39-56** • * REQUIRED TO START FROM BACK OF GRID AS CAR MODIFIED IN PARC FERME ! DISQUALIFIED FOR EXCESSIVE SKID BLOCK WEAR • !! 5S PENALTY FOR EXCEEDING TRACK LIMITS

// MEXICO CITY GP

Sergio Perez made a bold bid to rescue his awful campaign by lunging for the lead into the first corner, but a clash with Charles Leclerc ended his race, leaving Max Verstappen to score yet another win, chased hard to the finish by Lewis Hamilton.

Charles Leclerc was surprised when he secured pole position, but Ferrari had clearly done their sums correctly, as he was joined on the front row by team-mate Carlos Sainz Jr, both just a fraction of a second ahead of Max Verstappen.

Yet, when the lights turned to green, and the field streamed down the long run to the first corner complex, Leclerc found his car to be the meat in a Red Bull Racing sandwich, with Sergio Perez to his left and Verstappen to his right. As the cars turned into the first part of this three-part complex, Perez began to pull across, but Leclerc couldn't go right as Verstappen was there, and so he couldn't avoid contact, with Perez's car tipped up into the air. And that was that for Perez, his hopes of rescuing a troubled season with not just a win, but a home win, ended as his car was too damaged to continue.

Verstappen was able to edge away in the lead while Lewis Hamilton became bottled up behind Sainz Jr and only claimed third by pitting before the Spaniard.

Then, on lap 32, it appeared that the suspension broke on Kevin Magnussen's Haas, pitching it off at the esses. The Dane was uninjured, but his VF-23 most certainly was not. The safety car came out but soon the race was stopped so that the barriers could be repaired.

Verstappen led away on the restart and Hamilton, on softer tyres, soon passed Leclerc for second, but that was as high as he would climb.

Daniel Ricciardo had shown mixed form at COTA on his return from a hand injury, but was magnificent here, qualifying a very competitive fourth in his AlphaTauri and racing to seventh. While, yet again, Alex Albon worked wonders for Williams and rose from 14th to bag a couple of points.

Sergio Perez's bid for glory in his home grand prix was a brief one, going out at the first corner.

MEXICO CITY ROUND 19   DATE: **29 OCTOBER 2023**

Laps: **71** · Distance: **189.738 miles/305.354km** · Weather: **Hot & bright**

Pos	Driver	Team	Result	Stops	Qualifying Time	Grid
1	**Max Verstappen**	Red Bull	2h02m30.814s	3	1m17.263s	3
2	**Lewis Hamilton**	Mercedes	2h02m44.689s	2	1m17.454s	6
3	**Charles Leclerc**	Ferrari	2h02m53.938s	2	1m17.166s	1
4	**Carlos Sainz Jr**	Ferrari	2h02m57.968s	2	1m17.233s	2
5	**Lando Norris**	McLaren	2h03m04.080s	3	1m21.554s	17
6	**George Russell**	Mercedes	2h03m11.834s	2	1m17.674s	8
7	**Daniel Ricciardo**	AlphaTauri	2h03m12.384s	2	1m17.382s	4
8	**Oscar Piastri**	McLaren	2h03m13.918s	2	1m17.623s	7
9	**Alex Albon**	Williams	2h03m19.387s	2	1m19.147s	14
10	**Esteban Ocon**	Alpine	2h03m33.963s	1	1m19.080s	15
11	**Pierre Gasly**	Alpine	2h03m37.022s	2	1m18.521s	11
12	**Yuki Tsunoda !**	AlphaTauri	2h03m49.796s	2	no time	18
13	**Nico Hulkenberg**	Haas	2h03m51.123s	2	1m18.524s	12
14	**Zhou Guanyu**	Alfa Romeo	2h03m52.490s	2	1m18.050s	10
15	**Valtteri Bottas !!!**	Alfa Romeo	2h03m56.411s	2	1m18.032s	9
R	**Logan Sargeant ***	Williams	70 laps/fuel pump	2	no time	19
R	**Lance Stroll !!**	Aston Martin	66 laps/crash damage	3	1m19.227s	20
R	**Fernando Alonso**	Aston Martin	47 laps/withdrew	3	1m18.738s	13
R	**Kevin Magnussen**	Haas	31 laps/accident	1	1m19.163s	16
R	**Sergio Perez**	Red Bull	1 lap/crash damage	0	1m17.423s	5

FASTEST LAP: HAMILTON, 1M21.334S, 118.373MPH/190.503KPH ON LAP 71 · RACE LEADERS: VERSTAPPEN 1-19 & 32-71, LECLERC 20-31 · • 10-PLACE GRID PENALTY FOR OVERTAKING UNDER YELLOW FLAGS · ! REQUIRED TO START FROM REAR OF GRID FOR USING ADDITIONAL POWER UNIT ELEMENTS · !! REQUIRED TO START FROM PIT LANE AS CAR MODIFIED IN PARC FERME !!! 5S PENALTY FOR CAUSING COLLISION WITH STROLL

SAO PAULO GP

Max Verstappen chalked up win number 17 of his 2023 campaign ahead of Lando Norris's now regularly competitive McLaren. It was a race in which the recent form of both Ferrari and Mercedes deserted them and Aston Martin came good again with Fernando Alonso taking his first podium for seven races.

There was a glimmer of hope that Lando Norris might score a first win for McLaren when he qualified on pole for the sprint race, but Max Verstappen immediately quashed that hope and raced on to grab the eight points for victory.

In the Grand Prix itself, the Dutch ace made a good enough start to protect his lead into the opening corner, and that was the safest place to be, as all hell broke out behind him: Nico Hulkenberg tagged Alex Albon's Williams, which spun into Kevin Magnussen's Haas which, in turn, damaged Oscar Piastri's rear wing. Fellow Australian Daniel Ricciardo also had his rear wing damaged by a tyre carcass thrown from Magnussen's car.

Verstappen was never troubled from there and Norris advanced from seventh to second place thanks to a couple of events. Firstly, Charles Leclerc's awful luck resurfaced as his Ferrari failed on the formation lap and then Mercedes endured what team boss Toto Wolff described as the team's 'worst performance in 13 years' and fell down the order, with Lewis Hamilton able to finish only eighth and George Russell retiring.

The most memorable battle of the race was over third place, with Sergio Perez and Fernando Alonso having a great scrap before the Aston Martin driver got ahead to take the final spot on the podium. Lance Stroll showed how Aston Martin's form had returned by finishing fifth, comfortably ahead of Carlos Sainz's Ferrari, suggesting that Ferrari's form had also evaporated.

Alpine helped its championship cause with a double helping of points, with Pierre Gasly coming seventh and Esteban Ocon 10th. Ocon was helped when Alfa Romeo's likely run to points was brought to a halt when both of its cars were made to retire with unspecified technical issues.

INTERLAGOS ROUND 20   DATE: 5 NOVEMBER 2023
Laps: 71 · Distance: 190.064 miles/305.8789km · Weather: Hot & bright

Pos	Driver	Team	Result	Stops	Grid	Sprint
1	Max Verstappen	Red Bull	1h56m48.894s	4	1	1
2	Lando Norris	McLaren	1h56m57.171s	4	6	2
3	Fernando Alonso	Aston Martin	1h57m23.049s	4	4	11
4	Sergio Perez	Red Bull	1h57m23.102s	4	9	3
5	Lance Stroll	Aston Martin	1h57m29.739s	4	3	12
6	Carlos Sainz Jr	Ferrari	1h57m39.082s	4	7	8
7	Pierre Gasly *	Alpine	1h57m44.987s	4	15	13
8	Lewis Hamilton	Mercedes	1h57m51.753s	4	5	7
9	Yuki Tsunoda	AlphaTauri	1h57m58.774s	4	16	6
10	Esteban Ocon *	Alpine	70 laps	5	14	14
11	Logan Sargeant	Williams	70 laps	4	19	20
12	Nico Hulkenberg	Haas	70 laps	4	11	18
13	Daniel Ricciardo	AlphaTauri	70 laps	4	17	9
14	Oscar Piastri	McLaren	69 laps	4	10	10
R	George Russell *	Mercedes	57 laps/overheating	4	8	4
R	Valtteri Bottas	Alfa Romeo	39 laps/technical	3	18	19
R	Zhou Guanyu	Alfa Romeo	22 laps/technical	3	20	17
R	Kevin Magnussen	Haas	0 laps/accident	0	12	16
R	Alex Albon	Williams	0 laps/accident	0	13	15
NS	Charles Leclerc	Ferrari	Clutch	-	2	5

FASTEST LAP: NORRIS, 1M12.486S, 132.976MPH/214.005KPH ON LAP 61 · RACE LEADERS: VERSTAPPEN 1-56 & 60-71, NORRIS 57-59
* 2-PLACE GRID PENALTY FOR FAILING TO FOLLOW RACE DIRECTOR'S INSTRUCTIONS

The battle of the race was late on over third place between Fernando Alonso and Sergio Perez.

LAS VEGAS GP

Not even a five-second penalty and a damaged front wing could deny Max Verstappen his 18th win of the season, while third place after a last lap demotion by Ferrari's Charles Leclerc was enough for Red Bull team-mate Sergio Perez to become the championship runner-up.

The celebs were out in force at the glamour-packed Las Vegas Grand Prix. Qualifying had juggled the grid, with the notable ten-place grid penalty applied to second-fastest qualifier Carlos Sainz Jr, who had to have extra power unit elements fitted after his floor-wrecking contact with a drain cover. This elevated Verstappen to second and he dived inside Charles Leclerc, pushing him wide into turn 1. Behind them, Fernando Alonso had a spin, while Sergio Perez tapped Valtteri Bottas, forcing the Mexican to pit for repairs.

Two laps later, Lando Norris's McLaren hit a bump at turn 11 and crashed into the wall. This brought out the safety car and several of those who had started low down, including Sainz Jr and Lance Stroll, pitted. This would transform their fortunes.

Verstappen then heard that he had been given a five-second penalty for his move at the start. George Russell and Pierre Gasly got closer to Leclerc, but then the Ferrari set off after Verstappen. Leclerc passed him on lap 16 and the Dutchman pitted, serving his penalty, before rejoining in 11th.

Leclerc's lead was now 14 seconds over Perez, who had already pitted. When Leclerc did pit, there was a problem changing a wheel and he rejoined third, albeit still clear of Verstappen.

Then Russell and Verstappen clashed at turn 12, for which Russell was given a five-second penalty. The safety car was redeployed and Verstappen pitted, but his damaged front wing was left on to save time and he rejoined fifth. The timing of this second safety car probably cost Leclerc victory, as it brought Verstappen closer. Perez passed Leclerc on lap 32, but three laps later Leclerc went back ahead. Then Verstappen grabbed second from Perez and took the lead on lap 37. Leclerc was demoted to third but regained second on the last lap.

LAS VEGAS ROUND 21

DATE: 18 NOVEMBER 2023

Laps: **50** · Distance: **192.599 miles/309.958km** · Weather: **Cool & dry**

Pos	Driver	Team	Result	Stops	Qualifying Time	Grid
1	Max Verstappen	Red Bull	1h29m08.289s	2	1m33.104s	2
2	Charles Leclerc	Ferrari	1h29m10.359s	1	1m32.726s	1
3	Sergio Perez	Red Bull	1h29m10.530s	2	1m33.855s	11
4	Esteban Ocon	Alpine	1h29m26.954s	1	1m34.834s	16
5	Lance Stroll !	Aston Martin	1h29m28.356s	2	1m34.199s	19
6	Carlos Sainz Jr !!	Ferrari	1h29m29.123s	2	1m32.770s	12
7	Lewis Hamilton	Mercedes	1h29m30.044s	2	1m33.837s	10
8	George Russell *	Mercedes	1h29m31.380s	2	1m33.112s	3
9	Fernando Alonso	Aston Martin	1h29m34.253s	2	1m33.555s	9
10	Oscar Piastri	McLaren	1h29m37.785s	2	1m34.850s	18
11	Pierre Gasly	Alpine	1h29m42.559s	1	1m33.239s	4
12	Alex Albon	Williams	1h29m51.687s	1	1m33.323s	5
13	Kevin Magnussen	Haas	1h29m53.114s	2	1m33.537s	8
14	Daniel Ricciardo	AlphaTauri	1h29m56.814s	1	1m34.308s	14
15	Zhou Guanyu	Alfa Romeo	1h29m58.451s	1	1m34.849s	17
16	Logan Sargeant	Williams	1h29m59.171s	1	1m33.513s	6
17	Valtteri Bottas	Alfa Romeo	1h30m33.639s	2	1m33.525s	7
R	Yuki Tsunoda	AlphaTauri	46 laps/power unit	2	1m36.447s	20
R	Nico Hulkenberg	Haas	45 laps/power unit	2	1m33.979s	13
R	Lando Norris	McLaren	2 laps/accident	0	1m34.703s	15

FASTEST LAP: PIASTRI, 1M35.490S, 145.263MPH/233.779KPH ON LAP 47 · RACE LEADERS: VERSTAPPEN 1-15 & 37-50, LECLERC 16-21 & 27-31 & 35-36, PEREZ 22-26 & 32-34 · ! 5-PLACE GRID PENALTY FOR OVERTAKING UNDER YELLOW FLAGS · !! 10-PLACE GRID PENALTY FOR USING ADDITIONAL POWER UNIT ELEMENTS · * 5S PENALTY FOR CAUSING A COLLISION

Charles Leclerc separates the Red Bulls on the streets of Las Vegas as Verstappen heads for win 18.

ABU DHABI GP

Twenty-two Grands Prix, 19 wins, 12 poles, nine fastest laps, 575 points and a third title in succession was Max Verstappen's final tally from his most remarkable season. Only Charles Leclerc got close to him in Abu Dhabi, and that was only on the opening lap.

It would have felt wrong if anyone other than Max Verstappen had won the final race of the 2023 campaign, as it really has been all about him and his record-breaking domination.

The main point of interest was going to be which team would end the year as runner-up. Mercedes had travelled to the Las Vegas GP with a 20-point lead over Ferrari, but their poor run there meant that they arrived in Abu Dhabi with that slashed to just four. Leclerc boosted Ferrari's hopes by qualifying second, but this was negated by Carlos Sainz Jr failing to find a clear lap, which left him starting 16th. It wasn't all smiles at Mercedes, though, as although George Russell would line up fourth, Lewis Hamilton was at a loss with the car's handling and qualified only 11th.

By dint of Yuki Tsunoda opting for a one-stop strategy, there was the rare sight of an AlphaTauri leading, with the Japanese driver in front for five laps from lap 18 before Verstappen motored past into a lead he would keep.

With Verstappen well clear, Leclerc focused on making sure that he kept Russell behind him, which he did, but both were passed by Sergio Perez as he brought the second Red Bull up from ninth. However, both he and Russell were happy to let him past, as the Mexican had been given a five second penalty for contact with Lando Norris, and they knew that he didn't have time to make that up.

Sainz Jr knew that he couldn't go the distance on two sets of hard tyres, so had to pit near the end, dropping out of tenth place. In fact, he pulled off with a lap to go with a power unit problem. By then, though, Ferrari's bid to outscore Mercedes had failed.

Charles Leclerc, Max Verstappen and George Russell filled the year's final podium after 22 rounds.

YAS MARINA ROUND 22   DATE: **26 NOVEMBER 2023**

Laps: **58** • Distance: **190.253 miles/306.183km** • Weather: **Hot & dry**

Pos	Driver	Team	Result	Stops	Qualifying Time	Grid
1	Max Verstappen	Red Bull	1h27m02.624s	2	1m23.445s	1
2	Charles Leclerc	Ferrari	1h27m20.617s	2	1m23.584s	2
3	George Russell	Mercedes	1h27m22.952s	2	1m23.788s	4
4	Sergio Perez *	Red Bull	1h27m24.077s	2	1m24.171s	9
5	Lando Norris	McLaren	1h27m26.908s	2	1m23.816s	5
6	Oscar Piastri	McLaren	1h27m34.111s	2	1m23.782s	3
7	Fernando Alonso	Aston Martin	1h27m42.136s	2	1m24.084s	7
8	Yuki Tsunoda	AlphaTauri	1h27m45.712s	1	1m23.968s	6
9	Lewis Hamilton	Mercedes	1h27m47.048s	2	1m24.359s	11
10	Lance Stroll	Aston Martin	1h27m58.256s	2	1m24.422s	13
11	Daniel Ricciardo	AlphaTauri	1h27m58.853s	2	1m24.442s	15
12	Esteban Ocon	Alpine	1h28m08.997s	1	1m24.391s	12
13	Pierre Gasly	Alpine	1h28m12.984s	2	1m24.548s	10
14	Alex Albon	Williams	1h28m15.808s	2	1m24.439s	14
15	Nico Hulkenberg	Haas	1h28m26.320s	2	1m24.108s	8
16	Logan Sargeant	Williams	1h28m30.415s	2	no time	20
17	Zhou Guanyu	Alfa Romeo	1h28m32.046s	2	1m25.159s	19
18	Carlos Sainz Jr	Ferrari	57 laps/power unit	3	1m24.738s	16
19	Valtteri Bottas	Alfa Romeo	57 laps	1	1m24.788s	18
20	Kevin Magnussen	Haas	57 laps	2	1m24.764s	17

FASTEST LAP: VERSTAPPEN, 1M26.993S, 135.795MPH/218.541KPH ON LAP 45 • RACE LEADERS: VERSTAPPEN 1-16 & 23-58, LECLERC 17, TSUNODA 18-22 • * 5S PENALTY FOR CAUSING A COLLISION

// FINAL RESULTS 2023

POS	DRIVER	NAT		CAR-ENGINE	R1	R2	R3	R4	R5	R6
1	MAX VERSTAPPEN	NED		RED BULL-HONDA RB19	1P	2F	1P	2	1F	1P
2	SERGIO PEREZ	MEX		RED BULL-HONDA RB19	2	1P	5F	1	2P	16
3	LEWIS HAMILTON	GBR		MERCEDES F1 W14	5	5	2	6	6	4F
4	FERNANDO ALONSO	SPA		ASTON MARTIN-MERCEDES AMR23	3	3	3	4	3	2
5	CHARLES LECLERC	MON		FERRARI SF23	R	7	R	3P	7	6
6	LANDO NORRIS	GBR		McLAREN-MERCEDES MCL60	17	17	6	9	17	9
7	CARLOS SAINZ JR	SPA		FERRARI SF23	4	6	12	5	5	8
8	GEORGE RUSSELL	GBR		MERCEDES F1 W14	7	4	R	8F	4	5
9	OSCAR PIASTRI	AUS		McLAREN-MERCEDES MCL60	R	15	8	11	19	10
10	LANCE STROLL	CDN		ASTON MARTIN-MERCEDES AMR23	6	R	4	7	12	R
11	PIERRE GASLY	FRA		ALPINE-RENAULT A523	9	9	13	14	8	7
12	ESTEBAN OCON	FRA		ALPINE-RENAULT A523	R	8	14	15	9	3
13	ALEX ALBON	GBR/THA		WILLIAMS-MERCEDES FW45	10	R	R	12	14	14
14	YUKI TSUNODA	JPN		ALPHATAURI-HONDA AT04	11	11	10	10	11	15
15	VALTTERI BOTTAS	FIN		ALFA ROMEO-FERRARI C43	8	18	11	18	13	11
16	NICO HULKENBERG	GER		HAAS-FERRARI VF-23	15	12	7	17	15	17
17	DANIEL RICCIARDO	AUS		ALPHATAURI-HONDA AT04	-	-	-	-	-	-
18	ZHOU GUANYU	PRC		ALFA ROMEO-FERRARI C43	16F	13	9	R	16	13
19	KEVIN MAGNUSSEN	DEN		HAAS-FERRARI VF-23	13	10	R	13	10	R
20	LIAM LAWSON	NZL		ALPHATAURI-HONDA AT04	-	-	-	-	-	-
21	LOGAN SARGEANT	USA		WILLIAMS-MERCEDES FW45	12	16	16	16	20	18
22	NYCK DE VRIES	NED		ALPHATURI-HONDA AT04	14	14	15	R	18	12

SCORING

1st	25 points
2nd	18 points
3rd	15 points
4th	12 points
5th	10 points
6th	8 points
7th	6 points
8th	4 points
9th	2 points
10th	1 point
Fastest lap	1 point*

*if in top 10 finishers

SPRINT RACE POINTS

1st	8 points
2nd	7 points
3rd	6 points
4th	5 points
5th	4 points
6th	3 points
7th	2 points
8th	1 point

POS	TEAM-ENGINE	R1	R2	R3	R4	R5	R6
1	RED BULL-HONDA	1/2	1/2	1/5	1/2	1/2	1/16
2	MERCEDES	5/7	4/5	2/R	6/8	4/6	4/5
3	FERRARI	4/R	6/7	12/R	3/5	5/7	6/8
4	McLAREN-MERCEDES	17/R	15/17	6/8	9/11	17/19	9/10
5	ASTON MARTIN-MERCEDES	3/6	3/R	3/4	4/7	3/12	2/R
6	ALPINE-RENAULT	9/R	8/9	13/14	14/15	8/9	3/7
7	WILLIAMS-MERCEDES	10/12	16/R	16/R	12/16	14/20	14/18
8	ALPHATAURI-HONDA	11/14	11/14	10/15	10/R	11/18	12/15
9	ALFA ROMEO-FERRARI	8/16	13/18	9/11	18/R	13/16	11/13
10	HAAS-FERRARI	13/15	10/12	7/R	13/17	10/15	17/R

ROUND 1	BAHRAIN GP	ROUND 7	SPANISH GP	ROUND 13	DUTCH GP
ROUND 2	SAUDI ARABIAN GP	ROUND 8	CANADIAN GP	ROUND 14	ITALIAN GP
ROUND 3	AUSTRALIAN GP	ROUND 9	AUSTRIAN GP	ROUND 15	SINGAPORE GP
ROUND 4	AZERBAIJAN GP	ROUND 10	BRITISH GP	ROUND 16	JAPANESE GP
ROUND 5	MIAMI GP	ROUND 11	HUNGARIAN GP	ROUND 17	QATAR GP
ROUND 6	MONACO GP	ROUND 12	BELGIAN GP	ROUND 18	UNITED STATES GP

ROUND 19	MEXICO CITY GP
ROUND 20	SAO PAULO GP
ROUND 21	LAS VEGAS GP
ROUND 22	ABU DHABI GP

D DISQUALIFIED   **F** FASTEST LAP   **NC** NOT CLASSIFIED   **NS** NON-STARTER   **P** POLE POSITION   **R** RETIRED   **W** WITHDRAWN

R7	R8	R9	R10	R11	R12	R13	R14	R15	R16	R17	R18	R19	R20	R21	R22	TOTAL
1PF	1P	1PF	1PF	1F	1	1P	1	5	1PF	1PF	1	1	1P	1	1PF	575
4	6F	3	6	3	2	4	2	8	R	10	4	R	4	3	4	285
2	3	8	3	4P	4F	6	6	3F	5	R	D	2F	8	7	9	234
7	2	5	7	9	5	2F	9	15	8	6	R	R	3	9	7	206
11	4	2	9	7	3P	R	4	4	4	5	DP	3P	NS	2P	2	206
17	13	4	2	2	7	7	8	2	2	3	2	5	2F	R	5	205
5	5	6	10	8	R	5	3P	1P	6	NS	3	4	6	6	18	200
3	R	7	5	6	6	17	5	R	7	4	5	6	R	8	3	175
13	11	16	4	5	R	9	12F	7	3	2	R	8	14	10F	6	97
6	9	9	14	10	9	11	16	NS	R	11	7	R	5	5	10	74
10	12	10	R	R	11	3	15	6	10	12	6	11	7	11	13	62
8	8	14	R	R	8	10	R	R	9	7	R	10	10	4	12	58
16	7	11	8	11	14	8	7	11	R	13	9	9	R	12	14	27
12	14	19	16	15	10	15	NS	R	12	15	8F	12	9	R	8	17
19	10	15	12	12	12	14	10	R	R	8	12	15	R	17	19	10
15	15	R	13	14	18	12	17	13	14	16	11	13	12	R	15	9
-	-	-	-	13	16	W	-	-	-	-	15	7	13	14	11	6
9	16	12	15	16	13	R	14	12	13	9	13	14	R	15	17	6
18	17	18	R	17	15	16	18	10	15	14	14	R	R	13	20	3
-	-	-	-	-	13	11	9	11	17	-	-	-	-	-	2
20	R	13	11	R	17	R	13	14	R	R	10	R	11	16	16	1
14	18	17	17	-	-	-	-	-	-	-	-	-	-	-	-	0

R7	R8	R9	R10	R11	R12	R13	R14	R15	R16	R17	R18	R19	R20	R21	R22	TOTAL
1/4	1/6	1/3	1/6	1/3	1/2	1/4	1/2	5/8	1/R	1/10	1/4	1/R	1/4	1/3	1/4	860
2/3	3/R	7/8	3/5	4/6	4/6	6/17	5/6	3/R	5/7	4/R	5/D	2/6	8/R	7/8	3/9	409
5/11	4/5	2/6	9/10	7/8	3/R	5/R	3/4	1/4	4/6	5/NS	3/D	3/4	6/NS	2/6	2/18	406
13/17	11/13	4/16	2/4	2/5	7/R	7/9	8/12	2/7	2/3	2/R	2/R	5/8	2/14	10/R	5/6	302
6/7	2/9	5/9	7/14	9/10	5/9	2/11	9/16	15/NS	8/R	6/11	7/R	R/R	3/5	5/9	7/10	280
8/10	8/12	10/14	R/R	R/R	8/11	3/10	15/R	6/R	9/10	7/12	6/R	10/11	7/10	4/11	12/13	120
16/20	7/R	11/13	8/11	11/R	14/17	8/R	7/13	11/14	R/R	13/R	9/10	9/R	11/R	12/16	14/16	28
12/14	14/18	17/19	16/17	13/15	10/16	13/15	11/NS	9/R	11/12	15/17	8/15	7/12	9/13	14/R	8/11	25
9/19	10/16	12/15	12/15	12/16	12/13	14/R	10/14	12/R	13/R	8/9	12/13	14/15	R/R	15/17	17/19	16
15/18	15/17	18/R	13/R	§4/17	15/18	12/16	17/18	10/13	14/15	14/16	11/14	13/R	12/R	13/R	15/20	12

STARTS

DRIVERS

377	Fernando Alonso	(SPA)	**183**	Nick Heidfeld	(GER)	**128**	Mario Andretti	(USA)
349	Kimi Raikkonen	(FIN)	**180**	Ralf Schumacher	(GER)		Adrian Sutil	(GER)
332	Lewis Hamilton	(GBR)	**179**	Romain Grosjean	(FRA)	**126**	Jack Brabham	(AUS)
325	Rubens Barrichello	(BRA)	**176**	Graham Hill	(GBR)	**123**	Charles Leclerc	(MON)
306	Michael Schumacher	(GER)	**176**	Jacques Laffite	(FRA)	**123**	Ronnie Peterson	(SWE)
306	Jenson Button	(GBR)	**171**	Niki Lauda	(AUT)	**118**	Pierluigi Martini	(ITA)
299	Sebastian Vettel	(GER)	**163**	Jacques Villeneuve	(CDN)	**115**	Damon Hill	(GBR)
269	Felipe Massa	(BRA)	**163**	Kevin Magnussen	(DEN)	**114**	Jacky Ickx	(BEL)
257	Sergio Perez	(MEX)	**163**	Thierry Boutsen	(BEL)		Alan Jones	(AUS)
256	Riccardo Patrese	(ITA)	**161**	Mika Hakkinen	(FIN)	**114**	Keke Rosberg	(FIN)
252	Jarno Trulli	(ITA)	**161**	Ayrton Senna	(BRA)		Patrick Tambay	(FRA)
246	David Coulthard	(GBR)	**160**	Johnny Herbert	(GBR)	**112**	Denny Hulme	(NZL)
239	Daniel Ricciardo	(AUS)	**158**	Martin Brundle	(GBR)	**111**	Jody Scheckter	(RSA)
229	Giancarlo Fisichella	(ITA)	**157**	Olivier Panis	(FRA)	**111**	Heikki Kovalainen	(FIN)
222	Valtteri Bottas	(FIN)	**156**	Heinz-Harald Frentzen	(GER)		John Surtees	(GBR)
215	Mark Webber	(AUS)	**152**	John Watson	(GBR)	**110**	Daniil Kvyat	(RUS)
210	Gerhard Berger	(AUT)	**149**	Rene Arnoux	(FRA)	**109**	Philippe Alliot	(FRA)
208	Andrea de Cesaris	(ITA)	**146**	Derek Warwick	(GBR)		Mika Salo	(FIN)
206	Nico Rosberg	(GER)	**146**	Carlos Reutemann	(ARG)	**108**	Elio de Angelis	(ITA)
204	Nelson Piquet	(BRA)	**145**	Eddie Irvine	(GBR)	**106**	Jos Verstappen	(NED)
203	Nico Hulkenberg	(GER)	**144**	Emerson Fittipaldi	(BRA)	**104**	Jo Bonnier	(SWE)
201	Jean Alesi	(FRA)	**143**	Lance Stroll	(CDN)		Pedro de la Rosa	(SPA)
199	Alain Prost	(FRA)	**134**	Jean-Pierre Jarier	(FRA)		Jochen Mass	(GER)
194	Michele Alboreto	(ITA)	**133**	Esteban Ocon	(FRA)		Lando Norris	(GBR)
187	Nigel Mansell	(GBR)	**132**	Eddie Cheever	(USA)		George Russell	(GBR)
185	Max Verstappen	(NED)		Clay Regazzoni	(SWI)	**100**	Bruce McLaren	(NZL)
183	Carlos Sainz Jr	(ESP)	**130**	Pierre Gasly	(FRA)			

CONSTRUCTORS

1,074 Ferrari	**566** Sauber (including BMW Sauber and Alfa Romeo II)	**227** March
946 McLaren		**197** BRM
815 Williams	**503** Red Bull (*née* Stewart then Jaguar Racing)	**166** Haas
737 Alpine* (*née* Toleman then Benetton then Renault II, Lotus II & Renault III)	**491** Lotus	**132** Osella
	468 Mercedes GP (*née* BAR then Honda Racing then Brawn GP)	**123** Renault
691 AlphaTauri (*née* Minardi then Toro Rosso)	**430** Tyrrell	
601 Aston Martin II (*née* Jordan then Midland then Spyker then Force India then Racing Point)	**409** Prost (*née* Ligier)	
	394 Brabham	
	382 Arrows	

MOST WINS

DRIVERS

103	Lewis Hamilton	(GBR)	16	Stirling Moss	(GBR)		Jody Scheckter	(RSA)
91	Michael Schumacher	(GER)	15	Jenson Button	(GBR)	9	Mark Webber	(AUS)
54	Max Verstappen	(NED)	14	Jack Brabham	(AUS)	8	Denny Hulme	(NZL)
53	Sebastian Vettel	(GER)		Emerson Fittipaldi	(BRA)		Jacky Ickx	(BEL)
51	Alain Prost	(FRA)		Graham Hill	(GBR)		Daniel Riccardo	(AUS)
41	Ayrton Senna	(BRA)	13	Alberto Ascari	(ITA)	7	Rene Arnoux	(FRA)
32	Fernando Alonso	(SPA)		David Coulthard	(GBR)		Juan Pablo Montoya	(COL)
31	Nigel Mansell	(GBR)	12	Mario Andretti	(USA)	6	Tony Brooks	(GBR)
27	Jackie Stewart	(GBR)		Alan Jones	(AUS)		Jacques Laffite	(FRA)
25	Jim Clark	(GBR)		Carlos Reutemann	(ARG)		Riccardo Patrese	(ITA)
	Niki Lauda	(AUT)	11	Rubens Barrichello	(BRA)		Sergio Perez	(MEX)
24	Juan Manuel Fangio	(ARG)		Felipe Massa	(BRA)		Jochen Rindt	(AUT)
23	Nelson Piquet	(BRA)		Jacques Villeneuve	(CDN)		Ralf Schumacher	(GER)
	Nico Rosberg	(GER)	10	Gerhard Berger	(AUT)		John Surtees	(GBR)
22	Damon Hill	(GBR)		Valtteri Bottas	(FIN)		Gilles Villeneuve	(CDN)
21	Kimi Raikkonen	(FIN)		James Hunt	(GBR)			
20	Mika Hakkinen	(FIN)		Ronnie Peterson	(SWE)			

CONSTRUCTORS

243	Ferrari	17	BRM		Wolf	
183	McLaren	16	Cooper	2	AlphaTauri (including	
125	Mercedes GP (including Honda Racing, Brawn GP)	15	Renault		Toro Rosso)	
		10	Alfa Romeo		Honda	
114	Williams	9	Ligier	1	BMW Sauber	
114	Red Bull Racing (including Stewart)		Maserati		Eagle	
			Matra		Hesketh	
79	Lotus		Mercedes		Penske	
50	Alpine (including Benetton, Renault II, Lotus II & Renault III)		Vanwall		Porsche	
		5	Aston Martin (including Jordan & Racing Point)		Shadow	
35	Brabham					
23	Tyrrell	3	March			

The first of Max Verstappen's wins came at the 2016 Spanish GP on his maiden outing after his promotion to Red Bull Racing.

DRIVERS

19	Max Verstappen	2023
15	Max Verstappen	2022
13	Michael Schumacher	2004
	Sebastian Vettel	2013
11	Lewis Hamilton	2014
	Lewis Hamilton	2018
	Lewis Hamilton	2019
	Lewis Hamilton	2020
	Michael Schumacher	2002
	Sebastian Vettel	2011
10	Lewis Hamilton	2015
	Lewis Hamilton	2016
	Max Verstappen	2021
9	Lewis Hamilton	2017
	Nigel Mansell	1992
	Nico Rosberg	2016
	Michael Schumacher	1995
	Michael Schumacher	2000
	Michael Schumacher	2001
8	Mika Hakkinen	1998
	Lewis Hamilton	2021
	Damon Hill	1996
	Michael Schumacher	1994
	Ayrton Senna	1988
7	Fernando Alonso	2005
	Fernando Alonso	2006
	Jim Clark	1963
	Alain Prost	1984
	Alain Prost	1988
	Alain Prost	1993
	Kimi Raikkonen	2005
	Michael Schumacher	2006
	Ayrton Senna	1991
	Jacques Villeneuve	1997
6	Mario Andretti	1978
	Alberto Ascari	1952
	Jenson Button	2009
	Jim Clark	1965
	Juan Manuel Fangio	1954
	Damon Hill	1994
	James Hunt	1976
	Nigel Mansell	1987
	Felipe Massa	2008
	Kimi Raikkonen	2007
	Nico Rosberg	2015
	Michael Schumacher	1998
	Michael Schumacher	2003
	Ayrton Senna	1989
	Ayrton Senna	1990
	Jackie Stewart	1969
	Jackie Stewart	1971

CONSTRUCTORS

21	Red Bull	2023
19	Mercedes GP	2016
17	Red Bull	2022
16	Mercedes GP	2014
	Mercedes GP	2015
15	Ferrari	2002
	Ferrari	2004
	McLaren	1988
	Mercedes GP	2019
13	Mercedes GP	2020
	Red Bull	2013
12	McLaren	1984
	Mercedes GP	2017
	Red Bull	2011
	Williams	1996
11	Benetton	1995
	Mercedes GP	2018
	Red Bull	2021
10	Ferrari	2000
	McLaren	2005
	McLaren	1989
	Williams	1992
	Williams	1993
9	Ferrari	2001
	Ferrari	2006
	Ferrari	2007
	McLaren	1998
	Mercedes GP	2021
	Red Bull	2010
	Williams	1986
	Williams	1987
8	Benetton	1994
	Brawn GP	2009
	Ferrari	2003
	Ferrari	2008
	Lotus	1978
	McLaren	1991
	McLaren	2007
	Renault	2005
	Renault	2006
	Williams	1997
7	Ferrari	1952
	Ferrari	1953
	Lotus	1963
	Lotus	1973
	McLaren	1999
	McLaren	2000
	McLaren	2012
	Red Bull	2012
	Tyrrell	1971
	Williams	1991
	Williams	1994

Above: The last of Jim Clark's F1 wins came at Kyalami in 1968.

Opposite: Lewis Hamilton pushed in 2016, but Nico Rosberg won.

MOST POLE POSITIONS

DRIVERS

104	Lewis Hamilton	(GBR)		Nelson Piquet	(BRA)		James Hunt	(GBR)
68	Michael Schumacher	(GER)	23	Charles Leclerc	(MON)		Ronnie Peterson	(SWE)
65	Ayrton Senna	(BRA)	22	Fernando Alonso	(SPA)	13	Jack Brabham	(AUS)
57	Sebastian Vettel	(GER)	20	Valtteri Bottas	(FIN)		Graham Hill	(GBR)
33	Jim Clark	(GBR)		Damon Hill	(GBR)		Jacky Ickx	(BEL)
	Alain Prost	(FRA)	18	Mario Andretti	(USA)		Juan Pablo Montoya	(COL)
32	Nigel Mansell	(GBR)		Rene Arnoux	(FRA)		Jacques Villeneuve	(CDN)
32	Max Verstappen	(NED)		Kimi Raikkonen	(FIN)		Mark Webber	(AUS)
30	Nico Rosberg	(GER)	17	Jackie Stewart	(GBR)	12	Gerhard Berger	(AUT)
29	Juan Manuel Fangio	(ARG)	16	Felipe Massa	(BRA)		David Coulthard	(GBR)
26	Mika Hakkinen	(FIN)		Stirling Moss	(GBR)	10	Jochen Rindt	(AUT)
24	Niki Lauda	(AUT)	14	Alberto Ascari	(ITA)			
				Rubens Barrichello	(BRA)			

CONSTRUCTORS

249	Ferrari	14	Tyrrell		Matra		
156	McLaren	12	Alfa Romeo	3	Shadow		
137	Mercedes GP (including BAR, Honda Racing & Brawn GP)	11	BRM		Toyota		
			Cooper	2	Lancia		
128	Williams	10	Maserati	1	AlphaTauri (including Toro Rosso)		
107	Lotus	9	Ligier		Arrows		
96	Red Bull (including Stewart GP)	8	Mercedes		BMW Sauber		
39	Brabham	7	Vanwall		Haas		
36	Alpine (including Toleman, Benetton, Renault II, Lotus II & Renault III)	5	March		Lola		
31	Renault	4	Aston Martin (including Jordan, Force India & Racing Point)		Porsche		
					Wolf		

Michael Schumacher made his name with Benetton in 1992, gathering points then wins and fastest laps at the start of his F1 career.

MOST FASTEST LAPS

DRIVERS

77	Michael Schumacher	(GER)	21	Gerhard Berger	(AUT)	13	Alberto Ascari	(ITA)
65	Lewis Hamilton	(GBR)	20	Nico Rosberg	(GER)		Jacky Ickx	(BEL)
46	Kimi Raikkonen	(FIN)	19	Valtteri Bottas	(FIN)		Alan Jones	(AUS)
41	Alain Prost	(FRA)		Damon Hill	(GBR)		Riccardo Patrese	(ITA)
38	Sebastian Vettel	(GER)		Stirling Moss	(GBR)	12	Rene Arnoux	(FRA)
30	Nigel Mansell	(GBR)		Ayrton Senna	(BRA)		Jack Brabham	(AUS)
	Max Verstappen	(NED)		Mark Webber	(AUS)		Juan Pablo Montoya	(COL)
28	Jim Clark	(GBR)	18	David Coulthard	(GBR)	11	Sergio Perez	(MEX)
25	Mika Hakkinen	(FIN)	17	Rubens Barrichello	(BRA)		John Surtees	(GBR)
24	Fernando Alonso	(SPA)	16	Daniel Ricciardo	(AUS)	10	Mario Andretti	(USA)
	Niki Lauda	(AUT)	15	Felipe Massa	(BRA)		Graham Hill	(GBR)
23	Juan Manuel Fangio	(ARG)		Clay Regazzoni	(SWI)			
	Nelson Piquet	(BRA)		Jackie Stewart	(GBR)			

CONSTRUCTORS

259	Ferrari		Benetton, Renault, Lotus II & Renault III)	12	Matra
164	McLaren	41	Brabham	10	Prost (including Ligier)
133	Williams	20	Tyrrell	9	Mercedes
100	Mercedes GP (including BAR, Honda Racing & Brawn GP)	18	Renault	8	Aston Martin (including Jordan & Force India)
		15	BRM		
95	Red Bull		Maserati	7	Sauber (including BMW Sauber & Alfa Romeo II)
71	Lotus	14	Alfa Romeo		
56	Alpine (including Toleman,		Cooper	6	Vanwall

MOST POINTS (this figure is gross tally, i.e. including scores that were later dropped)

DRIVERS

4,639.5	Lewis Hamilton	(GBR)	658	Rubens Barrichello	(BRA)	329	Ralf Schumacher	(GER)
3,098	Sebastian Vettel	(GER)	633	Lando Norris	(GBR)	310	Carlos Reutemann	(ARG)
2,586.5	Max Verstappen	(NED)	614	Ayrton Senna	(BRA)	307	Juan Pablo Montoya	(COL)
2,267	Fernando Alonso	(SPA)	535	David Coulthard	(GBR)	289	Graham Hill	(GBR)
1,873	Kimi Raikkonen	(FIN)	530	Nico Hulkenberg	(GER)	281	Emerson Fittipaldi	(BRA)
1,797	Valtteri Bottas	(FIN)	485.5	Nelson Piquet	(BRA)		Riccardo Patrese	(ITA)
1,594.5	Nico Rosberg	(GER)	482	Nigel Mansell	(GBR)	277.64	Juan Manuel Fangio	(ARG)
1,566	Michael Schumacher	(GER)	469	George Russell	(GBR)	275	Giancarlo Fisichella	(ITA)
1,486	Sergio Perez	(MEX)	422	Esteban Ocon	(FRA)	274	Jim Clark	(GBR)
1,317	Daniel Ricciardo	(AUS)	420.5	Niki Lauda	(AUT)		Robert Kubica	(POL)
1,235	Jenson Button	(GBR)	420	Mika Hakkinen	(FIN)	268	Lance Stroll	(CAN)
1,167	Felipe Massa	(BRA)	394	Pierre Gasly	(FRA)	261	Jack Brabham	(AUS)
1,074	Charles Leclerc	(MON)	391	Romain Grosjean	(FRA)	259	Nick Heidfeld	(GER)
1,047.5	Mark Webber	(AUS)	385	Gerhard Berger	(AUT)	255	Jody Scheckter	(RSA)
982.5	Carlos Sainz Jr	(SPA)	360	Damon Hill	(GBR)	248	Denny Hulme	(NZL)
798.5	Alain Prost	(FRA)		Jackie Stewart	(GBR)	246.5	Jarno Trulli	(ITA)

CONSTRUCTORS

9,642	Ferrari	2,026	Aston Martin (including Jordan, Midland, Spyker, Force India & Racing Point)	433	BRM
7,727.5	Mercedes GP (including BAR, Honda Racing & Brawn GP)			423	Prost (including Ligier)
				342	Cooper
7,344	Red Bull (including Stewart, Jaguar Racing)	1,368	Lotus	312	Renault
		1,014	Sauber (including BMW Sauber & Alfa Romeo II)	278.5	Toyota
6,291.5	McLaren			249	Haas
3,626	Williams	864	Brabham	173.5	March
3,496.5	Alpine (including Toleman, Benetton, Renault II, Lotus II & Renault III)	847	AlphaTauri (including Minardi & Toro Rosso)	167	Arrows (including Footwork)
		621	Tyrrell	163	Matra

CHAMPIONSHIP TITLES

DRIVERS

7	Lewis Hamilton	(GBR)		Jenson Button	(GBR)
	Michael Schumacher	(GER)		Giuseppe Farina	(ITA)
5	Juan Manuel Fangio	(ARG)		Mike Hawthorn	(GBR)
4	Alain Prost	(FRA)		Damon Hill	(GBR)
	Sebastian Vettel	(GER)		Phil Hill	(USA)
3	Jack Brabham	(AUS)		Denny Hulme	(NZL)
	Niki Lauda	(AUT)		James Hunt	(GBR)
	Nelson Piquet	(BRA)		Alan Jones	(AUS)
	Ayrton Senna	(BRA)		Nigel Mansell	(GBR)
	Jackie Stewart	(GBR)		Kimi Raikkonen	(FIN)
	Max Verstappen	(NED)		Jochen Rindt	(AUT)
2	Fernando Alonso	(SPA)		Keke Rosberg	(FIN)
	Alberto Ascari	(ITA)		Nico Rosberg	(FIN)
	Jim Clark	(GBR)		Jody Scheckter	(RSA)
	Emerson Fittipaldi	(BRA)		John Surtees	(GBR)
	Mika Hakkinen	(FIN)		Jacques Villeneuve	(CDN)
	Graham Hill	(GBR)			
1	Mario Andretti	(USA)			

CONSTRUCTORS

16	Ferrari			Renault
9	Williams		1	Benetton
8	McLaren			Brawn
	Mercedes GP			BRM
7	Lotus			Matra
6	Red Bull			Tyrrell
2	Brabham			Vanwall
	Cooper			

NB. The Lotus stats listed are based on the team that ran from 1958–1994, whereas those listed as Lotus II are for the team that ran from 2012–2015. Those marked as Alpine are for the team based at Enstone that started as Toleman in 1981, became Benetton in 1986, then Renault II in 2002, Lotus II in 2012 and Renault III in 2016. The Renault listings are for the team that ran from 1977 to 1985, the stats for Red Bull Racing include those of the Stewart Grand Prix and Jaguar Racing teams from which it evolved, and those for Mercedes GP for the team that started as BAR in 1999, ran as Honda GP from 2006 and then as Brawn GP in 2009. Aston Martin II's stats include those of Jordan, Midland, Spyker, Force India and Racing Point, while Scuderia AlphaTauri's include those of its forerunner Minardi and Scuderia Toro Rosso. Alfa Romeo II's figures are for the team created in 2019 from Sauber, with no connection to the two iterations of the works team that ran from 1950–1951 and 1979–1985.

DRIVER	TEAM	Round 1 – 2 March BAHRAIN GP		Round 2 – 9 March SAUDI ARABIAN GP	Round 3 - 24 March AUSTRALIAN GP	Round 4 – 7 April JAPANESE GP	Round 5 – 21 April CHINESE GP	Round 6 – 5 May MIAMI GP	Round 7 – 19 May EMILIA ROMAGNA GP	Round 8 – 26 May MONACO GP	Round 9 – 9 June CANADIAN GP	Round 10 – 23 June SPANISH GP
MAX VERSTAPPEN	Red Bull											
SERGIO PEREZ	Red Bull											
LEWIS HAMILTON	Mercedes											
GEORGE RUSSELL	Mercedes											
CHARLES LECLERC	Ferrari											
CARLOS SAINZ JR	Ferrari											
LANDO NORRIS	McLaren											
OSCAR PIASTRI	McLaren											
FERNANDO ALONSO	Aston Martin											
LANCE STROLL	Aston Martin											
PIERRE GASLY	Alpine											
ESTEBAN OCON	Alpine											
ALEX ALBON	Williams											
LOGAN SARGEANT	Williams											
YUKI TSUNODA	'AlphaTauri'											
DANIEL RICCIARDO	'AlphaTauri'											
VALTTERI BOTTAS	Sauber											
ZHOU GUANYOU	Sauber											
NICO HULKENBURG	Haas											
KEVIN MAGNUSSEN	Haas											

SCORING SYSTEM: 25, 18, 15, 12, 10, 8, 6, 4, 2, 1 POINTS FOR THE FIRST 10 FINISHERS IN EACH GRAND PRIX & 1 POINT FOR FASTEST LAP SET BY A DRIVER FINISHING IN TOP 10 & 8, 7, 6, 5, 4, 3, 2, 1 POINTS FOR THE FIRST 8 DRIVERS IN EACH SPRINT RACE

Round 11 – 30 June AUSTRIAN GP	Round 12 – 7 July BRITISH GP	Round 13 – 21 July HUNGARIAN GP	Round 14 – 28 July BELGIAN GP	Round 15 – 25 August DUTCH GP	Round 16 – 1 September ITALIAN GP	Round 17 – 15 September AZERBAIJAN GP	Round 18 – 22 September SINGAPORE GP	Round 19 – 20 October UNITED STATES GP	Round 20 – 27 October MEXICO CITY GP	Round 21 – 3 November SAO PAULO GP	Round 22 – 23 November LAS VEGAS GP	Round 23 – 1 December QATAR GP	Round 24 – 8 December ABU DHABI GP	POINTS TOTAL

The publishers would like to thank the following sources for their kind permission to reproduce the photographs and artwork in this book.

Max Verstappen is greeted by his father Jos and Red Bull's motorsport consultant Helmut Marko after adding the Hungarian GP to his long list of 2023 victories.

GETTY IMAGES: Rudy Carezzevoli 41L, 46L, 47L, 51L, 52; Chris Graythen 20; Stefano Guidi 50L; Kym Illman 16L, 17L, 22L, 27L, 32L, 33L, 36L, 40L; Qian Jun/MB Media 26L; Clive Mason 30; Buda Mendes 24; Vince Mignott/MB Media 37L; Dan Mullan 23L; Michael Potts/BSR Agency 34, 54L; Clive Rose 14; Edmund So/Eurasia Sport Images 55L; Mark Thompson 12L, 13L; Leo Vogelzang/ATPImages 38

GRAPHIC NEWS: 11T, 12R, 13R, 15T, 16R, 17R, 21T, 22R, 23R, 25T, 26R, 27R, 31T, 32R, 33R, 35T, 36R, 37R, 38T, 40R, 41R, 45T, 46R, 47R, 49T, 50R, 51R, 53T, 54R, 55R, 64, 65, 66, 67, 68, 69, 70, 71, 72, 73, 76, 77, 78, 79, 80, 81, 82, 83, 84, 85, 86, 87, 88, 89

MOTORSPORT IMAGES: 8-9, 31B, 35B, 39B, 57B, 59TL, 59TR, 61TL, 61TR, 61C, 123, 124; Sam Bloxham 53B, 100, 105; Charles Coates 15B; Ercole Colombo 25B, 49B, 61BL; Glenn Dunbar 6-7, 97, 116, 128; Rainer Ehrhardt 57TR; Steve Etherington 18-19, 101, 104, 113; Andrew Ferraro 95; Simon Galloway 90-91, 106; Jake Grant 62-63, 98-99, 117; Andy Hone 74-75, 92, 96, 107, 108-109, 114; Zak Mauger 5, 28-29, 48, 93, 111, 112, 115; Lionel Ng 42-43; David Phipps 57C; Rainer Schlegelmilch 21B, 121, 122; Sutton 11B, 45B, 59C; Mark Sutton 2, 10, 44, 59B, 61BR, 94, 102, 110; Steven Tee 57TL, 103

Every effort has been made to acknowledge correctly and contact the source and/or copyright holder of each picture. Any unintentional errors or omissions will be corrected in future editions of this book.